The

CONSPIRACY SUMMIT DOSSIER

AN IN-DEPTH WHISTLE-BLOWER'S GUIDE TO THE STRANGEST AND MOST BIZARRE COSMIC AND GLOBAL CONSPIRACIES!

Newly Added Revelations From:

- Adam Gorightly—Ritual Magic, Mind Control & UFOs
- Commander X—Mind Control In The 21st Century
- Kenn Thomas—Wilhelm Reich, Eisenhower And The Aliens
- Terry Melanson—Sulphur Enigma Of Paranormal Visitation

CONSPIRACY JOURNAL / GLOBAL COMMUNICATIONS

Conspiracy Summit Dossier

Special Updated Material
by
Adam Gorightly, Commander X, Kenn Thomas, Terry Melanson,
William Cooper, Jessica Cooper

ISBN: 1-60611-056-X
EAN: 978-1-60611-056-0

Nonfiction

Timothy Green Beckley: Editorial Director
Carol Rodriguez: Publishers Assistant
Sean Casteel: Associate Editor
Tim Swartz: Editorial Assistant

Printed in the United States of America
Cover Art by William Kern

For free catalog write:
Global Communications
P.O. Box 753
New Brunswick, NJ 08903

Free Subscription to Conspiracy Journal E-Mail Newsletter
www.ConspiracyJournal.com

Contents

Based on transcripts recorded
at the National Alien Agenda and
Conspiracy Summit
Phoenix, AZ & San Diego, CA.
NOTE: Minor editing has been done for clarity
sake. We apologize for any misquotes
or misspellings that might have occurred during
the making of this transcript.
We DO NOT necessarily believe or advocate the nature
of some or all of this material but provide an open forum.

UPDATED WITH NEW MATERIAL
MARCH 2009!

Contributors

Adam Gorightly

A self described "crackpot historian", Adam Gorightly has been chronicling fringe culture and conspiracy politics in an illuminating manner for more than two decades now. An active contributor to the zine revolution of the late '80s and early '90s, Adam's byline was a familiar sight in many cutting-edge magazines of the period where he sharpened his literary teeth penning articles on the paranormal, conspiracies, and fringe culture. His explorations into these arcane waters eventually led to his first book, published in October 2001,The Shadow Over Santa Susana: Black Magic, Mind Control and the Manson Family Mythos, which has been described as the mother of all Manson family tomes. This was followed in November 2003 by The Prankster and the Conspiracy: The Story of Kerry Thornley and How He Met Oswald and Inspired the Counterculture, the first bio of the legendary counterculture figure, chronicling Thornley's amazing and tragic life. Adam's latest offering, The Beast of Adam Gorightly: Collected Rantings 1992–2004, features many articles from Adam's formative years in the zine scene and onward into the new millennium.

Terry Melanson

In his career as a conspiracy historian and archivist, Terry has written over 120 articles on just about every conspiracy you can name -- some well known, others obscure. He has been a guest on numerous talk shows including the Swedish based Fire and Ice program and he contributed to the 3 volume set which is the UNIVERSAL SEDUCTION. His postings and a great deal of other material can all be found on www.ConspiracyArchive.com including a great interview with the editor of this volume Timothy Beckley.

Commander X

Commander X is the pseudonym for a retired military intelligence official who is the author of numerous books and articles detailing some of the world's most mysteries secrets and conspiracies. Commander X felt that it was important to reveal the inner sanctum of the secret movers and shakers who not only control the government, but also our very lives.

As well, Commander X was concerned that the public had the right to know the truth about the global UFO phenomenon and the devastating arrangements made by the secret government with hostile extraterrestrials. These treaties have enabled the UFO entities known as "the grays" to freely abduct unwilling humans subjects for unholy genetic experiments, all with the approval of the secret world government.

Some of Commander X's books include: The Commander X Files, The Ultimate Deception, The Controllers, Underground Alien Bases, Mind Stalkers, Incredible Technologies of the NWO, William Cooper: Death of a Conspiracy Salesman, Reality of the Serpent Race and the Subterranean Origin of UFOs, Commander X's Guide to Incredible Conspiracies, Time Travel: A How-to Insiders Guide, Invisibility & Levitation: A How To Guide To Personal Performance, Teleportation How to Guide : From Star Trek to Tesla.

KENN THOMAS

Conspiracy buffs everywhere applaud Kenn Thomas for his continued efforts to break the back of the establishment elite and their attempts to turn the public into mind controlled guinea pigs.

For several decades he has published the Steamshovel Press, a para political magazine full of the latest information that Big Brother would like us to take giant steps away from.

A highly respected speaker and author, Thomas has written or co-authored the following titles

The Octopus: Secret Government and the Death of Danny Casolaro
Parapolitics: Conspiracy in Contemporary America
Popular Alienation: A Steamshovel Press Reader
Nasa,Nazis & JFK:The Torbitt Document & The Kennedy Assassination
Maury Island Ufo: The Crisman Conspiracy
UC Conspiracy Files: The Evidence Behind the World's Most Notorious...
The Octopus: The Secret Government and Death of Danny Casolaro

Go to his web site
www.SteamShovelPress.com

William Cooper

The Bush administration once identified William Cooper as the most dangerous man in broadcasting. His controversial short wave show was aired daily, helping to stired up a hornets nest of controversary. With a lengthy background in several branches of the military, Cooper's earliest notoriety among conspiracy buffs developed among UFO enthusiasts, as he promoted UFO conspiracy theories, Kennedy assassination theories, and theories about a New World Order. Cooper claimed that he had actually seen papers identified as Majestic 12 which stated that our government had in his possession wreckage taken from the site of UFO crashes and that this information was being kept from the American public. He claimed that the military had established a trade agreement with the aliens and that they were here with our full consent and knowledge. Later in his career, Cooper spent less time talking about UFOs and more and more time claiming that the IRS was NOT empowered to collect taxes. This ultimately lead to a confrontation with federal authorities to tried to get Cooper to come down from his fortified retreat and face the consequences' . He would not and a shootout with the local sheriff's office resulted in an injured deputy and Cooper being fatally wounded. His shows have been archived and his book Beyond A Pale Horse remains a best seller among conspiracy buffs and freedom fighters.

ILLUMINATI: THE LORDS OF DARKNESS

Secret extension of high-Freemasonry worships Satan as The Lord of Light and Truth and has a goal of world domination under the New World Order

Founded in Ingolstadt, Bavaria on 1 May 1776 by Adam Weishaupt, a prominent Freemason, The Illuminati was a secret Satanic order, an extension of high, or Illuminized, Freemasonry, existing as a special order within an order. Its operations were closely connected with the powerful Grand Orient Masonic Lodge of France. The order's name, meaning "the enlightened ones," signified that its members had been initiated into the secret teachings of Lucifer who, according to the doctrines of Illuminized Freemasonry, was the lightbearer and source of enlightenment.

The Illuminati had been designed specifically to carry out the plans of high Freemasonry to create a New World Order by gaining complete control of key policy-making circles of European governments and attempting to influence the decisions of Europe's leaders from within through these advisory positions.

Referring to the various governmental leaders which the Illuminati had targeted for subversion, Weishaupt remarked:

"It is therefore our duty to surround them with its (the Illuminati's) members so that the profane may have no access to them. Thus we are able most powerfully to promote its interests. If any person is more disposed to listen to Princes than to the order, he is not fit for it and must rise no higher. We must do our utmost to procure the advancement of Illuminati into all important civil offices.

"By this plan we shall direct all mankind. In this manner, and by the simplest means, we shall set all in motion and in flames. The occupations must be so allotted and contrived, that we may, in secret, influence all political transactions."

For the order's strategy to succeed, its activities and the names of its members had to remain confidential. Initiates were therefore sworn to secrecy, taking oaths describing what would happen to them if they ever defected from the order or revealed its plans. As another measure of security, the order's correspondence would be conducted through the use of symbols and pen names. Weishaupt's pseud-

onym was Spartacus.

The power of the order was dramatically increased at the Masonic Congress of Wilhelmsbad, on 16 July 1782. This meeting included representatives of all the secret Societies—Martinists as well as Freemasons and Illuminati—which now numbered three million members worldwide. It enabled the Illuminists to solidify their control over the lodges of Europe and to become viewed as the undisputed leaders of the One World Movement.

What passed at that Congress will never be known to the outside world, for even those men who had been drawn unwittingly into the movement, and now heard for the first time the real designs of the leaders were under oath to reveal nothing. The Comte de Virieu, a member of a Martiniste lodge at Lyons, returning from the Congress of Wilhelmsbad could not conceal his alarm and when questioned on the tragic secrets he had brought back with him, replied, "I will not confide them to you. I can only tell you that all this is very much more serious than you think. The conspiracy which is being woven is so well thought out that it will be, so to speak, impossible for the Monarchy and the Church to escape from it."

From this time onwards the Comte could only speak of Freemasonry with horror.

It was decided at the Congress that the headquarters of Illuminized Freemasonry should be moved from Bavaria to Frankfurt, which was already becoming the stronghold of the Rothschilds (Red Shield) and the international financiers. The ensuing cooperation between the Rothschilds and the Illuminati would prove to be mutually beneficial, multiplying the influence of both throughout Europe.

After some ten years in existence, the Illuminati was discovered and exposed by the Bavarian government as a result of tips received from several of the order's initiates. The leaders of Bavaria moved quickly to confiscate the order's secret documents. These original writings of the Illuminati were then sent to all the leaders of Europe to warn them of the plot. However, some of these leaders had already fallen under the influence of the order and those who had

ILLUMINATI • PAGE TWO

not yet succumbed to the Illuminati found its plans to be so outrageous they didn't believe something like this possible they refused to take the warning seriously.

Disbelief remains as the single biggest factor working in Freemasonry's favor. Decent people tend to find it difficult to believe that there could be individuals so evil in nature as to actually try to take control of the world on behalf of Lucifer (Satan). However, as difficult as it may be to believe, the plot to create a Luciferic New World Order, is a fact that will soon destroy all civilized nations.

Although several members of the order were ultimately prosecuted by the Bavarian government, most of the initiates managed to get away and were taken in by various European leaders. Weishaupt for example, took up refuge with the Duke of Saxe-Gotha where he remained until his death in 1811.

By the time the Illuminati had become exposed, its efforts had already spread into more than a dozen countries, including the United States. Since 1776, at least three U.S. presidents have warned the public of the Illuminati's activities in this country. One of those presidents was George Washington.

"I have heard much of the nefarious and dangerous plan and doctorates of the Illuminati. It was not my intention to doubt that the doctrine of the Illuminati and the principles of Jacobinism had not spread in the United States."

Washington went on to denounce the order in two separate letters written in 1798, and would once again warn America against foreign influence in his farewell address. Concerned that the American people might fall under the sway of these corrupt powers, he said:

"Against the insidious wiles of foreign influence (I conjure you to believe me fellow citizens), the jealousy of a free people ought to be constantly aware; since history and experience prove that foreign influence is one of the most baneful foes of republican government. But that jealousy, to be useful must be impartial, else it becomes the instrument of the very influence to be avoided, instead of a defense against it. Excessive partiality for one foreign nation and excessive dislike for another, cause those whom they actuate to see danger only on one side, and serve to veil and even second the arts of influence on the other. Real patriots, who may resist the intrigues of the favorite, are liable to become suspected and odious, while its tools and dupes usurp the applause and confidence of the people, to surrender their interests.

"The great rule of conduct for us, in regard to foreign nations, is, in extending our commercial relations, to have with them as little political connection as possible. So far as we have already formed engagements, let them be fulfilled with good faith. Here let us stop."

Although the Illuminati officially ceased to exist in the 1780s, the continuation of its efforts was ensured through the Grand Orient Lodge of France. Working through the Grand Orient and the network of Illuminized Masonic lodges already put in place by Weishaupt, high-Freemasonry would continue with its plans to build a New World Order.

One of the factors working in Freemasonry's favor is that it rarely does anything covert in its own name. In order to advance its agenda it establishes other organizations, such as the Illuminati, to which it gives special assignments. That way, if anything goes wrong and the operation gets exposed, Freemasonry remains relatively unscathed, claiming it had nothing to do with the matter.

Well into the early 1900s, Illuminized Freemasonry would continue to operate in this fashion, creating new organizations to advance their cause of worldwide domination.

The first major step of the Illuminati was to incite the French Revolution through the Jacobin Society and Napoleon Bonaparte, who was one of their men. Illuminized Freemasonry would also receive help from Voltaire, Robespierre, Danton and Marat, all of whom were prominent Masons. The Jacobin Society's motives and connections were revealed when it named Weishaupt as its "Grand Patriot."

The U.S. had barely declared its independence when these same European forces began efforts to bring America's young banking system under their control. Alexander Hamilton was at the forefront of this drive. President Thomas Jefferson, keenly aware of the plot, argued:

"If the American people ever allow private banks to control the issue of their currency, first by inflation and then by deflation, the banks and the corporations that will grow up around them will deprive the people of all property until their children wake up homeless on the continent their fathers conquered."

During the mid 1800s, the Illuminati would be partly responsible for inciting the U.S. Civil War.

ILLUMINATI • PAGE THREE

Charleston, South Carolina, where the Successionist Movement began, also happened to be the American headquarters of Scottish Rite Freemasonry, a little known fact which Freemasonry has successfully kept from the public. The headquarters of the Scottish Rite were later moved to Washington, DC, where they remain to this day.

Abraham Lincoln strongly resisted efforts by Illuminist forces to establish a privately controlled central bank. His foresight and wisdom would prevent the establishment of such a system for another forty-eight years. Shortly before his assassination, he warned:

"As a result of war, corporations have been enthroned and an era of corruption in high places will follow and the money power of the country will endeavor to prolong its reign by working on the prejudices of the people until wealth is aggregated in the hands of a few and the Republic is destroyed. I feel at this moment more anxiety for the safety of my country than ever before, even in the midst of war."

In 1913, the persistent efforts of Illuminized Freemasonry paid off with the creation of the Federal Reserve System, ensuring European Illuminists a permanent role in America's finances, along with providing them more money with which to further their cause of worldwide domination and establishment of the New World Order. Some of this money would eventually go toward financing the Council on Foreign Relations, formation of which was influenced by Edward Mandell House.

Colonel House was an Illuminist agent committed to the one-world interests of the Rothschild-Warburg-Rockefeller cartel, serving as their point-man in the White House. He first gained national prominence in 1912 while working to get Woodrow Wilson nominated as president. After Wilson's election, he became the president's most trusted personal advisor. House was to Wilson what Henry Kissinger would later be to Richard Nixon. Without question, he was the dominant force in the White House, exerting his influence particularly in the areas of banking and foreign policy.

His accomplishments as Wilson's chief advisor were many. Among other things, he successfully persuaded Woodrow Wilson to support and sign the Federal Reserve Act into law. Later, realizing what he had done, President Wilson remorsefully declared, "I have unwittingly ruined my country!"

During World War 1, which began within a year after the Act's passage, House made secret missions to Europe as Wilson's chief foreign diplomat. It didn't take long before he managed to drag the United States into the war (April 1917). As the war came to an end, House worked diligently to help plan the League of Nations. Funded in part with Rockefeller money, the League was to serve as the first political step toward forming a One World Government.

President Wilson, as a result of House's counsel, became the leading spokesperson for the League of Nations. Wilson was publicly accepted as the League's chief architect, despite the fact that House was actually in charge.

Much to Wilson's dismay and embarrassment, however, he could not even persuade his own country to join the organization. The American people strongly resisted this move toward globalization, placing heavy pressure on Congress to reject the treaty, thereby keeping the U.S. out of the League.

The non-entry of the United States into the League of Nations represented a huge setback for Colonel House and the internationalists. There could be no world government without the participation of the world's leading power. But it was only a temporary setback. The globalists would learn from this incident and would never again underestimate the power of the American people or of Congress. To ensure that a similar incident didn't occur, the cartel, working through House and his Socialist accomplices, would establish the Council on Foreign Relations.

Introduction By Timothy Green Beckley

Today we know that the government covers up a heck of a lot of things, not just UFOs. Some of the things they cover up for National Security reasons, but many of the things they cover up for no reason at all. Tonight we're going to go beyond UFOs, although that certainly is part of the discussion, and we're going to get some of the theories and some of the ideas and some of the research that some of our speakers have collected on various government conspiracies. It will cover a wide range of subjects, and should be very fascinating. Each speaker will give a short opening address on their beliefs and give some of their ideas, and then we'll open it up to questions from the audience. We'll be on our way in a few minutes.

Welcome to the final session of the Sixth Annual National New Age Alien Agenda and Cosmic Conspiracies Conference. Tonight we're having a Conspiracy Panel with six leading experts on various aspects of the Great Cosmic Conspiracy. Our guest host this evening, and MC and moderator, is a gentleman who has had a great deal to do with conspiracies and cover-ups as far as the UFO mystery goes. He was a recognizable name in the UFO field for many years, working under cover, formerly in the military. And along with the military, he had very, very many strange things happen to him.

He was probably the first individual from military intelligence to talk openly about what had happened to him in the military. Guy Kirkwood—you might recognize the name that he used for many years while speaking on the UFO platforms at Giant Rock and other places—Mel Noel. He will be our moderator tonight. He will start the discussion and then pass the microphone to the panelists here. They'll have about ten minutes to discuss their expertise in the area of the cover-ups and conspiracies and so forth, and then we'll open it up to questions and debate. Then Guy will tell a little bit about his experiences.

So with that, I will pass the microphone over to Guy Kirkwood, aka Mel Noel.

Guy Kirkwood Begins The Introductions

Kirkwood: Thank you, Tim. I, as I'm sure many of you, have some limited, or maybe some considerable knowledge, concerning each one of the speakers here this evening. But so that we might bring everyone in the audience up to speed, if you will, we're going to allow each one to give you a thumbnail sketch outline of their background, experiences, and some of the knowledge that they bring with them this evening.

So then we can open the floor to questions, because that's the only way that you're going to learn what you're looking for. We'll just start on the right with Vance Davis.

Vance Davis

Davis: Okay, thank you, Guy. My name's Vance Davis. I served seven years in the National Security Agency, but being paid by and for the Army. When I was eighteen years old I joined the government, took its tests, and I worked with communications and crypto, though I didn't do that most of my time in the military. But I learned a lot while at Fort Mead. Then got out for a year, got back in, then got sent to Oxford to finally do my job. And started doing some parapsychology research. I found some information that we were being given, found some facts and some information that dealt with some conspiracies, some cover-ups.

Alien information. Also how the government works and how it doesn't work, which I learned from practical experience, not from reading books. We went AWOL and got caught in Gulf Breeze, Florida. About a week and a half later, on July 14, 1990, right before the Gulf War, which we knew a lot about, we were released with Honorable Discharges by orders of the White House. For some reason. We don't know that reason, but again that's another conspiracy. And here I am after about three years of being underground.

Now I'm here talking and trying to inform the public about how the government does work, just as Guy did and does now, I'm sure. There are many other people who aren't in the military or were in the military that are coming out and talking about how it really works in the intelligence field, how it works in the government. And you guys are all seeing a great show. By what you see on TV, you don't see the real power going on behind the scenes. So that's what we're here to do, and I'm open for any questions. If I don't know, I'll tell you. Thank you very much.

Jordan Maxwell

Maxwell: My name is Jordan Maxwell. My mother had an uncle when I was a child who worked in the Vatican Secretary of State's Office. Every few years, he would come home to visit the family and would sit and talk with my father and his brothers and family friends about the intrigue going on throughout the world behind the scenes of religion. So I grew up in that kind of an environment.

Also, my great-grandfather was a Senator from the state of Florida. I had two federal judges in my family. The late Senator Claude Pepper, before he died, was a family friend. So I grew up in a family listening to politics and religion from behind the scenes. And I waited for many years to have someone expose the connections behind the scenes of government, money and religion. Since nobody had done that to my satisfaction, I'm going to try to do it myself.

I believe that there is a conspiratorial apparatus working in the world. And I think everyone's pretty well come to that conclusion. That nothing is happening by chance. But when you understand how Adolph Hitler was financed, when you understand how the

Soviet Union was financed, how New York and Washington, D.C., London, England—I used to listen, as I said, to my mother's uncle talking about how the Vatican was operating throughout the world and I got a very good idea about what was going on in the Catholic Church.

I have to say that there are two facets to the Catholic religion and to Western religion in general, all of Judeo-Christianity in general. There is the world of theology and religion, which everyone can join in arguing back and forth as to the right way to understand scripture. And then there is another whole world behind the scenes called The Religio-Political-Economic Establishment of the West. Now what we're talking about is Big Government, Big Business, and Big Lies.

I've seen enough, heard enough, and had enough of the exploitation of ignorant and uninformed people. So it's my purpose in life to show the connections between secret societies, fraternal orders, banking families who are financing our churches, our religious organizations, Jehovah's Witnesses, Seventh-Day Adventists, the Mormon Church, Worldwide Church of God, all of them. All of these cults, movements, religious orders. The people themselves are fine people. I know many of them. But I'm not talking about the people.

I'm talking about the organizations and how they're financed and how they were started and how the government and Big Money are party to this conspiratorial apparatus. And if there is a God, and believe me, I don't feel like an expert, because I have far more questions than I do answers, but if there is a divine essence or presence in the universe, there is no doubt in my mind that it has nothing whatsoever to do with man-made organizations. And that somewhere along the line, we're going to find out that we're out of balance and out of synch with the creative force in the universe.

I'm very big on the Goddess, though I don't talk about it a whole lot. I believe that there has been an out-of-balance since the Roman Empire when the emphasis was taken off of the Goddess and the female principle in the universe and was put solely into Man's hands to govern the world. I think until such time as we appreciate the feminine contribution to the human race, we're not going to get away from this Man-dominated world which gives us rape, crime, manipulation, exploitation and all of the manly things of the world. And when we understand that the earth is our mother, that it is a feminine principle of creation, I think we can then get back and understand who we are as humans.

We've all been exploited by religion, by politics, Big Money, Big Business, and it is my purpose to try and wake people up to see who these people are and what they've been doing to us. Thank you.

Wendy Wallace

Wallace: My name's Wendy Wallace. Jordan and I have a similar calling. I guess we all do. It's that wake-up call. My name, not too coincidentally, means White-Brown Wanderer, Seeker of Truth. Had my mother known, she wouldn't have named me that.

It's been a problem ever since. And that has been all my life. When I was about ten years old, I looked around and realized everything was stark raving mad. People were nuts, the world was upside down and backwards. Nothing made any sense at all. And I started getting real curious about what in the world this was all about.

And I started, about the age of ten, started studying comparative religions. The politics thing, by about the time the Viet Nam War came along, I knew that was a farce. I mean, everybody voted for LBJ because Goldwater was going to bomb them flat. Remember that? Well, that was the end of my voting career or even thinking about it. I knew that had to be a farce somehow.

And economics, I never had much to do with that. But the search for truth led me of course to—well, I got conked on the forehead by numerous gurus and all kinds of self-actualization classes. The Berkley Psychic Institute. You name it, I was there. You name a guru, I had him. Looking for that something that I knew I was missing. And I always studied the conspiracies. All throughout the seventies. Gary Owens' wonderful little book "None Dare Call It Conspiracy." And I just went, "Whoa, does that make sense."

And I started looking at it. And someone said, "Oh, that's a John Birch Society publication. You don't want to read that." So I set it down for five years or something. "Oh, well, then okay." Then later I picked it up again. "This stuff's still right." I kept on looking and of course found out that there's a whole big scene behind the scenes that most of us are not often aware of.

I always read anything anybody gave me. They said, "Here, read this." I would. So I came by lots of information that I would have otherwise logically just screened out. Because we like to read what agrees with us. So I found myself getting a pretty broad range of information and points of view. And every three or four years, I would find myself in a Brave New World, in 1984, and the Book of Revelations. And that book is an unusual book in the Bible. It's the only one that promises a blessing. It's a mixed blessing, but it's a blessing.

So about two years ago, all this came together in my head. All the studying that I had done. And the garbage just kind of flew away, and the parts that were real all kind of fit together. I was Born Again. Which I didn't even know what it was until sometime later. Except that I just totally changed. I'd been sort of mildly drunk for twenty-five years, then the desire for alcohol just went away. I'd never been able to say a sentence without swearing, and it was two weeks before I realized that I hadn't said a swear word. My hobby had been looking to get laid, and it just neutered me in a second. It was absolutely amazing. And that's all in the Bible, it turns out. All those effects are right there.

About two weeks after that, I was alerted to the fact—because I didn't know Revelations like I knew "1984" and "Brave New World"—George Bush announced that he was going to triple the tariff on oil and wine. And it was going to stop international trade wars. It was going to be something else. And then two weeks later he said he would not triple the tariff on oil and wine, on oil and wine only. Well, that clicked me into the Book of Revelations, Chapter Six, which says, "See thou hurt not the oil and the wine," in regard to commodities and prices.

I said, "Whoa." And it took about eight or nine months to figure out I had been given what the Bible calls "the gift of prophecy." It's not the same as being a prophet in the Old Testament. They got their heads cut off if they were wrong once. It's different in the New Testament, where we only try to "prophesy in part." But all of a sudden, I was just seized. And what you'll see out there is a book of eight hundred pages that started out as a two and a half page letter to the people that I thought would want to know, which was the, quote, "Christian Church." I mean, they're the ones who are supposed to be interested in the Bible, right?

So I sent this letter off to all of these pastors, you know, and meanwhile someone gives me a computer. I'd been doing all this on a $20 typewriter. Someone gives me a computer and a printer, so it sort of keeps expanding. When it was about sixteen pages, I spent half my life's savings to fly to Ontario and see Hal Lindsey and Peter LeMan and Grant Jeffries and all these wonderful Christian prophets and show them, you know, "Hey, here we are. We're in Chapter Six, right here. It's on the clock. It's happening." By that time, the other seals had filled in. And the Four Horsemen went to the first four of the seven seals.

And Hal Lindsey denounced me from the stage. He said, "Anybody who tells you we're in the seals is trying to start a cult." Well, after that, none of the two thousand people there would hear a word I had to say. And the Lohan brothers said, "We can't be in Chapter Six. We're raptured out of here in Chapter Four." And that's the delusion that accompanies the Pre-Tribulation stance, "This can't be it because we're still here." And that's what they're going to be saying when the Antichrist arrives. "This can't be it, because we're still here."

So that gives you the basics. That's what my book's about. That's where I'm coming from. The only question is whose side you end up on. We know who wins.

Bridget Woundenberg

Woundenberg: Hi, I'm Bridget Woundenberg. And I don't know if I'm really a conspiratologist, but I am a UFO abductee and I've been probably surrounded by conspiracy most of my life. As far as I know, just about everyone I've ever met at least has wanted to deny that there is a conspiracy. Most of the time, when I talk to people in the general public, you mention the word "conspiracy" and they laugh. "Uh-oh, you're a paranoid." And they don't want to talk about it, they don't want to deal with it, and don't want to accept it as a reality.

It's taken me a long time to accept it as a reality, but in reality I've had to deal with conspiracies since I was old enough to know what the word meant. In my research into UFOs and extraterrestrials and any kind of paranormal phenomena, I've found conspiracy after conspiracy after conspiracy. If it wasn't in the attitudes that people assumed, personality changes once they got into something and came back, or were approached by people, or something strange would happen and I'd see strange personality changes. People would vanish that I used to know. Never been found again.

I've known some interesting people. I've listened to a lot of stories. I got real crazy in my research and I wrote a lot of letters and I made a lot of phone calls. I got a lot of, "You better leave this one alone." With no explanations. Just left me in the dark. And that was real frustrating. So I've had to decide, "Well, is this a conspiracy or is it that people just don't want to deal with me?" And after it went on and on and on like that, I just finally had to accept the fact that the conspiracies were going on.

The way I look at it is, and I agree with Jordon Maxwell and Wendy Wallace, also, to some extent at least, that we're truth seekers. There's two choices. There's a light and a dark, whatever you want to call it. I've heard so many names for it, but the way that I see it is that anytime that any group is out there trying to learn or trying to start a new religion or make a movement in something they believe in, it seems as though something is trying to hold them back. After a while, it gets to the point where you have to start wondering, "What is this power? What is so powerful that it spends so much money and so much resources to keep it back? And why? Why aren't we allowed to learn? Why are we sent in so many different directions? We're given so many ideas. Now why is that?"

It seems to me like it's a real easy way to keep people confused and keep them in the dark. Give them so many ideas that they don't even know what's up anymore. And you really have to go into your own heart and you have to listen to your heart. I do research into DNA and genetics, and I got into crop circles, and I just went into kind of an intuitive phase with this thing. I started listening to my own heart and just shut everything else out. Or, I didn't shut everything out. I took everything in, and I took it into my heart. I kept all the voices out, and I listened to my own voice.

I started weeding out what I believed was right and what I didn't believe was right. And when I approached people and I asked questions, depending on the way that they responded to me, I kind of could get an idea of where they were coming from. Were they trying to keep something from me, were they of the light or of the dark, were they of the government? I mean, you name it.

I have a real personal scenario as far as the conspiracy. My father's been missing for a long time. And I have done just about everything imaginable to find him. Now I'm not saying my father was abducted and taken up to Mars or the Pleiades—that's a possibility, too. But talking about conspiracy, I know what conspiracy feels like. It's reached me a real personal level, and it's a real frustrating thing. When you get out here in this community and you're searching for answers, for what's right—you're searching for some spirituality and you want some answers. You want something positive in your life that's going to make you grow to be a better person, and when you're denied that, that's real frustrating. It's a reality, and it's something you've got to drive beyond.

And I believe that. I believe you've got to go for those answers. And I believe that we need to network and I believe that we need to establish some kind of trust between us, and decide who we can trust and who we can't. Like I said, the best advice that I have is you have to love your own heart and you have to listen to your own heart, because sometimes people can put on a good show. I know the government's real powerful. They can accomplish anything. And what I haven't seen, I've heard plenty of stories about. I've heard too many stories for it not to be real. So, that's all I have. Thank you.

Vladimar Terziski

Terziski: I'm Vladimar Terziski. Coming from Eastern Europe, you should realize that conspiracies are in my blood. In talking about snow, you should talk to an Eskimo. Talking about conspiracies, you should talk to somebody coming from Eastern Europe. Actually, I am extremely proud to present the next continuation of our evolution of the conspiratorial viewpoint of the universe. It was exactly, about, two and a half years ago when we did the first conspiracy panel on a major event like this. It was a big Los Angeles Whole Life Expo. However, it was considered too "politically incorrect" at the time so we were kicked out of the Expo.

I improvised some ads and we rented a room at a nearby hotel. And we had about fifty people until about three in the morning. We have come a long way because this time we talk with Tim Beckley and he agreed that, "Yes, it's high time." This is an historical moment to do an official conspiracy panel. I want to thank all of you for being here and to thank also the panelists who are sharing this conspiratorial viewpoint of mine on the universe.

As a physicist, I have concentrated on my efforts to unravel the conspiracies in the official academic sciences. With my first two books, and a lot of videos—most of these theories are reflected in this big video set of two-day long seminar that we did about two years ago. In my first two books, I talk about the most politically incorrect topic one can talk about in physics, namely anti-gravity. Secret societies have said a long time ago that two things that they don't want to reveal to the masses are the secret of anti-gravity and the secret of the origin of the human race.

So with my presentation—I've been talking on the speakers' circuit for three years in the United States—if they would accept me I would go through the front door. If they would not accept me, I go through the back door. Rent my conference room on my own, tell them it's a Fourth Amendment infringement if they tear my posters down from the public areas, and then we do an underground conspiracy seminar until the early morning hours.

Anyway, my goal number one is to reveal the politically incorrect sciences. The secret sciences that have been developed in private by the secret elite. By the secret societies. That also happens to be the World Bankers. Anti-gravity has been researched for more than 130 years. And the first anti-gravity landing on the moon happened in the 1890s. This was the topic of my next book. And in this book, called "Encounters of the Foo-Fighter Kind," I have studied in great detail the emergence of close to fifty models of anti-gravity devices in World War II Germany with every existing engine in the German arsenal. Car engines, aviation turbo jets, rocket engines, electric motor-type drives—all of these were internal combustion-type engines. Free energy drives, many of a little more advanced stages.

All of this information came two years ago from a designer-leaked revelation by a German secret society in Vienna, which, after the unification of Germany had gotten bolder and had decided to tell their part of the story in contradistinction to the American part of dealings with the little base said to fit this on. The most fascinating story that I got from my trip in Germany in May for the $1 million budget documentary on the German secret anti-gravity program, was a story that one of the craft built by the Brill secret society departed in April 1945 from Germany, near Berlin, on a trip to a star system 68 light years away, where one of the two home planets of the Shumerian Alien Federation is located. Aliens looking like us. Tall, blonde, blue-eyed Nordics.

And they made the first warp speed flight in our terrestrial history. With a terrestrially built craft with alien technological know-how. In about twenty years, they covered sixty light years, so they traveled at about Warp Three, I would say. My own suspicion is that the "Star Trek" series is nothing more than an educational designer-leak of the secret anti-gravity research and development projects of the Rockefeller Foundation and other private entities have been going on for more than fifty years and that first warp speed flight that I know about was the beginning of these incredible inventions.

Back to the political conspiracies, which, how should I say? Conspiracies have many hierarchical levels to them. Talking about the lowest levels, the people at the top try to occupy our time and to prevent our attention from focusing on the higher and more interesting levels of conspiracies. "The Clinton Chronicles" is an incredible documentary film about the thirty or so alleged murders that happened in Little Rock, Arkansas, around the Mafia and dope smuggling friends of Clinton. It has been the most widely talked about documentary film on the Christian Radio Network. I'm listing important conspiracies. A tape cannot make it on the video tape marketplace against the power of the academy of politically incorrect sciences unless it is extremely politically incorrect.

"Report From the Iron Mountain" is an incredible revelation about the ecological hoax and the destruction of the environment. It is done on purpose. It is done by the government as a hasty substitute for the disappearance of the Russian Bear Threat. When the threat of the Russian invasion disappeared, the government needed a hasty substitute that would rationalize the continuation of the very existence of the government. We need a strong government to defend our weakling population, of "sheeple" as some researchers call us. From the arrogant, brutal, big-time government by gaining the destruction of the world. I have the feeling that the whole ecological crisis is a skillfully created smoke screen and a hoax.

"The Magical Money Machine" talks about the creation of money out of paper and ink, out of nothing. And the whole focus of the banking system. I deeply admire the work of Jordon Maxwell, myself personally, because I've never found on my travels on four continents anyone who has gone deeper into the secret symbology of the secret societies than Jordon. I was literally astonished. He's got extreme gems of revelation for me that we are a fascist country.

I come from Eastern Europe, from under the shadow of the dreaded Red Star that caused close to one hundred million people to die in revolutions. Concentration camps in Russia and China. The Cultural Revolution in China cost twenty million people. The Russian concentration camps killed millions of people. All of these happenings were not coincidental. In fact, they were all quietly whispered down through the years of the Russian secret societies by the advisors from the West. And they are part of the global campaign for reduction of the population. That is the number one policy issue of the secret government and the Illuminati.

Read the publications of the Club of Rome and you will realize what urgency they give to that—the requirement to reduce the population. The New World Order has the Third Reich order. This is probably the shortest sentence that summarizes what is prepared for America. The ugliest possible combination of films like "Metropolis," "1984," "Brazil" and "The Philadelphia Experiment, Part 2" and many other films that reveal what has been prepared for us.

"Crisis Creation" is a beautiful tape on the riot-engineering, on the artificial instigation of the riot in Los Angeles by government agents. The 666 tape is a made-for-television film on the bar-coding technology and the upcoming bar-coding, the numbering of missing pets, missing children, and later on, all of us. One of the most interesting tapes that we have done, and with this I'm concluding basically, two more sentences, is the "Occult National Socialism." Which is probably the only tape on the market that goes over five or six levels, hierarchical levels of conspiracy. Taking one country in question: World War II Germany. We talk about half a dozen German secret societies that were pulling the strings of the National Socialism behind the scenes. About half a dozen alien races above the secret societies that were working shoulder to shoulder with the Germans. All of these, both aliens and German secret societies, were under the spell of the Dark Star, which in turn was fighting with the Metaphysical Center of Light, Shambala, for control of the planet.

We have these multi-hierarchical levels of terrestrial secret societies, their different competing sets of aliens working with them. The Americans, through the Allies, were working with a different set of aliens, contacting them through the American and British Freemasonry and Illuminati.

If we are to study "conspiratology," the higher we look at these hierarchical levels, the easier it becomes for us to understand what is going on. The main purpose of the government, the secret government, is to direct our attention on the contrary, to the

14

lowest level to confuse us with the technicalities and the inconsequential stuff. And contrary to the trembling lady sitting next to me, and her conclusion that the government is all-powerful and that they can do anything they want, I say this is one of their biggest "stink-controlling" efforts that they have done. To present the picture that they control all the terms of the equation.

On the contrary, they can control less than half of the terms, and we the people, without any arms, without any organization, are a lot more powerful than the government. All we have to do is just spread the word around. The moment you shine the light on the ugly conspiracy, it starts melting like last year's snow. And by having millions of people meditating or praying, or simply believing that none of their ugly plans will come to pass, then they would never materialize.

I think that we are all powerful, and this is the strongest, most optimistic message that I have to give. We have to concentrate our efforts to spread the word around and to have everybody dutifully meditating, praying, or simply sending out positive thoughts that now these plans won't materialize. Thank you very much.

Alexander Collier

My name is Alexander Collier, and I want to say it's a real pleasure for me to be on the panel with such distinguished people. You are all so unique, and I feel privileged to be here.

As far as blowing one conspiracy, the origin of the human race came from Lyra, so there's one that they don't have secret. Ladies and gentlemen, I'm an Andromeda contactee for almost thirty years now. I'm talking about face-to-face physical contact as well as telepathic. It started for me in Woodstock, Michigan, in 1964 and has continued until the present time. As far as the conspiracies, the whole thing that we're involved in to some degree or another is a conspiracy.

I'm aware of a lot of the government conspiracies, the New World Order, but I'm also aware of other conspiracies—to keep us, as a race, from knowing who we are. That is the biggest secret they want to keep from us. And according to the Andromedans, every single soul on this planet is royalty. The regressive ETs, those who want to control, simply do not want you to know.

At least twenty-two different extraterrestrial races have colonized the earth in our history. We have been genetically altered and manipulated by at least those same twenty-two. We are the only race in our galaxy that can make that claim. And when you add the fact that we are in fact spiritual beings, parts of God, they—the Andromedans, and those other benevolent races—consider us "royalty." Even though we're not acting like royalty. Much of the behavior that we have on the planet, from what I understand, we have been taught by these ET gods, who also have been here controlling and manipulating us as a race.

As far as there being a God, according to the Andromedans, there is. They have said that if you have to put a gender to it, it would be female. Basically, it is neutral, but how we perceive ourselves, and the belief systems that we have regarding ourselves and our reality, is how we use that energy.

There's a lot going on. The single most important thing that I would like to say is that everything, everything, everything in our lives is based on belief systems. And if you want to change your life, you change your belief systems. There is nothing that can stop you from being what you want. And if the governments can convince you that you're just this lowly "sheeple," as Vladimar put it, then that's exactly what you'll be. And he's right when he says that we are more powerful. We are. There is no question about it.

And unless we as a race take back our power, and rise to the occasion, we're really going to get screwed. By a small group of human beings who sold us out, who have totally sold us out, to a group of regressive extraterrestrials from Orion, the grays. And that's all I have to say.

Guy Kirkwood, aka Mel Noel

I'll give you a quick overview of some of my few experiences dealing with the United States government. My background was—as a teenager, I raked leaves, shoveled snow, mowed lawns, babysat, saved my money, lied to my parents and took flying lessons. And from my seventeenth birthday on, I've been driving airplanes. For the most part, it's an occupation of, as one author put it, endless hours of sheer boredom spiced with moments of sheer terror.

In 1954, I was with the 191st Fighter Interceptors Squadron in Salt Lake City, Utah. And in August of that year, three of us were sent TDY to Denver, Colorado, Lowery Air Force Base, and briefed on aerial photography there. After that, we were sent back to Salt Lake City where the program, which was at that time scheduled for ninety days, was to fly BFR conditions daily between Salt Lake City and another Air Force Base in Idaho in the hunt for flying objects, Unidentified Flying Objects.

It was unfruitful for the first eighteen days, and on the nineteenth day we had our introduction. On that occasion, and two others, we exposed approximately 33,000 frames of film. That film was evaluated back on the east coast, and ironically—and totally by coincidence—here in Phoenix, three years ago, I met a gentleman who just walked up to me and said, "You know, I can confirm your Air Force assignment." I said, "Oh, how is that?" He said, "I was at home at the time." And I remember thinking, "Well, that's better than being at a bar. But what's that have to do with it?"

And he explained that he was based at the Air Force Base in Idaho. He had processed the film. He was the first one to see what we had on film. Because we were never privy to it. And I said, "I'll be darned. Did we get anything good?" And he said, "Oh, yeah, a lot of it was really good." At the time of such an assignment, you find out about the control factors in the military. The instructions that, if and when anything occurs, "Thou shalt not discuss, divulge, reveal, relate any aspect of the assignment to anyone, including yourself." I mean, it was almost that bizarre.

And to do so is punishable by a fine of up to $10,000 and imprisonment for up to ten years. Of course, in the interests of National Security. At that time, we had no reason to argue with such reasoning.

Once you're introduced to this subject, it doesn't go away. It doesn't leave you alone. It haunts you for all time. For every question that you seek an answer for, when you find that answer, it only creates ten more questions. What starts off as being privy to a mystery, as you will, becomes, over a period of time, the most complex, compound, study you're ever going to be involved in. It is confusing, and if you haven't already found this out, you're going to find out that from time to time, what you think you really need is a good cerebral laxative.

In 1966, I was with United Airlines. And one day, just east of Albuquerque, on a scheduled passenger flight, we had one alongside of us. These are the pictures that we took right from the flight deck of that airplane. It's interesting, once again, how the powers that be deal with something like that. It was not without a note of humor. I was what they call "side saddle," flight engineer on the flight. The co-pilot was flying the airplane. The captain was just sitting and monitoring. I noticed that he was distracted or had taken an interest in something off to the left side of the aircraft.

We were at that time at a cruise altitude of 30,000 feet. Everything, as we say, was "fat, dumb and happy." After a moment of his evading whatever it is without saying anything, he turned and tapped the co-pilot on the shoulder. When he had the co-pilot's attention, he just pointed out the window. The co-pilot looked, apparently didn't see anything, resumed his duties. A minute later, the captain once again tapped him on the shoulder. At that point, the co-pilot looked a second time. This time there was a reaction. His eyes turned to ping-pong balls. And all he said was, "I don't believe it."

About that time, the senior cabin attendant came forward and she said, "Captain, I know that you're very busy, but the passengers want to know what they're looking at out there." He gave it a moment's thought and gave her a classic answer. He said, "Miss, you go back there and you tell them that they're looking at the same thing we're looking at." As she started to leave, he stopped her and asked, "To your knowledge, does anybody in the crew have a camera on board?" She said, yes, she had a Kodak in her flight bag. He said, "Please make your announcement, then please bring the camera forward in the flight bag. I don't anyone to be aware of its presence on the flight deck. Please expedite."

As she did that, he motioned to me and said, "Do you want to have a look?" And I got up to a better vantage point and this is what we saw. What is in this picture is roughly twenty percent of the length of this thing. By comparison, it was approximately three times longer than this room. In height, it was roughly double the height of the room. There is, as you look closely, but you can't see it from there, a light on the aircraft. We lucked out, as the saying goes, in the background, beyond the object, what you see is a cloud formation which we refer to as an anvil. It is a formation of a thunder storm which as it towers, as it climbs into the jet stream, the high-speed winds aloft carve the cloud and it trails out and it forms the profile of an anvil. That documented our altitude. That phenomenon does not occur typically below 24,000 feet.

This is a photograph that was broadcast back from Phebos, the Russian Mars shot. As you see, the long, narrow, white item in the photo. That is a UFO that according to Maureen O'Popivich, who presented me with this photo, is approximately nine miles in length. It flew between the space shot and the artificial moons of Mars. Shortly after this photo was relayed back to earth, that shot failed. Two succeeding space shots by the United States, by NASA, to Mars also failed. Approximately two years ago, the powers that be decided that they did not like what I was saying. My noise level was too high.

They decided that I did not currently exist, but that my history in aviation didn't exist. It's interesting, because there's a scenario that's going on right now that is testing their mythology. This is an article from a Southern California newspaper and it reads, "El Cahon Pilot Averts Crash." I'm the pilot. It had to with the loss of an engine and a Rockwell Commander flight that we were making back from Baker, California, two weeks ago Thursday. The airplane became a glider. And in the ensuing minute and a half, on the flight day the engine failed, a minute and a half later we were all sitting safely on Freeway 67 in Southern California.

It was interesting. The first official on the scene was a Highway Patrol officer. And he had a sense of humor. He said, "I have to get a picture of this. This is the most exotic traffic stop of my career." Now, the other interesting aspect of this, following such an incident, there is an incredible amount of paperwork and investigation by the National Transportation Safety Board, the Federal Aviation Administration—the interrogation goes on for five hours. Not just myself, but all my passengers.

And you have to haul in everything. "Here's my license, here's my medical, here's my bi-annual, here's my flight checks, here's my log books for 180 years." And they're sitting, tabulating all this up, and they're going through all these records, and they're saying, "When did you get your license?" I'm saying, "Why are you asking me?" And they said, "My God, you've got almost 23,000 hours." I said, "That's not a record." And they said, "No, but you have all these ratings and all this experience, and Oklahoma City says you don't exist!" Right? I'm not there.

It's a can of worms. Because these agencies don't talk to each other. Right? It's going to be very interesting where it goes from here. Because here's all these United Airlines flight records. Here's all these Air Force flight records. Here's all these instructors with their credentials signed off in these log books. And they're saying, "Hey, this is real history. I wonder what happened? How come you don't exist?" As one guy put it, "You have a pilot's license that looks about as old as when Christ was a corporal." I said, "Well, I can't explain that. You know, you'll have to figure it out." So, it goes on.

And like I said earlier, once you're introduced to this subject, it doesn't leave you alone. Whether you're looking at a UFO in curiosity or looking at questions concerning them, all of a sudden, it's not just a UFO. All of a sudden, you're looking at government and control. You're looking at controls beyond the government. You're questioning your disciplines and beliefs. Most everything you've been taught is being challenged. And it's highly disconcerting. It's going to bother the hell out of you.

I notice even now, just one small example—how many people in this room believe that the flag to your right is the flag of the United States of America? About half? It's not. It is the flag of the Admiralty. It's identified by the gold fringe around the outside. Only a flag of the same design and without that fringe is the true flag of the United States of America. You're being put on, and they're secretly saying, "Ha, ha. We fooled you."

How many people have looked at the symbols on a dollar bill? How many people know what they mean? And you're saying, "What the hell does this have to do with a UFO?" It's control. These are the symbols. They're flagrant symbols. You're looking at them daily and you have no idea what they mean. And you're getting little ones. There's thousands more. It's not a nice picture. It's not a pleasant picture. It's not things we'd like to think. And unfortunately, if it's going to change, it's only because of people like everyone of us that are going to make it happen. Don't wait for somebody else. They're not going to do it for you. It's not part of the plan.

You are well controlled, and have been since the day you were born. And without getting into a lot more detail, there is one thing going for us. And it's called "The Window of Opportunity," because it's working against them. There's only a couple more years left for them to pull off a dastardly plan. If we get through that portion of it, then much of the troubles are going to be going away. But you've got to uncover every stone and become educated beyond belief in the meantime.

Now we're going to open it up to questions, and you can direct them at the individuals as you will.

The Blue Berets

Question: (Repeating question from audience member) In 1962, there was a group created that used the title "The Blue Berets." His understanding is that the group was wiped out. He's looking for clarification. Anybody? Jordan, you nodded.

Maxwell: I have a friend in the Air Force, and he mentioned that to me. I wasn't there, so I don't know. But he mentioned that the Air Force had a secret team called "The Blue Berets" and they went out on downings of UFOs and that kind of thing. Or anything that had to do with extraterrestrials or something of that nature. The Blue Berets were sent out by the Air Force to cordon off the area, to seal it off. He didn't say that much about it, but this was just an in-passing conversation. That's all I really know about it, but I do recall him mentioning the Blue Berets, and they were Air Force, according to what he was saying.

Davis: It's also interesting that Blue Berets—you still see Air Force personnel sometimes in certain areas wearing Blue Berets. They're very rare when you do see them. I've seen them in Europe. I don't know what they're doing. I don't know who they are. But I was told by a friend that they're kind of "recon" forces. The Air Force name is the same as the Army. Because I was at multi-force bases and you'd see them. They worked with us sometimes. They didn't talk much. They were very quiet people. So that's all I know about them, and they're still around. They're doing something.

Two Kinds Of Grays?

Question From Audience Member: I've heard two definitions of the grays, the little guys who are three to four feet tall. And the grays, that are like us, that supposedly are the grays that we made a treaty with, and are occupying the underground bases at the Ant Hill, Dulce, Area 51 and Los Alamos. Does anybody know if there's a difference between the two? Are they one and the same or what?

Collier: From my research and my understanding, first of all, I don't think there's any of them at Area 51 anymore. They're all gone, and they've been gone for years. What everybody is seeing at Area 51 is our own technology. It's a big testing base. In Albuquerque, I think it's called Area 76. As for the grays' difference, the smaller ones are basically what you might call your workers. They're pretty well controlled. They're telepathically controlled. You can do the same thing to them. If you're abducted and you know you're being abducted, tell them what to do and they'll do it. Okay? They're given certain jobs to do, and that's about it.

The other ones are very sentient. Some of them can be good, and some of them can be bad. There are many, many races and many varieties of races. There may be other ones that we don't even see, or a few people have seen and never talked about.

Wallace Also Tackles The Question

Wallace: I would just like to add a little broader perspective. The Bible has a lot about EBEs and UFOs in it. What it says is, "As it was in the days of Noah, so it will be in the End Times." And what we know, if we go back to Genesis, is that in the days of Noah, what were called "the sons of the gods" mated with the daughters of the earth. What we're talking about here is that Satan has had the run of the heavens since he took a third of the angels with him. They don't get booted out of heaven until Revelations 12. In other words, all these bases on all the planets and so on.

He's had a great deal of freedom to simply use the DNA that God created. He can't create anything himself, but boy can he synthesize. He is an imitator. His line is, "I will be like the Most High." So he's been out there banging together all kinds of grotesqueries. Whether they're this tall, or this tall, what color they are. Bird-reptiles. Whatever. And in going back to the days of Noah in Genesis, you'll also find the word "cockatrice." We hear it in both Jeremiah and Isaiah, that cockatrices will be sent in the Last Days.

It also refers to the "web," which is not only the web of the cryptocracy, but also the web of the satellite that has us pinned down now to ten foot squares. Okay? So it talks about putting your trust in the web and anybody who messes with it is going to get bit. Anybody who messes with these things is going to die.

And the reason we know that cockatrice refers to genetic manipulations is because a cockatrice is said to come from a cock's egg. And cocks don't lay eggs. We hear constantly about how these supposedly superior races from other planets are master genetic manipulators. And we hear about the bird-reptile they've created and all that sort of thing—how these are our "gods." Well, they would sure like us to think so.

Terziski's Turn At Bat

Terziski: The little gray question is one of the most important and interesting for me personally. I've been investigating UFOs for close to twenty years, and I'll probably start teaching about them in some of the Los Angeles universities pretty soon. I have a feeling that they're probably thousands, God knows how many, little gray races in the universe existing. Some of them have never heard about earth.

I've also heard that the government presently works with 170 different races. A lot more than they are willing to reveal. On top of that, earth itself is visited every year by plus-minus 3,000 different races. A lot of them would never come again. They just travel around the universe doing their learning. However, the genetic experiments in the underground bases are done in conjunction with our secret government, working in cooperation with the secret governments of Russia. The Russian genetic research center, I have heard, is on an island north of the Northern Arctic Circle. Close to the Bering Straits, very conveniently close to Alaska, and quite probably connected with an underground, gravity-levitated tube shuttle in the United States secret underground cross-continental tube shuttle system.

And many other countries take part in this research in the same vein as neutral countries like Sweden or pacifistic Japan, which took part in the mind-control research twenty years earlier, as it was revealed in the mind control conspiracy papers. But my biggest suspicion is, in spite of the existence of plenty of little gray races around the universe, on top of that, the genetic knowledge of the secret government and of the Illuminati has reached such a level. In my research I have discovered that what H.G. Wells wrote in his book "The Island of Dr. Moreau" was not science-fiction but was an account of the first genetic research on the planet done almost a century ago. And the first cross-breeding of humans and animals.

I have talked personally to a famous producer in Los Angeles who saw himself a German documentary film from the concentration camps. Cross breeds between humans and animals—living, walking, breathing cross-breeds. A horrific film about the genetic research program of a foundation in Germany. The goal of the Germans was to create the Master Race, which was the same goal as the Illuminati Nazis behind them. Nazi Germany, fascist Italy, Bolshevik Russia—these were all creations of the global secret Illuminati government. They are trying out different modes of social management.

The rumor is that even Orwell's "1984" is not a prophetic warning of what may happen, but another of the Illuminati's blueprints for possible management of our planet. It is extremely high on their agenda. Basically higher than the necessity to eliminate the excess population and to bring down the population. It's to create the new Super Race, and this genetic research has been going on for more than a hundred years. From the German concentration camps, where they did it on thousands of inmates, they moved the whole genetic research to the Germans' south polar colony. It's a huge polar colony. The rumor goes that it has a population of close to a million. Probably even more.

A new genetically engineered type of Super Man, the tall, blonde, blue-eyed Nordics. Which we funnily enough have seen present in so many of the little gray abductions scenarios as the "string-pullers" of these scenarios. The grays are given the orders. Even from the film "Fire In The Sky" by Travis Walton, it was greatly distorted, the whole story, and only in the old "UFOs Are Real" documentary do we see most of the real story. Where Travis meets this tall, blonde, blue-eyed Nordic, who probably speaks English with a heavy German accent. That's why they are not allowed to speak.

My suspicion is that the little grays, or some of them, are nothing more than genetically engineered clones, biological robots, cyborgs, that are used to do the abductions on a grander, national scale. On all the population of the United States. When major researchers—I don't want to name names—claim that it's a global phenomenon, it's a total lie. There are no abductions in Africa, because nobody is interested in the genes of the black race to be included in the new, future, Nordic-type, blonde Super Race.

No abductions in Asia for the same reason. No abductions even in the Slavic countries where I come from because the Illuminati have long since decided that even the Slavs are not good enough or "white" enough to make it into the Nordic race. What Hitler planned to do with the Slavs was to turn them into the fertilizer for the agricultural field of the Thousand Year Reich. It's not much different than the abduction policy in Eastern Europe. There are no abductions in Eastern Europe. Period.

In Russia, they don't even have a word for abduction. On the contrary, Russian contacts with aliens are totally on the positive side. These are healing, teaching, and joy-riding contacts. This is my feeling, that basically a lot of what is going on in the little gray abduction scenario is run by the government. And the little grays, as biological robots, are conveniently used, because if you have government scientists in white smocks or military personnel abducting these people, and if we end up with anywhere from 200,000 to 400,000 missing children a year—just call the milk carton 800 number on the missing kids and try to get some information from the lady on how many of them are missing a year.

My first and last call yielded a 200,000 number yesterday by the lady. I've heard a rumor as high as 400,000 a year. Where do these children go? Some of them become genetic fodder in these ugly underground Frankenstein factories. A lot of them are probably taken to the Evacuation and Survival Colonies. To the South Pole, to the moon, Mars and beyond. And to many other places.

But my feeling is that everything that is "revealed" to us by the major researchers in the field is everything but the truth. It's a cleverly crafted smoke screen which covers up the true story behind it.

The Hybrid Exercise

Kirkwood: I've been close to one experience of a hybrid exercise, in I think it was 1977, when they brought out the film "Close Encounters Of The Third Kind." The film was premiered in Las Vegas. They had asked Dr. Allen Hynek, who at that time had some of the most important credentials involved in the UFO study. They had asked him to come to Las Vegas to address the opening night audience. Unfortunately, his calendar wouldn't permit it. And in turn he contacted me in Los Angeles and he asked if I would do him a favor, if I could pinch hit for him and go to Las Vegas that evening and address the audience. I said, yes, I could handle it for him.

He said, "Fine, I'll put you in touch with a fellow named Gene Marvin in Las Vegas." And Gene Marvin was a local television personality. He had a show that he broadcast out of Las Vegas on numerous subjects, a great area of interest, not just UFOs. Anyway, we became friends and I visited with him in Vegas a number of times, and likewise when he came to Los Angeles on industry business.

And one day, probably about eight to ten months after I'd met him, he called and said, "Mel, you and I have worked a lot of this stuff, but I've got a matter going on right now that's curling my hair. How soon can you get over to Las Vegas?" I said, "Oh, a week or ten days?" He said, "All right, fine, let me know. I want to set up an appointment for you to listen to a couple of people."

I went over there and he introduced me to a young, 28- to 29-year-old, sheriff's deputy and his wife. And I listened to his story. The incident that the deputy referred to had taken place about a year and a half before. And on a given evening, he had to serve some papers at the state line. He went out there, and he accomplished that task. He was driving back toward Las Vegas—and those of you who have driven that road, which is Route 15—it's pretty much a lonely, straight, desolate piece of highway.

It was nearing midnight at the time, he said, and as he drove along his attention was drawn to a bright, large, pulsing light some miles north of the highway. And he attempted to satisfy his curiosity by saying to himself, "Well, it's the light of a locomotive." But, no, that didn't work. "Oh, it's a helicopter zone. There are military operations in the area." Anyway, his curiosity grew and he decided to take it upon himself to have a closer look.

He took the next paved road to the north, and as he did so, he realized that the object was moving slowly but not parallel to his line of traffic. It was moving towards the southwest. As a result, he took a dirt surface road and traveled west bound to intercept the line of travel of the object. He said he proceeded to a point where he could no longer see it through the windshield. At that time he stopped the car. He got out with his flashlight, and he's looking around at a typical Nevada night sky with a million stars. And no object.

He said he was standing there feeling kind of foolish. "Oh, boy, was this a stupid thing to do, drive all the way out here on this wild goose chase." Then he said about that moment, he could feel the hair on the back of his neck going up. He turned around, and the object was about 200 to 300 feet away from him on the ground. He was literally transfixed. Things were going from bad to worse.

He could see two forms coming toward him. They were very slender and they didn't even seem to walk on the ground. They seemed to float about six inches above the ground. What he described today we would identify as a typical gray, or two of them. He said there was no evidence of body hair. There were no ears, just openings. No nose, just openings. A narrow slit for a mouth. He said they were communicating apparently between each other in humming sounds. They were discussing what they should do with him.

The deputy was transfixed. He said he could not move. He said at that point they both took him by one arm apiece, lifted him up with little effort, and took him back into the object. They then put him into a rather small room and he said that whereas there were never any words exchanged, there was never any verbal communication, he said he had no problem in understanding what they wanted.

In this case, they wanted him to disrobe. They wanted him to take his clothes off. And he said he would be damned. He said if this were his last night on earth, he wasn't going to go along with it. And he successfully, for the moment, fought them off. They then left him in this chamber, and a minute or so later, five of them came back. And at that point, there was no longer any discussion. As you will, they just stripped him.

He said they then placed him on a gurney and they rolled him around what was obviously a circular hallway and into a large room where he said there was an apparatus which the closest thing he could identify it with was an X-ray machine. He said he could see on the wall of this thing, what he would call a screen. They moved this machine over him, and he could see his skeletal outline, his vital organs, his circulatory system.

And this man is in terror. He really believes that these are his last hours. He said they took samples of his hair, scraped his tongue and his teeth, they took skin samples, they drew blood, urine, and fecal samples and semen samples. He said one approached him with a needle that must have been about fourteen inches long. And he said he understood the critter to say, "We're sorry for the discomfort. But what we must do, we must do." They then placed this needle into his naval, and he understood them to say, "At this point in time, we are altering your genetic structure."

Shortly afterwards, they completed their orders or whatever you might call it. They placed him outside still naked and threw his clothes out and his flashlight. He scooped everything up and ran as fast as he could. He said it became apparent that they had actually gone somewhere. He had no idea where, because when they picked him up, the object was 200 to 300 feet from the car, and when they let him out, he said the car was closer to a half mile away.

He got dressed and he arrived at the car. He noticed by the clock radio that two hours and ten minutes had gone by. He then proceeded to drive back to the sheriff's station in Las Vegas. In route, he decided that his job was tough enough as it was and that he was never ever going to tell anybody anything about this. He was just going to let it go away with time.

There was one problem, however. He discovered in the ensuing days that he had a headache. A head cracker that wouldn't go away. Day and night. He took all the shelf remedies, and they didn't have any effect. He finally contacted a doctor, and the doctor performed a physical. The doctor examined him, and he had a lot of questions about these marks on his body. He made up answers like, "I burned myself at the barbecue" or things like this. The doctor said, "Well, you're in excellent health. I can't find any physiological explanation for your headaches. I'm sorry I couldn't help you anymore." And that's it. And he left. But the headache didn't.

Several more weeks went by with the headache, and he contacted a second doctor, thinking there must be something that was causing this. The second doctor examined him, and with similar questions as to what are these marks about and how did this happen, and also pronounced him fit. He said, however, there was some hope in a technique. He said that he worked with a clinical hypnotist from UCLA, and they had discovered through regressive hypnosis sometimes the sources of trauma, many times going back to childhood, that created the stress situation. And the individual not being able to rationalize or reasoning the event away, can harbor it and it had become a subconscious stress source and i.e., the headache source.

And having discovered that, it succeeded many times in relieving the stress/headache condition. Of course, the sheriff wasn't about to allow this. Weeks went by and the headaches persisted. He finally gave in and he called the doctor and said, "I don't care what it takes, let's make that appointment with that psychiatrist." He lucked out. This woman psychiatrist at UCLA had at that time studied 68 abduction cases. So this was not virgin territory to her. It was not fresh ground.

Under hypnosis, of course the event came to the surface. Not only that, but being a law enforcement officer, his observational abilities were better than average. He was a keen observer. And he gave such detail, notations and testimony of the object and the critters and the interior, the instrumentation, and other things. But the woman, on her own, brought in a professional artist-type of person who does police renderings for suspects. Over a period of time, the artist produced 36 illustrations of what this man was describing.

In the meantime, he had what he thought was some good news. One day his wife says, "Honey, guess what? We're going to be a family! I'm pregnant!" Oh, boy, he thought, maybe some normalcy back into my life. The wife went over term. At ten and a half months, the doctors decided to induce labor. She was taken to Presbyterian Hospital in Las Vegas and the doctors delivered the child by Cesarean Section. The child was identical to the aliens.

The child lived four and a half hours. The vital organs were undeveloped and misplaced. As this man told this story to me, I turned to Gene and said, "Gene, have you talked to these doctors? Have you interviewed these doctors?" He said, "No, I haven't." I said, "Well, look, I'm in Las Vegas now. Let's go. I mean, this is of vital importance to this event." So we made it to the hospital, and both doctors were on duty. We were discussing it with them in the hallway, at which time they vehemently denied that the event ever happened. "We don't know what you're talking about. This is absolute nonsense. This is somebody's pipe dream. I don't care who the testimony's coming from, it's just too bizarre."

At that point, whether by bluff or serious intent, Gene Marvin lowered the beam on them. He said, "Doctors, one moment. We have enough documented evidence to place this deputy and his wife in this hospital on this date, and the evidence that you delivered a child from this woman at that time. It is enough evidence that I will have you all over Channel such-and-such News at ten o'clock tonight. It's up to you." And they said, "Let's step into the office."

They brought out the autopsy report, photographs of the child, and the other data that they had. It was an actual event. Now, no matter how you look at it, this is a very cruel invasion of a people. It's one thing to deal with the problems that mankind visit on each other. It's another thing to attempt to deal with something we have no control over. At least not known to me.

Collier's Rebuttal To Terziski

Collier: I would just like to add, in less than twenty words, the aliens, the grays, are not clones. Some of them are clones, but they are an alien race. If the Germans were behind this, or the humans, that would be one thing. We would be lucky if that were the case. But it isn't the case. We have real problems here. We have different races that are coming here that have completely different agendas. They don't really give a damn about us because they see how we treat each other, and their attitude is "What's their value outside of genetic material?"

They also see us killing ourselves and destroying our environment. So basically they figure that we're going to go anyway, so what's the point? So, Vladimir, I wish I could agree with you, but that just simply isn't my experience or my reality.

Collier And The Andromedans

Collier: The Andromedans have said, early in the 1950s, that the grays gave certain scientists in our government information regarding what we were doing to the planet. Not only that, but the Pleidadians themselves and a group from Sirius A had also told our scientists in their limited contacts what we were doing to our planet with industry. And I know there are some people who think that the environmental situation is not real, that they're going to try to create a religion out of it. Well, the fact is the earth is really sick, and it's a lot sicker than we've been led to think.

And according to the Andromedans, if we don't change what we're doing by the year 2001, I mean really start making some changes, not only on a physical level but a conscious level, as it stands right now, we have forty-one years of oxygen left in the environment. For the human species to exist, we need fifteen percent oxygen in the atmosphere. Right now, we have less than eighteen. And I'm correct as hell. Go out there and prove me wrong. I dare you. I dare you to go out and research this and prove me wrong.

Thirty-eight hundred years ago, the oxygen content was thirty-eight percent. That's why people lived to be hundreds and hundreds of years old. There was no disease. There was nothing. The reason that we have the cancers and all the other diseases that we have is because we have successfully been destroying our environment, or allowing it to happen. And private industry, hiring thugs like our government, who is totally under control by these big businesses, to police them. So it's like the fox watching the chicken coop. That's exactly what we've done. We're going to pay for it unless we start making some changes right away.

Alternative Three is a reality. There was a face on Mars. Actually, part of it still exists. It was called Adam and Eve. It was invaded in March of 1989, which is the photographs that this gentleman here held up. That's why our satellites, the Russian and the American satellites, have been shot down. Because they don't want us to know what's going on out there. The World Government had plans to move there and allow the earth to just die out. Well, now they have a problem. Now they can't get to Mars because they were double-crossed again. Which is their just come-uppings.

So instead of taking all of this energy, and doing something then about healing the planet, this elite, this conspiratorial group, decided they will create a whole new race, a whole new world, and just basically hand pick who it is they want. And all I can tell you is this: From what I've learned from the Andromedans, the only personnel on the moon were Aryan by birth. Period. They're Aryans. There's no blacks. There's no Hispanics. Only Aryans.

And I haven't pursued it because I already knew what that meant. So we have a real genuine mess on our hands. And the bottom line is, it's going to come down to all of us taking responsibility and making the changes. Don't look for a savior to save you. Don't look for Scotty to beam you up. It isn't going to happen. We have to make the changes. Because you don't evolve if somebody comes down and fixes your problems. You only go out and recreate it. Which is what we've done over and over and over again.

Wendy Wallace

Wallace: Just a little comment on that. Andrew Tomby is a physicist, and I went to one of his seminars about eight years ago. At that point, he was interested in measuring the ozone. As a matter of fact, he was the one who discovered that NASA had the computers set to reject as garbage anything over three percent depletion. At that point, eight years ago, he said that within fifteen to twenty years, the ozone would be depleted at the rate it was going at the time. The ozone would be depleted to about twelve or fifteen percent.

At that level of depletion, what happens is that all the vital plankton will die. They're already mutating and dying in many areas of the ocean. We're probably very close to that ten, eleven, twelve percent. What's interesting, too, about this is that, again, we go back to the Bible. And right around what would look like to be the year 2002, in the vial judgments, it says that the sun is given power to scorch the earth. I mean, I agree with you so totally. All you have to do is go out and stand in the sun to know that the planet's sick. You know, this whole idea of saying it's all just a farce. Please. Stand in the sun at noonday.

Terziski Dissents

Terziski: I would present a very quick dissenting opinion. As a physicist, I have a feeling that this planet is grossly under-populated. And I cannot help getting this feeling. I've taken one of the longest possible air routes from Moscow, flying over nine time zones. There are two more time zones to the eastern most part of Russia, and two more from Moscow to the west, also. Anyway, nine hours of flight. Not a single city underneath. Not a single village. Not a single road. Not a single railroad. Not a single electrical transmission line. Not a single hint that man exists on this planet.

Endless Siberian forests. Cold, of course, but not much colder than the northern Canadian towns. I have a suspicion that what we see on "Seaquest" is not science-fiction, but it is the history of the Illuminated exploration of the underwater world. I've heard stories that there are huge cities underwater on probably a dozen major locations. The biggest one is under the Bermuda Triangle, and all these freak physical phenomena are nothing more—of course it is a major vortex point on the planet—but I think the biggest players in the Bermuda equation are these constant, never-ending experiments with these new physical theories and gadgets that bring these freak phenomena to the surface.

On the energy crisis, I could talk for a day on these new technologies that are being used by the secret societies for 130 years. From the free energy, anti-gravity dirigibles of the 1860s and 1870s, to the free energy sources that Tesla built in the late 19th and early 20th century. To the free energy Hans Koler converters that were powering these incredible German inventions. On and on and on. Even careful reading of official Navy publications between the lines reveal that the Navy is busily working on 20,000 to 50,000 horsepower free energy propulsion units for the Navy ships. They're looking for subcontractor companies to build these free energy propulsion units that would not use nuclear energy, that would not use oil and that would not use coal. So what else is left for the American Navy? Rowing power? Or wind power? Obviously, this is free energy.

Number three, destruction of the environment. I heard several stories about the jerk who came with a nasty, vicious invention—a transmutational radiation transmitter, a beam that transmutes radioactive matter into non-radioactive just by sending a beam like you would shine with a projector. Mounting many such projectors on airplanes flying around Chernobyl would clean all of that piece of Ukraine in a month, maybe five months, big deal. All of the radiation around American plants, because of which the cattle mutilations are done to measure the advancement of that radiation into the food chain through the animal and into the human chain eventually, can be dealt with in the same way.

Not only that, but that jerk realized that if you shine this radiation at the tip of a nuclear missile, it transmutes the fissionable material inside and it ceases to be able to explode anymore. So, it's natural that this guy and his invention disappeared, never to be heard of again, because he would have pulled the carpet out from under these very cozy arrangement of the Mickey Mouse Cold War and the nuclear threat from the Russians that was needed to keep the secrecy of these projects going on. And, behind the scenes to work on all these secret projects on the moon, underwater and elsewhere.

The ozone hole, I'm saying as a physicist, it's a total hoax. There has never been a major paper on the ozone connection to the chloral fluorocarbons. Actually, a huge volcano on the South Pole, 115 miles upwind from the major measuring place for the ozone depletion, spews out more chlorine compounds, maybe a hundred times more than all the other chloral fluorocarbons around the world. Heating the chloral fluorocarbon manufacturing chain, the chloral fluorocarbons are the major refrigeration unit. That will make refrigerators in the Third World cost ten times as much as before.

And hitting the Third World in their weakest point, namely preservation of food from rotting, would bring deaths into tens of millions, maybe even hundreds of millions, just by increased rotting of the food. And on and on and on. I have a feeling that all of the destruction of the environment, if these free energy technologies, if these free transmutational technologies are brought to the surface, it can be taken care of in about a month or so. I'm even getting information that what we see on "Star Trek, The Next Generation" namely manifesting materialized matter—food or other products—is also technology that has been developed here by the secret societies.

I know from alien reports that on nearby planets how they produce their flying saucers. They have an oyster shell, open like a shell, and there comes a dump truck and pours garbage, dirt, junk, anything inside and the shell closes. You hear some funny, suspicious noises and then the shell vibrates. And then the thing opens and you have a gleaming saucer inside. It is a decomposition and transmutational unit where all this junk is broken into elementary particles that are rebuilt into whatever you want to make. It's like a copy machine for products, like if I had a paper copier.

Such technologies exist. But these would be the most politically incorrect technologies to be brought into our world because they would pull the pin from this carefully crafted scenario of the overpopulation. The overpopulation myth and hoax is needed in order to explain why we have to begin the reduction of the population. And when this becomes necessary, this reduction begins not from the First World, not from the Second, but from the blacks in Africa, from the yellows in Asia. This is my feeling, that they need the overpopulation hoax to explain why they have to start cutting off from these unwanted races. To bring a one-race planet, a New World Order.

It's an excellent thing. It's a great thing. The moment it happens on our planet, all wars cease. You have one language, one currency, one race, one everything. But on other planets, it happens the humane way. On other planets, through slow intermarriage and interbreeding and mixing. On our planet, our secret societies have decided to give it a crash course, physically eliminating the other races and stressing one of the white races, the Nordic race, as the one to remain.

More From The Andromedans And Collier

Collier: I would just like to make two comments on that. Number one, according to the Andromedans, we could easily support a population of eleven billion. Easily, if we had our act together. Number two, the idea that we need just one race and that all wars stop and everything else will come to bliss is just crap. The best example I can give you is the Pleideian culture themselves, they've had more civil wars there than we could ever think to have. And it's just one race and one language. They have different political views. So the point is, it doesn't matter what color we are. It doesn't matter what religion we are. Or what language we speak. We can all learn to live together. Period.

Wallace Speaks On Global 2000

Wallace: The Global 2000 Plan that wants half of us dead under the Club of Rome and the Carter administration—their projections are that they want half of the world's population

Space Shuttle to put it on and send it up there. They're building something up in outer space, a space station. Well, now we know they are. It's public knowledge.

But the point I'm making is that here in New Mexico they have something called a "bio-sphere." They were trying to figure out how to enclose humans inside of its own ecological system and see if they could get everything to work like it normally does on the earth in that very enclosed area or bio-sphere. Why is the question. And of course it didn't work too well. However, there was a movie made, and if you understand what Hollywood is all about, Hollywood and motion pictures tell you three things. They tell you what they've already done, what they're doing now, or what they're getting ready to do.

And if you go back a few years ago, Hollywood made a movie called "Silent Running." And I think that's just what the masters are doing. They're getting ready to run, but they're keeping it silent. It's a silent running. They're getting ready to get out of here. And they're going to take a bus. It's called a shuttle. They're going to take a bus out of town. They want a bio-sphere up there so they can live. And if you remember the James Bond movies, because Ian Fleming was privy to all the things going on in MI-5 and MI-6. And the James Bond movie "Moonraker," where the Space Shuttle was involved in a space station which was Stealth and hidden from radar, and they took young people up there to procreate the new human race, and in the movie, they dropped something like 37 canisters the mad scientist, Drac was his name, and I think that was a very Promethean name, it means something, but they dropped down 37 canisters of the most highly toxic poison to kill off the human race because they had their young people on the space station.

When the Space Shuttle Challenger blew up out there, they cordoned off the Atlantic Ocean and sent out the Navy or whatever to pick up the pieces. "The L.A. Times" had a profoundly incredible article in the paper. They said the reason why the military and the government sealed off the Atlantic Ocean is because there were 37 canisters of the most highly toxic poison ever developed on the earth in the Space Shuttle, and that's what they were trying to retrieve. If any one of them ever broke—they were sealed in case of a problem—but if any one of them broke under pressure in the ocean, it would kill all things in the ocean period. In all oceans. That's how totally toxic one canister could be.

When I read that I thought that's what's in the James Bond movie. That's what was in "Moonraker," that there were 37 canisters of the most toxic poison. And you turn around and find out in "The L.A. Times" that that's exactly what was on the Space Shuttle. It's an incredible story.

But getting back to the original point of what would they do—I think they know what's coming on the earth. Because they have an inside track on what's going on. I think they're getting ready to leave here in the event that something happens and the people wake up, and there's a mess of revolutionary movement in the world against that. They'll just quietly take their families and go on out there to the space station. And let the earth go its own way. So I think they're planning something. I think they're getting ready to run and they're keeping it silent.

You Will Curse Your God

Wallace: I would agree that's very likely, however, there are going to be foiled again. There's a verse I was just looking for, it's in Job, about how they put their faith in that web and how that faith will fail them. There's another verse that says that in the End Times, "You will curse your God and look upward for salvation." That sort of thing. You look down into the earth, tunnel under it, and stay safe there. And all you can see is darkness relating to further darkness.

And I think that's what's going to happen to these dudes. They're all going to be looking for rocks to hide under during that sixth seal.

Evacuation And Survival

Terziski: I would very quickly say several words about the evacuation and survival scenarios. I think that it is a multi-pronged strategy that has been developed to cover many different ways of making sure that the hierarchical elite would survive. The Alternative Two is a massive underground city-sized bases all over the United States connected with a tube shuttle. All over the Soviet Union, connected with a tube shuttle through the Bering Strait. All over South America. All of them connected. That one I know. I wouldn't be amazed if the South American system is connected to the North American.

What the Pleidians did about 200,000 years ago on this planet, connecting with giant spelunker type tunnels, the whole continent with their underground bases. Sometimes even these same old tunnels are used into this massive system. A friend of mine called a radio program where a university professor was talking about a revolution going on right under our feet. And that professor gave him a 1-800 number of the underground developers association of the city of Kansas. This guy called that association, posing as an enthusiastic proponent of the underground evacuation scenario.

And the enthusiastic guy on the other side sent him a glossy brochure about the ten-member sites of these underground shelters under the city of Kansas alone. You look at this glossy color pamphlet and you see underground shopping malls the size of a normal above-ground shopping mall. You don't see the end of it on the photograph. An underground convention center the size of the L.A. Convention center. Underground three-lane freeways. Underground railroads. Storage facilities. Computer rooms. The whole nine yards necessary for an autonomous underground economy to exist under the city of Kansas.

And they say "member sites," which means there are many other known members, private or secret societies sites. This is only under one American city. Probably a similar picture exists under every American city. That is Alternative Two.

Alternative Three is the moon, Mars, and other evacuational survival bases. I have a deep suspicion that what we see on "Star Trek," the new spin-off series, the "Deep Space" and "Babylon Five" is nothing more than just that. The Deep Space colonies are part of the Illuminated Empire. I've heard that in spite of the fact that they've been doing time machine experiments for more than a hundred years, Professor H.O. Schuman was the genius behind the German time machine effort.

The first gyroscopic time machine was built in 1922 by the Brill Secret Research Society in Germany with the personal calligraphic signature of Professor Schuman. Despite their time machine experiments for more than a hundred years, they have been creating an artificial wall around the earth. 2011, which they cannot penetrate. And they desperately need to do that to figure out how we are going to do in the future. Are they still going to be the rulers of the planet or what?

And not knowing what is coming, what is in store for them, they have made sure that they have plenty of evacuational survival options. I even have a suspicion that what we have seen in some of the science-fiction films is probably true.

I have the feeling that the secret government has either gained access to one of these realities, or created their own, if we read carefully. And as a physicist, I'm very interested in the physics of these phenomena. Some alien revelations talk about the possibility of creating an artificial reality through the spreading of generations stations along the normal points of the DEW line. Basically creating their own reality, and powering it by energy siphoned off the virtually limitless energy of the planet.

A lot of the missing scientists and children have been moved, not into underground bases and not into the South Pole colony that the Germans use, but into another totally different reality. The more time goes by, the more proof I get that this may be the case. So if eventually the Final Judgment as revealed by the Bible comes—and another interesting book where I found incredible information about these questions of the highest conspiracies in the universe, and this is not the only one. There are very many important revelatory sources. But in the book it says simply that Lucifer's rebellion has not been adjudicated, but it is about to be adjudicated.

And when that happens, probably the exploration opening and colonization of a parallel reality is a needed face-saving move by the Lucifer presence on the planet. As by the independent angelic presence on the planet. I don't want to start too much Christian Fundamentalist talk here. So, okay, let's leave this reality for the forces of the Trinity, if they ever come. And we get the other reality for our experiments. We can do there whatever we want. Procreate with humans and animals, the new Superman, the Brave New World, the New World Order, the Thousand Year Reich. We can have everything we want.

This is my suspicion. That's all I have to say.

Jordan Maxwell On The Dollar Bill

Maxwell: I have to be leaving soon, but there was a point I did want to bring up with the audience. In relation to occult symbolism, I have been involved in that kind of research for many years. I think it's something interesting that I'd like for you to know. When you hear so much talk about the symbolism on the dollar bill, and it's connection with secret societies, in particular of course is the pyramid with the all-seeing eye. And above it the words "Annuit Coeptis," which basically means, "Our enterprise is now a success," or "Our project has been crowned a success." The project itself is "Novus Ordo Seclorum," which is "The New Order of the World."

The pyramid with the all-seeing eye is a very interesting symbol, and there has been much written about it. However, when you look in the Book of Psalms in the Old Testament, in Psalms the messiah is once referred to—the messiah, not Jesus—is referred to as the chief cornerstone the builders rejected. Then twice in the New Testament, Jesus is referred to as the chief cornerstone that the builders rejected. The word "chief cornerstone" in the New Testament is a Greek word which corresponds directly with the Hebrew word in the Old Testament. The word "chief cornerstone," which Jesus is referred to as and the messiah is referred to as, means in the language "a triangle which sits on top of a pyramid."

That's what the word "chief cornerstone" means. It's a pyramidal, a triangle sitting on top of a pyramid. And so when you understand that the messiah or the messianic concept is connected to a coming new order, a coming new kingdom—it's a very important study when you get into the words, the terminology.

There is a very good reason why the messiah is referred to as the chief cornerstone. It has to do with Egypt. It has to do with the pyramids. And it's a very exciting study. I have a lot of that on a two-hour video, which, if you're interested in occultism and mystical symbols and occult symbols, all of that kind of thing. It's a very important subject. It has to do with Christianity, the Bible, secret societies, and the fraternal orders that are preparing a new kingdom for us, a New World Order.

The Grays Are Doomed To Extinction

Collier: I wanted to answer the question asked about the grays. From the Andromedans, the grays are doomed to extinction. It's just their time to go. Other things will happen to them. Basically, what they'll do is get as much genetic material as they can and then they'll try to leave the earth. But there are forces that are out there that simply aren't going to let them go traipsing around the universe and continue to do what they're doing here.

There is a political force, a governmental force, that we have in our galaxy. Many others have it. They know the difference between right and wrong. And those forces that have been doing things to us, they've also been doing it to 21 other systems in our galaxy. Their day is coming. It is definitely coming. The only real threat that we have in our galaxy are the Alpha Draconans. Nobody knows what to do with them, because we haven't been able to do it yet.

They're the ultimate warriors. They're the bullies. They can't force them to move into the light. But there are other things that are going on in the universe as the universe itself is evolving to higher and higher levels and higher dimensions, that the essence we know as God will deal with that directly in her own way. Thank you.

Bridget Woundenberg

Woundenberg: First of all, I'd like to clarify something that was said earlier. I had made a statement when I first came in that the government is very powerful. I wanted to get it said that I guess I was misconstrued. I had not said at all that they're more powerful, and I wanted to clarify by saying that I don't believe they are. I believe that we have the ability to respond to what we are dealing with here.

And we need to wake up and we need to learn how to respond and that's what our responsibility is. I've heard it said that this is more or less like an experiment here and we're laying in the petrie dish. All I can say is we need to wake up and to respond to what we're being challenged with and we need to go into ourselves. Because if there's a God or if there's a hierarchical power, that's where we're going to find it. We're not going to find it anywhere else. And that's where we're going to find the ability to deal with what our options are here.

And as I've heard again and again through this whole panel, is that we are going through an evolutionary change. And each one of us needs to figure out what that means for us. I don't think we are being faced with a dead-end situation. I think there's hope for us. I don't think that we are being controlled. I think that there are people or beings or entities or forces that would like to, but I think that we have an option here. We just need to search out what that is for each of us. Thank you.

Another Audience Question

Question From Audience Member: From attending lots of expos, and I was involved in the FTA bill, and lots of conferences—I'm so used to coming to these conferences and hearing facts and information and how bad this is. And this fine. This is good. I want to hear this. But I'm finding that what I want to start hearing is strategies and ideas and questions something like, "If we have a big family of light across the planet and there's a lot of people who are waking up, does everyone on the panel feel that this is bad and we just have to live with how bad it is? Are the bad scenarios going to come up?" I mean, I'm not hearing anything, except little bits and pieces, and I'd like to hear any possible strategies that we as a family of light beings could get together. What can we do? We have great power. I'm just commenting on the lack of focus on "What can we do?" (Applause.)

In fact, I'm feeling more like I'd like to organize a conference that's oriented toward having brainstorming sessions. I want to hear every person's ideas as to what can we create? Now we have a foundation of what the truth is, what's going on and how bad it is, and I believe that we have something brilliant here. If we all got together, we might come up with something phenomenal. So I'd like to ask anybody on the panel, given an ideal picture and an ideal reality where we all come together, what can we do? What are some of the possible scenarios that could change this whole thing?

The Panel Responds

Terziski: Let this be the second part of the panel, the creative part. And I really thank you for putting an end to the first part.

Wallace: I'll just point out the new perspective again. That's exactly the question they were addressing at the Tower of Babel. Is how do we exalt ourselves? How do we get together and fix this thing. And God said, "You ain't gonna." It's the same story this time. It has to do with man's delusion that we are essentially good. What it says here is, "The heart is deceitful above all things and desperately wicked. Who can know it?" And that's our problem.

We're going to mess it up once again. And Christ is returning. If you want a happy ending, be on His side when He comes. It's going to be phenomenal.

Collier: I have maybe two things to say. Number one, it starts on an individual basis. It starts with individual consciousness. And what I would suggest is that starting tomorrow morning, every single one of you, when you wake up, just pretend that everybody can read your mind. That whatever thoughts you have inside your head, everybody else can see it. Because if you do that, then every day you have to be real. You've got to really be who you really are and stop pretending to be something you're not or what you think you might be.

The other thing is, on one of my contacts as I was getting off the craft, I was very upset. I didn't want to come back here. And I turned and looked at one of the Andromedans, and he looked at me and he said, "The love that you withhold is the pain that you carry." What do you think about that? (Applause)

Wallace: One quickie on that, from a different Bible, the Satanist Bible. One of the tenets of the Satanist Bible is, "Say to yourself in your heart, 'I am my own redeemer.'"

Terziski: This is an incredible discussion. We're just getting into the heathenist perspective. Well, I have been many times afraid. I remember when I first talked about German saucers at a 1991 conference in Tucson, it was so quiet in the room that you could hear a pin drop. And all the government agents were sitting at the front edge of their chairs. You could feel their bodies forward, trying not to miss a word of what was being said.

I personally believe that there is a higher entity in the universe taking care of us all. A creator and a universal Father. I pray to that entity all the time. I pray for protection. I go to a conference and I pray that my slides won't get stolen because they are the only ones. I pray that the videos won't disappear and that nothing will break down and so on. I've even had very comical dreams of being abducted by little grays, which are probably true. Like a lot of researchers, if you have dreams of being abducted, you're probably abducted.

There was a ball of light that came streaking down into my kitchen and hid in the space between the wall and the refrigerator. Then went down to the floor, crawled under the refrigerator. And funnily enough, there was a carpet in that dream in the kitchen. So I saw kind of a little bulbous protrusion under the carpet crawling towards me. And it occurred to me that this is a little gray disguised under my carpet that is coming to abduct me. And even in the dream, I prayed to Christ and that was it. That was the end. I've had several such dreams, and even inside my dream, I would pray to something, whatever it is, and the thing would stop immediately.

On a social level, I think that all of us, if we believe in a positive outcome, we can bring such an outcome. The thought-forms of today literally shape our future. A lot of metaphysical researchers have pointed to that, as have alien contactees. If we believe that an End of the World will come, we are all going to end at Armageddon. If we believe that there will be an alien race who will come and pick us up off the planet before that end, then that's probably exactly where we're going to end up, in a scenario where there will be a massive lift-off off the planet.

If we believe that it will be a rosy, smooth transition to a New Age environment, maybe that's where we're going to end up. All of us. I have a nagging suspicion that probably the reality we live in is a little bit more complicated than it has been revealed to us in all of these revelations. That probably it is a multiple, parallel reality that exists with different timelines, with different outcomes. Each of us who believes that the Judgment Days of the End will come are going to end exactly in these Judgment Days. And those who have been true believers will be saved. It is a very "multiple" and schizophrenic viewpoint, paradigm, of the world. I just have a feeling that the universe is a lot more complicated than any one of us believes it is.

Finally, I do not channel. I am not a contactee. I get all my information from literary sources. One of the most interesting sources for conspiratorial information is a little booklet published by Rudolph Steiner in Switzerland. He was obviously contacted by and was channeling the White Brotherhood, and that is why Hitler hated his guts. He was chased out and I think he was killed eventually. And in that book, he's talking about the incarnation of Prime Movers that do not belong to the Trinity.

According to Steiner, Lucifer incarnated 2,000 years before Christ in ancient Babylon. That's why Babylon is such a catch phrase for the New World Government. "Babylon Five," "Star Trek, The Next Generation," maybe these things are not coincidences. Again, according to Steiner, the next incarnation that is going to happen around the year 2000 is of even a darker nature than is associated with the White side of the Force. All the German secret societies were under the spell of the Black Magic Star, which was struggling for control of the planet. But I think that we all, with our positive powers, can change that.

Another Audience Question

Question from audience member: First of all, in the words of George Carlin, the planet's not in any danger. We're in danger of not being able to live on the planet, but the planet itself is not going to have any problems. If you'll look around the planet, I believe that blue-green algae does real well in high UV light. Blue-green algae is what we're seeding Venus with to make it habitable. The blue-green algae will cause an increase in the oxygen count in the atmosphere and so on. So some of the things that are being presented in terms of the human destruction that comes from being overpopulated I think are kind of being exaggerated here.

If you take a look at the strength of mankind, if there is a strength of mankind that you want to identify, historically, has been one thing and one thing only: the adaptability to the given challenge. I don't believe for one second that if I had a few half-ways reasonable people who had a head on their shoulders that we couldn't solve a problem with the tremendous amount of resources that we've got to work with. It seems a lot more reasonable to fix what you're on, dig a hole in it, seal the hole or something instead of send a spacecraft out to escape from it.

You have no resources with a spacecraft out there. That doesn't mean I don't want to explore the stars. I do, but I find it a little bit odd that someone would put a trillion dollars into putting up some frail "Moonraker" trip when they could have dug a hole on the planet and rigged the surface to explode when they got tired of everybody. It would just be a lot easier to keep it on the planet if we had a problem.

As I look down through history, and this is where my question's coming from, I see consistently where a problem is, just like the people in this room can't get together and agree on what should be done, the people in total on the planet are kept pointed in other directions. The whole point of legislating that some by race, by sex, by creed, whatever it is, people are a minority, and they ought to be given special treatment to be sure they'll be elevated but are now going to be hated by everyone else because now they're elevated above them, is to cause prejudice.

Why do we have to fight each other? Thanks to the government helping us end prejudice, instead of fighting the real problem, which looks a lot more like the government than it does your local different race, different sex, different creeds. I'd like to know how, and this is my question, and I'm not looking for religious answers, I'm looking for possibilities, how is that if I look back through history and I look at the works of Sitchin and people who have analyzed the Bible and the Kabala, why is it that consistently through history we've run around the periphery of all the problems and dealt with all the symptoms and never stopped to fix the real problems in the middle?

How can it have been so consistent unless there is some race or some particular entity that's living across that span of time and holding all this together?

Man Is Fallen

Wallace: By saying that you don't want any religious answers, I'm assuming you mean you don't want the truth. When was the last time you found a sane, decent group of people who could get together and agree on something and get something done? We have a fallen nature.

Management Levels In The Universe

Terziski: I get the biggest kick out of comparing incomparable things. Namely, different revelations coming from different sources. First I read the Billy Meier Chronicles, a revelation from the creation. They believe there is no universal Father and the Father has no personality. Straight out of the first paragraph of the Lucifer manifesto. Then I discovered the revelation of the universe according to the Trinity. Then I discovered the revelation of the universe according to Jehovah. And on and on. Other revelations. However, trying to figure out from the astronomical map where each of these different hierarchies belonged, Jehovah is a local hierarchy around planet earth.

There is also a hierarchy for the local group of a dozen galaxies. The presence of the independent angels, basically the Lucifer rebellion, and the independent angelic presence on the planet. These are several hundred planets in our chunk of the Milky Way galaxy. Anyway, the most important philosophical and religious revelations that give a paradigm of looking at the universe are all local creations around our planet, around our solar system, around our galaxy, around our local group of relatives. Which means that there are much higher levels of management in the universe.

The super cluster that our local group of galaxies belongs to has probably 50,000 to 60,000 galaxies. It obviously has a management of its own. And even that super cluster is a little grain of sand in the larger universe. There are higher management levels as we go up this hierarchy. Eventually, there's probably a big management level or database that we call God of the whole universe. But even that universe in itself is a little grain of sand. Because many aliens that specialize in traveling to other parallel universes claim that there are an infinite number—these are like eggs in a bigger basket.

And each egg is one universe. And when Billy Meier asks, "I want to know. How many exactly are there other universes?" He was told, "Don't worry. More than enough." But still, he said, "I want to know." And he was told ten to the power of 740,000 of other universes, of other eggs in a bigger basket.

Basically, my point is that all our terrestrial religions are small, local creations that are helping us as we go along. But I have no doubt in my mind as to the triumph of the positive beginning in the whole universe and to the triumph of the positive forces. We just have to give them a helping hand.

Audience Member

Audience Member: I would like for all of you to look at each other. The differences that exist between all of us is what you are here to learn. That is precisely the answer that everyone has been sitting here waiting for. We are here to learn from each other. Until we do, we can't get out. Regardless of whatever anybody tells you, until we learn from each other—that's why we have so many varieties of people. Look at you. All the white people here—none of you look alike.

Wallace: Not even to you?

Audience member: No. So, basically, you have to learn from one another. Everyone has their own answers and we're here to speak them to all of them. My message, according to how I heard and learned it, is the human race will not leave until we all learn. And we are living together. We may have many different lives, but the spirit is all of the same essence. Regardless of what God you believe in. It doesn't matter. It's all made of the same essence. There is no distinguishing difference between the energy to create a chair and to create a human. It's all the same ether. It's all there for you. We all have to learn from one another. Basically, all religions are pulling people apart. So abandon them.

(Applause.)

End of first conference transcript.

Another Phoenix Conspiracy Summit Panel

Introduction By Sean Morton

Morton: Greetings! Welcome to the Conspiracy Panel. This has all been thrown together at the last minute. My name is Sean Morton. Thank you for coming. For those of you who went to my workshop and are now sitting through this, thank you for taking even more punishment. I want to introduce our wonderful panel. This is probably more brains on the subject of UFOs and government conspiracies than has ever been assembled at one table before.

I'd like to introduce a gentleman who's been a friend of mine since 1991 when the two of us were standing out in the freezing cold together watching flying saucers fly around over our heads out at Area 51. He's a terrific researcher. He's very much been responsible for blowing the lid off places like Tahachapee and he's been on KROK radio in Los Angeles a number of times. He's been on lots of national radio shows. I'd like to introduce Mr. Gary Shultz.

The lovely lady to his right is a registered nurse, has been a nurse for many, many years. She claims to have actually had various medical experiments done on her with lasers in the 1950s and 1960s. She is now an author and a researcher in the field of medical conspiracies and cover-ups. I'd like to introduce Carol Stoffer.

The next gentleman many of you have heard of. He's got a new book out now. He was the subject of a book called "The Montauk Project." And a brand new book is out called 'Montauk Revisited." He claims to be one of the survivors from the Philadelphia Experiment from the U.S.S. Elridge in 1943. He is a very accomplished scientist and physicist. I'd like to introduce Mr. Alfred Bielek.

And last but certainly not least on our panel is a man who can actually speak for half an hour at a time while never taking a breath. He speaks fluent Japanese and fluent Russian. The only language he doesn't speak is English. (Laughter.) He studied at the University of Japan. He has degrees in chemistry and physics. He's one of the most brilliant individuals I know. A very good friend of mine, Mr. Valdimar Terziski.

Once again, I am a great believer in dialogues. I think monologues are totalitarian and eventually fascist. So hopefully we can get all of you to ask questions. You have these people here before you now. This whole thing is designed as a question and answer session.

Many of you have heard a great deal about what the Clinton administration is doing regarding the multi-jurisdictional task forces, about the reworking of the American government. Everything from weather devices to monkeying with our weather to create natural catastrophes. To when and where aliens will actually invade earth.

So any question you would like to ask specifically about the topic of conspiracies, anything that's going on in the world right now, please feel free to ask this panel of experts. They are probably more knowledgeable in the field of medicine and political conspiracies than any other group I've ever come in contact with.

Let me ask Carol, now your basic expertise is in the field of medical conspiracies?

Stoffer: Yes.

Morton: Let me ask you something that was asked in my last workshop. Is there a cure for AIDS now? And is there some reason why various agents of the federal government are hiding it?

A Nurse Stumbles Onto A Conspiracy

Stoffer: Well, I'm not that tapped into the government that I can tell you there's a cure. But I know quite a bit about where it was worked on. I'm just a recent add-on to this illustrious panel and I feel just like a little chick on the block. I'm sort of new here. But I can just give you a little about my background.

I've had fifteen years of intensive care and emergency room nursing experience. My involvement in all of this occurred about 1971 when two patients came in to a local hospital here in Phoenix and told them in the emergency room that they had been chased across several states by someone shooting lasers. Eventually, that story turned out to be true. They were removed from the hospital in the middle of the night. There was a government cover-up in place at that time. Somebody showed up there impersonating a doctor. And we felt that we had been put under some kind of mind control.

I never found out what happened to those patients but it always was in the back of my mind because I myself am very Pro-Life, from the womb to the tomb. So what happened that night was not like my usual personality. I don't feel this is the place to go into it in detail. But from that incident, it started me digging, digging, digging for the truth. Because I realized that I had been a witness to a possible murder and/or kidnapping of these patients in the hospital.

After doing extensive research, years later I read an article in "The Arizona Republic" newspaper that the Pentagon had testified before the House Armed Services Committee that the Army had developed the laser for use as a weapon in battle. But it didn't say where these experiments were occurring or on whom. And this was a laser incident that occurred at the hospital I worked at.

So because of that article, I started contacting the federal government. HEW and other agencies. And ironically, the only thing that they wanted to know was did I ever tell the authorities? That's all they were concerned about. And I realized, "Oh, dear me, I better start telling them or I may end up being Karen Silkwood, too." So I contacted the local Phoenix police department, and they said, "Well, I believe your story and I think you should tell someone in the intelligence division." They patched me through to the director and I asked if he would please record my comments. He said, "We are."

Afterward, he said we'll give you a call back. So, in the meantime, after he recorded my comments, he must have spoken with someone, because he wanted to meet with me immediately the next day. I consented only on one condition—that he would bring me a written copy of my remarks. Because I didn't want to turn up dead, and I wanted proof. And I wanted to spread it around.

The day of the meeting came. He let me pick the place. I picked a restaurant near my home. We were sitting at a booth near the window facing the parking lot and I said, "Did you bring a copy of my remarks?" And he said, "No." I said, "Goodbye." I got up to leave, and he said, "No, no. I really want you to stay. If it will help, I'll write a little message for you on a card."

And because I was just Jane Q. Citizen, a trusting nurse wanting to look up to her police department, wanting to trust them, I graciously abided. Boy, that was a mistake. Anyway, he went on to say, "I know who you are. You're a very highly credible individual." In 1970, I ran for the state legislature. I had spoken out against abortion. I was involved in those kinds of activities. So he was aware of who I was because I used to interview Presidential candidates when they would come to town.

So he said, "We cannot give you a copy of your remarks for two reasons. One, the public is not ready for this. And two, it could get into the wrong hands." And that started me on my quest. And for years and years, since 1976, I've been involved in doing this research. I got my hands on some CIA/Pentagon documents which list every single city and state where our government has dropped biological and chemical weapons. I also uncovered a covert program called MK-Ultra which probably some of you may have heard of, along with MK-Delta, which is radiation experiments on American citizens.

But MK-Ultra includes not only biological, chemical experiments, but radiation, lasers, microwaves, para-military devices, harassment procedures—you name it, they use it. They worked in conjunction with the FBI, the narcotics bureau, the mental health bureau, any state health department that they feel they need. If they're conducting experiments, then those agencies, including HEW—and most of you people probably aren't aware, but the one government agency, since you're talking about conspiracies, the one agency that is now in charge of the biological chemical warfare program in the United States, on American citizens without their knowledge, is the Department of Agriculture.

The Frequency Of Telepathy

Question from Audience Member: In the book "The Montauk Project," the Navy figured out that the frequency of telepathy was 450 megahertz. Is that correct? And do they have plans at some point to present the American people with either a mind-control messiah or to actually use these weapons that they have to subdue major cities to enforce martial law?

Bielek: The answer to the question about whether or not they have a working system is yes. It's called the cellular phone system. Now, in case you don't know it, and I'm sure most of you don't, and I had intended to have a complete brochure here on the whole phone system and the backup technical data information regarding the frequencies and what effects they have on the brain, as measured and proven and with Congressional investigations of this subject. But unfortunately, the printer screwed up.

But basically, there are many systems. The most current, interesting one is the cellular phone system. Because in Southern California, starting in Orange County, and working forward to Los Angeles County, and it'll probably be over here next, they are converting, and have actually stated in the Los Angeles press, to a newer system which will have two functions. One, of course, the normal communications function. And the second one they would not elaborate on.

So we've done a little investigating and found they've raised the frequency from about 860 to now 980 megahertz. And 980 megahertz is in the region cited in the technical material they have as one of the hyperactive frequencies involving the brain. The intent here is not only to conduct normal traffic and in the normal mode for cellular phone use, but because the newer systems have all changed over from a kind of radiating antenna to both directions, receiving and transmitting, that now by using technology typical of the higher frequency—and everyone of these systems, even though in the same type of triangular tower, which you can see here in Phoenix, and in every major city except Flagstaff, Arizona—you can see what the towers look like.

And they're slowly converting the older systems. Every one of the newer systems has a huge band at its base. They have a chain link fence around it, an outer barbed wire fence, double locks and obviously locks on the band. And no indication of why they need such a big band. Well, private personnel that I know personally in Southern California made some measurements. The FCC power limit for transmission on the cellular phone system for the tower, not for the hand-held, is 30 watts. He personally measured that the towers had from three to ten kilowatts, which is far beyond the FCC limits.

And of course the FCC never objects to what another government agency will do. It doesn't make any difference whether you cite it or not. We have photos of the new installations. I've check further on this, and I've found that there is something even more sinister than just the mere matter of mind-control. It has been discussed in the interior of the government that these systems are being set up for riot control. Guess how they work?

The frequencies that are involved, approximately around 989 megahertz, interfere directly with the neurological inter-connections system, the neurological brain-firing frequencies, interior to the brain, which involve the receptor systems. And if you interfere with it, with a high end power signal, you swamp out the normal brain functions. What happens to the body when the signals from the brain telling it what to do cease?

The body freezes rigid. It doesn't die as a direct result of this, but it freezes rigid. This has already been discussed in the interior of the government. I have a friend who has connections. And I said, "Well, that's very interesting. What happens if this equipment is turned on a freeway while people are driving?" He said that is considered an acceptable risk. A few thousand car wrecks, etc.

I said that sounds a little bizarre. He said they consider it less of a risk than what would happen if they do not use this thing. It is intended for riot control. And of course the primary target now for controlling riots is the Los Angeles basin, including Orange County. This is only one aspect of many of mind-control and mind-modification. There are other systems that can be done telepathically by means of special, highly exotic radio equipment. Basically equipment that is operating beyond the electromagnetic spectrum which we call normally the first order of transmission. That is a standard radio signal which involves electric fields and a magnetic field at right angles.

You go to a second order system, a so-called "scaler" system, and you eliminate the magnetic and you have only electric fields. You can go to higher orders beyond this. But the interesting thing is that laboratory tests have proven that the human brain is a very good receptor of scaler, second order energy. It will receive it directly, without any hardware, and translate it directly. Whatever message content may happen to be in that transmission, they're for people who have been preconditioned, and I'm referring mostly to the Montauk boys, or anyone else who's been through a similar program, if they've been preconditioned to this, they can send out a radio message from a slightly modified transmitter that most new transmitters will easily transmit, into the second order domain and beyond.

Like, "If you get this message, call such and such a phone number." So the person gets this message, they call the phone number and then they get the rest of their instructions. It is perhaps a hypnotic control mechanism or who knows what? This is only two examples. There are many others. The government's means for mind-control and for controlling the population is very well advanced, believe me.

Electronic Warfare

Schultz: To quickly answer the lady's question about electronic warfare, I highly recommend the book "Cross Currents" by Robert O. Becker, MD. The subtitle is "The Promise of Electro-Medicine and the Perils of Elecro-Pollution." And he shows with a great amount of documentation the harm of the electromagnetic spectrum on human beings and living creatures. Published by Jeremy Tartar, Inc. 1990. "Cross Currents." And there are other writers as well. I'm not going to recite them now, but that will at least start you off on the road to understanding that.

Now as far as cancer goes, cancer is a gigantic fraud. I subscribe to another thesis of cancer, which says that cancer is simply a deficiency disease of nitrylocide. And therefore, stimulants and irritants do not cause cancer. They simply determine where it's going to occur. They simply are functional points of attack that set up this mechanism where the body's unable to respond in a natural way, and the cancer is a natural response, lacking a defense, that results.

Due to a nefarious cartel named I.G. Farben—how many people have heard of that? It was the major chemical corporation in Nazi Germany. They dealt in dyes stuffs. That's originally how they came on the scene. They quickly developed into a megalithic cartel. In 1926, a marriage took place between them and Standard Oil in this country. Then they designed to take over the medical schools and see to it that homeopathy, which was a natural competitor to aloe-pathic quackery, which is what most MDs today are—I'm sorry if you're one of those—what does MD stand for? Merchants of Death.

You have been brainwashed in the medical schools because they have co-opted the medical program to eliminate homeopathy and to institutionalize aloepathy only. So this mega-cartel, this Standard Oil/I.G. Farben cartel, virtually owns all of the major American chemical industry, the pharmaceutical industry, and so on. And they viciously eliminate any competition, and especially natural methods of competition because those are cheap methods, and they interdict their very high-priced fraudulent chemical remedies.

As you know, it takes about $100 million to bring one of these phony drugs onto the market place. So they don't want competition from ozone, which you can obtain for pennies a liter. And if ozone can wipe out AIDS, well that means the end of AZT. God forbid. So, it's mostly financial.

Governing Hierarchies

Terziski: Events on our little planet are governed by management hierarchies that are way far and above our little place in the galaxy. By analogy with my little home country of Bulgaria, where very few of the home events were decided from within the country in the last two centuries. All the strings were pulled from London, Paris, Moscow, Hungary and so on. So on a higher extraterrestrial and esoteric level, there is a powerful struggle, kind of an arm-twisting contest between several management structures for predominance and preeminence on our planet.

And a very important key issue of this struggle is the population of the planet. One of these management factions wants to eliminate to as low as 500 million and this is basically the Illuminati branch of the structure. The other one wants to maximize the population to even more than the five billion. The planet can sustain 50 billion.

Audience question: Why?

Terziski: It's a very esoteric reason given in a rare interview in the kitchen of Billy Meier, among many other sources, to Randy Winters, where he says that in an overpopulated planet, from the Pleidian concept—the Pleidians want our planet to become the same as their planet, with only 550 million people. Because the number of souls on a planet are fixed. So then, in an under-populated planet of 500 million people, when a person dies, the soul of that man spends 150 years on the average on the Other Side, in the schools of the Other Side.

In an overpopulated planet, when a soul dies, he spends only ten years in the schools of the Other Side. So basically the schools of this side belong to one hierarchy and the schools of the Other Side belong to the other hierarchy.

Audience question: So why do they want to kill everybody off?

Terziski: Well, you play under the rules. Because there are even much higher levels of overseeing hierarchies. You're allowed certain tricks, certain kicks, but—

Audience member: See, this is what confuses me. I'll put this out to you and I'll put this out to them, too. It seems to me we have a lot of medical advances at the beginning of the century which expanded the population. We had cures for polio and various other diseases. Which suddenly, right around the year 1914, which led to the expansion of the population to five billion and which will eventually be eight billion by the year 2000.

Now you have the same medical establishment that brought us the vaccines that cured everything are now introducing things like AIDS and electromagnetics to trim down the population. What, in your opinion, is the reason for that? Why do they want to kill us off?

Terziski: We live in a yin/yang universe. The dark side of the Force creates all the population elimination matters. The light side of the Force creates the Baby Booms after every major war. My feeling is that, despite the title of this panel as a conspiracy panel, still the universe is an evenly balanced affair of positive and negative, of good and bad, or whatever we call them. Yellow and pink. So whatever step one side does, the other side counteracts with a force of its own. It's a celestial chess game of a very high level.

Audience member: So you're saying it's all a matter of balance?

Terziski: It's all a matter of balance.

Audience member: Is there anyone else on the panel who want to answer that question? Why they contributed to the population and now why they're trying to kill us off?

Bielek: Yes. There is another view on this, and this was originally postulated by Charles Forte in the middle of the last century. His investigation as a newsman for a period of some fifty or sixty years, looking at all the strange incidents that he saw, categorizing them, cataloging them, and I think he wound up with about a hundred shoe boxes full of clippings. He came to the final conclusion in several books he wrote that the human race is the property of someone else.

They push it for a period of time into growth and expanding the population. Just like we grow a crop in the fields. We grow it for a period of time until it matures. They grow the human population as a crop until it matures, then they come in and harvest it.

Audience member: For what? For souls? For energy?

Bielek: That was something he could never answer completely. But he said it was for the possibility of food. Now food could be in the physical sense. It could also be in the soul sense. It could be both.

But there's one other aspect that we need to get back to—why does somebody want to reduce the population? As you go into the protocols of the New World Order, and the Global 2000 report, the general consensus is that the population here is beyond the possibility of this planet continually supplying the needs of five and a half or six billion people. They've got to reduce the population because they're running out of raw materials, air, a lot of things which are necessary for a minimum standard of living, much less the standard of living that we enjoy in this country.

This is one of the biggest problems. And there are those who want the population reduced partly for that reason and partly because a smaller population is much easier to control.

The Satanic Church

Stoffer: I'd like to say something real quick. How many of you know that the Head of the Satanic Church for the whole world lives in Scottsdale? Anton Levane. He lives in Scottsdale and if you look in the phone book, there's an association called The Flame. It's on McDonald Drive. And I'm just going to interject this because I know what kind of conference this is. But I feel I have to say this: In Scottsdale, allegedly, from what we hear, the Blessed Mother is appearing at a Catholic Church. And in the Bible it says, "Where evil abounds, grace abounds doubly."

Well, it just so happens at this church is right down the street from Anton Levane's place. Good ol' Anton's place. I just thought I'd interject that.

Souls As Building Blocks

Terziski: A soul is another important building block of the universe. The soul is the building block of the spiritual universe as atoms are the building blocks of the material universe. And my feeling is that more of these stories are probably a very cleverly implanted government thought control, basically a fear-creating propaganda measure as opposed to the actual reality. For instance, a lot of things ascribed to the little grays are grossly exaggerated in order to create massive waves of fear. Because fear in itself is the best mind-controlling method.

Fear shuts the high-level, paranormal abilities of the pineal gland and of the whole brain much better than anything else. And my personal feeling as a physicist is that the global warming is a hoax, the global freezing is a hoax, the shifting of the polar axis is a hoax, the coming earthquake in California is a hoax. The government has the technology to create earthquakes with technology created almost forty years ago.

They have the technology to control the weather and to create all these floods in the Midwest.

Back To The Bible

Schultz: Getting back to the Bible, as Carol mentioned earlier, it simply says about the soul, "The soul that's in it, it shall die." More about that later. Very quickly, I agree with Vladimar. Because we're more than a soul. Man is imbued with a spirit as well as a soul. A soul is simply the life that's in the blood.

Sean, if I may, since this is a conspiracy panel, and I've been studying various conspiracies for over two decades, I'd just like to make a quick orientational statement. I'm going to begin my platform statement with a quote. "Single acts of tyranny may be ascribed to the accidental opinion of a day. But a series of oppressions begun at a distinguished period and pursued unalterably through every change of ministers who plainly prove a deliberate, systematic plan of reducing us to slavery," –Thomas Jefferson. (Applause.)

Thank you. Now by the way, I just want you to know this is a very common element of our lives. And your city attorney and your district attorney use this term every day, don't they. And I'm going to give a definition then from their dictionary, "Black's Law Dictionary," "conspiracy, a combination or confederacy between two or more persons formed for the purpose of committing by their joint efforts some unlawful or criminal act, or some act which is lawful in itself, but which becomes unlawful by the concerted act of the conspirators."

How do you like that? See how slippery this is? How almost universal it is?

Manipulation By The Media

Terziski: This was a very important question of media manipulation of society, of totalitarian control of the media. Coming from Eastern Europe, I mean, people from Eastern Europe are probably the best qualified on the planet to sense an approaching totalitarian evil. Because they have lived their lives under this system. You'll be amazed at how often we comment with our Bulgarian and other Eastern European friends that this country not only smells of socialism, it reeks of socialism. In many ways, the totalitarian oppression here is even more sinister and more elaborate than the primitive one over there.

Because they didn't have the computers or the smart think tanks. And they didn't have all the money and all of the wonders that American money can buy. Back to information— over there it's one state-controlled radio. And you can never have a UFO story. There was a massive flap over Moscow. A giant mother ship flew slowly several hundred kilometers over several major cities, then slowly flew over Moscow and hanged for about fifteen minutes a few kilometers from the center of Moscow, near the Kremlin.

And there were small lights. This was in August, 1980. Small lights came. They were observed in apartment complexes hovering close to the second or third floor, and from the upper floor, they could see the guy pulling the handles in the craft. It was never mentioned in the Pravda paper. There was a major flap over Paris. There have been flaps over all the cities. The only one that was mentioned was in 1952 over Washington, the Capitol Building, and this was the only one that called for a major national press conference.

Because the party line slowly changes, my feeling is, as a totalitarian media observer, is that they're slowly building up for a politically correct landing that will happen probably in England. There will be a photo opportunity, maybe next summer if the time is right, where all the major world television stations will be given the chance to shoot a craft that will be there for a few minutes and then they would depart.

These are major events that are slowly being built up in Ufology. Especially the crop circles in England and the triangular shapes over Belgium. By carefully judging the media time, the attention given to some cases and completely ignoring hundreds of thousands of other cases, one realizes which are the politically correct aliens, which are the politically correct contactees, and which are the politically correct landings that we have to talk about.

They're slowly building up. And the little grays are the only politically correct alien race that probably exists in the universe. And the government and our foreign offices are all skillful in their galactic diplomacy to secure a diplomatic treaty with these aliens and our government. This is the slowly building party line. We are prepared for a major landing.

That's why any landing that's not authorized—and they don't know what to do. I mean, a ten-kilometer-long ship hanging over Long Island. How the hell would they report that if they weren't sure that it was from an alien race that's not from our federation at all?

In Defense of the Media

Audience member: In defense of the media, the media in the United States is much more controlled than the media in the rest of the world. There are 25,000 different forms of media in the United States, books, newspapers, television, what have you. And they're owned by a grand total of about thirty guys. They all know each other and they all play golf together. So it is very controlled. Now in our defense, at the same time, when you talk to people who are like station managers, they don't know anything. They just don't know anything.

Can Radiation Kill The Soul?

Another audience member: Is it possible, from your scientific perspective, that the soul can be killed through some sort of radiation?

Bielek: Some very heavy radiation, yes. It can be damaged from lesser radiation, but it would recover from that. Just as the body can be destroyed by excess of radiation. If you get a high enough level of radiation, you can destroy a soul. But that's taking something like a hydrogen bomb. Now a hydrogen bomb, of course, is something a little bit beyond the normal atomic bomb in many of its aspects. The power, the temperatures, and of course the reaction of fusion rather than fission. You have a very different animal there.

Terziski: A very important thing about the Pleiadians, though. They were asked who created AIDS and his ambassador Billy Meier at a Whole Life Expo in Los Angeles said, "Well, Billy, the Pleidians think that AIDS came from the Green monkey." Then there was a little "ah-hah-hah" in the room. And then I realized that the Pleidian population's prescription for our planet is exactly out of the pages of the Illuminati Club of Romers.

Question from Audience Member: How is the average working person supposed to defend ourselves from all of these conspiracies? There's no possible way to do it. I want some honest answers. There's no way that any of you in this room can defend yourselves from all the inevitable things that are coming about.

Schultz: Very quickly, are you feeding the monster? Are you filling out a 1040 form? Think about going underground. That's one solution. Stop feeding the monster. That's right, the IRSS. You're supposed to find ways to stop feeding the monster. Privacy engineering. Start doing war with the enemy. We are at war. If you haven't figured that out, as you just pointed out, we're at war. That's right. There are many conspiracies acting against you to grind you into fine dust.

Audience Member: So you're talking about in the next few years all of us belonging to basically a resistance?

Schultz: Exactly.

End of Second Conspiracy Summit Transcript

So there you have it. Do you sit back and do nothing while the various conspiracies slowly work toward their fruition? Or do you take a stand along with those who yearn to resist at all costs the coming New World Order?

The choice is yours!

More From Vance Davis

Introduction: Vance Davis is an Army Intelligence Specialist, and he's here tonight to answer several questions regarding whether or not the government is telling us the whole truth about UFOs. And I'm wondering whether to laugh or to cry. But it will be interesting to hear what this young man has to say. Let's give him a good hand. (Applause)

Davis Gives His Early History

Davis: How is everybody doing tonight? I haven't been in this field for very long, to be honest. Since 1990. How many people remember what happened in 1990? How many people know a little bit about our story? How many people know nothing? I like you guys. That means you haven't heard the garbage. I will tell you some of the garbage.

First of all, when we were arrested, one of the things that came out in the paper was that we were at Gulf Breeze to visit Jesus Christ coming down in a UFO. They even mentioned that on CNN. The second thing was, we were there to kill Ed Walters. Pretty wild. We were also part of a great cult called "The End Of The World Cult." How many people remember hearing those things? Well, let me remind you of the story. In July of 1990, six soldiers went AWOL from Augsburg. We got caught in Gulf Breeze, Florida, on July 14th. It hit the news. We didn't know it hit the news. We were in jail in solitary confinement. And I guarantee you that they were going to make us disappear.

They wouldn't let us call anybody. We had no lawyer. We were tied up and could not talk to anybody. Though we did. You know, you tell the guards not to talk to them. Guess what guards do? "Gee, how come we're not supposed to talk to you? Did you know you guys are Satanists?" Oh, really. "Tell us the true story." It's like telling a kid not to eat candy. How many of you were in the military or worked with the government? It's interesting that when you see something interesting, they say, "Oh, don't worry about that. You don't need to know." Doesn't that make you want to know more?

You're kind of like, "Oh, that was neat looking. Let's find out some more." And you usually find someone that will tell you, don't you? On some things. Okay? How many people know about Pollen, the guy who just got caught? Everybody says, "Well, how did he get the information?" He knew people. I guarantee, he knew people.

The Release of Davis And His Comrades

Well, we were released 21 days later with honorable discharges by orders of the White House. From what we understand from several people that we have met—and I've met one of the press aides of George Bush—we were a major topic in the White House during that time. At that time, they even knew Saddam Hussein was going to go into Kuwait. We didn't, but we let people know. And it actually leaked out. One of the first predictions in August leaked out. It came out in "The L.A. Times" that we went AWOL because there was going to be a war in the Middle East.

Presidential Politics And The NSA

How many people have read "The L.A. Times" from that time that remember that? You remember that little statement? Like one line. Well, guess what happened on August 18th? Saddam Hussein walked into Kuwait. "Oh, we can't let him do that." But under the table, we promised him that he wouldn't get hurt. I believe it was a ploy to boost the economy of the United States. Did it do it? Oh, yeah, big time. Did it almost get Bush reelected? Why didn't it? I guarantee you, Bush didn't want to win. Bush did not want to win. He knew things were going to change. And would you want the blame for it? Let Clinton have the blame, right? Let the Democrats dig their hole.

And it's not Clinton's fault either. Though he has made some funny moves. But he's told to make moves. Well, the government is interesting. I've been to talks in the past three years where I've heard people talking about the NSA. How many people know what the NSA is? The National Security Agency. How many people remember the book "The Puzzle Palace"? It came out in 1985. We had a heyday at NSA. The NSA came out with the official statement, "Oh, this story's old" and everything else. Do you know within a week we had all our code books changed? They were all in the book. He talked to somebody really high up. And we were told not to talk to the press.

Soon after that, Reagan dedicated two buildings at NSA. Do you remember that? NSA is black-funded, or was. Under the table funds. Like close to $30 billion, reported at one time, they got to do their work. Well, when Reagan dedicated the buildings, Senator Dole goes, "Well, where did they get the money to build two gold $30 million buildings? We didn't authorize it." Uh-oh. Guess what happened to NSA's black funds? It disappeared. But not really. I think they're given close to $20 million a year to do what they must do, and of course other people funnel money to them. In fact, other countries funnel money to them. They are the world's largest communications and listening agency.

FOIA Requests And "AVCs"

And they come out now in "Washington Technology" and actually admit it. They work on cryptography. They encrypt all the communications for banks, businesses, car dealers. Everybody. They're very, very civilianized. Now, if they're targeting communications, how do the aliens talk to each other? Communications, right? So who would copy or who would listen in on the aliens or UFOs communications? The NSA. And I guarantee you, the people that do FOIAs, guess who they always write to for information on UFOs and AVCs? NSA. By the way, the government calls them AVCs, not UFOs. If you go and ask the government, "Can you give me information on UFOs?"—how many people are researchers here and have sent in FOIA requests? Did you put the word UFOs in there?

You messed up. Did you get anything back? A flat denial. Exactly. There's no such thing as UFOs. The government knows and classifies everything. They give it a title. AVC is one title, if they know what type it is. It stands for Alien Visitation Craft. Very simple, isn't it? How many people know what H-PACs are? Human-Piloted-Alien-Craft. Reverse technology, all that good stuff.

Now, if you want to file, this is what you do. Make something up. I want you to test it. I want people to test this out. Write again, and put in 001CIG0135. A file name number, okay? Call it AV, etc. Guess what that stands for. Alien Visitation, file number one, cigar-shaped, sighting number 0135. See what kind of response you get back. If you get a denial, that's cool. But you may get a long explanation, "No such file." If you get a "No Such File," and it's taken six months for them to get back to you, that means somebody looked for a file. And they didn't find it. Guess what you just hit on. Because legally, by the Freedom of Information Act, feel free to correct me, if you have the file name and you know it and you ask for it, they have to release it.

The Government Plans To Tell The Public

It may take two years, but they have to release it. So what's happening, what I'm trying to teach you is you're not asking the right questions. I met a man who did ask the right questions one time, and the guy told him "No comment." Then he whispered to him, and I'm not going to give you his name, the person he was asking whispered to him, "Where'd you get the information from?" In other words, "How'd you find out what to ask me?" And believe me, before this happens, if you guys see what's going on now, the government, by the end—one of the predictions we were given, by the end of 1995, the government will admit there's other life forms.

You can see it in the news and in the press. Everything. They're going to admit it. They're playing big time with Roswell, because our Representative in New Mexico, Steve Schiff, from what I understand, Steve Schiff is a little upset. Because they put it out in the paper about the Mogul Project, but they never told him. He found out through the paper. So guess what he thinks? "Bullshit. You lied to me." Because they could have told him that. He's on their committee for some of this stuff. And now another representative in New Mexico is getting involved in cattle mutilations. How many people have heard that? They're getting involved in that, now.

Something's going on, and the government's going to tell you. The United States will tell you. Because they feel now the public may be able to handle it a little bit more. But it's the truth. How many people will believe what they tell you here in this room? Gee, we've got a good crowd here, Frank. Maybe an intelligent one, I tell you.

Davis Reveals Technology On The Moon

Well, I was what's called a 98KU1. It's a non-Morse intercept analyst. I was trained in Gulf Breeze, Florida and in Pensacola, Florida, Quarters Station. But I never did my job for the first four years. I worked with satellites. I worked with other things. We do have communications devices on the moon. In fact, one of them is called "The Earth Transmission Array" which was the last thing the Apollo missions left up there. It was originally left to basically measure the distance accurately. But they do turn it and pick things up. It's not facing Earth, people. They turn it to where it doesn't face us. And it still works. At least it did when I was still in.

Good And Evil Aliens

Aliens. Are they good? Are they bad? How many people believe there are evil aliens? I'd like to know your definition of "evil." Somebody stand up and tell me their definition of "evil." Who would like to do that? Okay, sir?

Audience member: I would define "evil" as enforcing your own will to harm others.

Davis: Very good. You thought about that for awhile, didn't you? It took awhile to get a good definition, didn't it? That's an acceptable definition, I think. They definitely have a different moral code, though. Well, what if you went and asked permission from your parents if you could do something to somebody? Are you allowed to do it? And every way you look at society, how many people would go ahead and do it? I "allow" you to shoot somebody. How many people in the civilian world out there—you see I've still got my military training, don't I? In the public, how many people would shoot?

The guy in Pensacola did, didn't he? So it's not hard. But the thing is, people say, "Well, abductions are good." How many people here believe abductions are good? You do, honestly? Do you like rape? I believe this. There are many, many races out there. Some have different moral codes. Some are controlled by pretty bad dudes. They're forced to do what they have to do. And there's some really good ones who are not interfering. They visit you in dreams. They may show up like an angel and tell you something before they leave. Then you turn around and they're gone. The good ones don't abduct. That doesn't mean the ones that abduct are really bad. They're told to do so. Plus, most of them have been given permission by people in our own government to do so.

The Government Under Duress

And they believe that they have the right to do it. Because in their eyes, the government has sole possession of the people. Do you all know that Europeans have no rights? The government has their rights. You have to report to the government every time you move. Tell them where you're going, what you're doing, what job you're changing to. How many people believe we have high taxes? Our taxes are doodley squat compared to Europe. Almost 50 percent of their paychecks go to taxes. We're at 20 percent. We're getting closer. I've added it up in my head. It averages 20 to 25 percent.

But it is increasing. And in some companies, you pay union wages. You have to pay everything else. No wonder some of the guys are making $25 an hour. They're only getting $12, actually. Well, in the aliens' sense, in how the government views it, I'm going to bring in a couple of theories for you. What if I were to tell you that our government is under duress? How many people would believe that? Our government's under duress. So why would they be allowing them to do things? Because probably they believe that the aliens can destroy this world and they're trying to protect the public.

A few lives to protect the many. That's a military idea. Acceptable losses. But do you know why the government and the military plays it? Because if you lose a few, that means you have many more to fight the bigger battle later. But people in power think they can have it both ways. There are two governments. And someone told me that because we went AWOL, we were this close to proving it. Just because we went AWOL. I believe there's good and bad aliens. And the only way you can tell between the good and the bad is by following your own heart and your own spirit. If you learn to listen to who and what you are, then you can never be misled.

Teaching Your Children

In society today, what are kids being taught in school? Listen to your teacher, listen to your government, listen to your elders. They know everything that's right. I'd rather have my children, and my children will not go to public school, thinking on their own two feet. To decide for themselves. Now, I can teach them morals. It's the parent's job to teach them morals, is it not? How many throw-away kids do we have in this country now? Why are they throw-away kids? Because both parents have to work to survive. The system is corrupt. All kinds of neat stuff.

The Government Within The Government

Now they're getting ready to mark people. A real fun subject. It's not my biggest subject, but it's one reason we went AWOL. And the way I look at it, maybe it's part of the big scheme of things. Maybe it was all planned. Possibilities. But see, saying the word "government," meaning everyone in the government. Certain individuals within the government. I was in the government. Am I a bad guy? How many people think I could be a plant? I could be myself without knowing it, couldn't I?

Who knows what they did to me? Maybe they set up the whole Ouija board thing and talked to us in a weird way. It's a possibility. How many people believe that we might be used in the future to put out real information? How many people listen to Art Bell? You know, he gave that theory over the radio when he did an interview with us. Because right now, we're pretty credible. We have here 700 pages of documents that INSCOM released. Statements, reports. They even have—do you want to see our notes from the Ouija board? (Holds up blacked out pages. Laughter.)

By the FOIA, they are not allowed to release the names unless the person it is about requests it. So they cross out names, Social Security numbers, addresses, unless a person signs a waiver and says you can release it. But when they do something like this, they still consider it fairly highly important messages.

Why Davis And His Comrades Were Released

Do you know why we were released? There's two reasons why we think we were released. One, if they'd taken us to court martial, what does court martial mean in this country? Court, right? Look at the O.J. Simpson case right now. And what are they trying to do to the media in the O.J. Simpson case? Kick them out, right? But the courts are supposed to be public, are they not? Court martials are too, aren't they? If they took us to a court martial with the stuff we had, the government would have to prove their case, would they not? Guess what they'd have to prove. And guess what they won't do? That means that the government would have to prove that what we know, they know, too.

The charges. They don't want that. Because then you know. They knew about the LA race riots. I guarantee you they knew something was going to set it off. They knew about the Gulf War. How many people remember Pat Robertson's book "New World Order"? It came out in May of 1990. He talked about the war in the Gulf, too. But you know, Pat Robertson is an insider. His Dad was a big Senator. So he had a lot of answers even before us.

That's interesting, too, some of the statements that are on here. You ought to read what people say after they know you and you think you know them. Boy, people really protect their butts. "Well, I only knew him a little bit." Hell, we were training buddies. And some people really protected themselves in here by not—you know we didn't tell everybody everything. But if everybody left that wanted to leave, there probably would have been 25 people. We have real information. We have high probability, like the predictions worked.

Back To The Aliens

Now, again, back to the aliens. We weren't really into it, but we received a lot of information. And one of the interesting things is that it all ties together, people. The spiritual, the physical, the alien, the metaphysical. It's all tied in. It's all one big picture. But they keep you off or on the UFO track. You're not going to think about the others. And if they get you on the metaphysical track, they're not going to get you to think about the others. If you keep thinking about O.J. Simpson, you're not going to worry about power. If you worry about something else, you're not going to worry about something over here. They try to keep you scattered. It's a psychological ploy.

Believe it or not, they do it in basic training. If you've been in the military, you know that. They scatter you in basic training. You don't know whether you're coming or going. It's messed up. By the time you come out, you're sort of brainwashed and you pretty well take orders as given. Four years later, it breaks. You can pretty well get back out of it. Except for the Drill Instructors. I think they're always into it. They like inflicting pain. And when mental pain is added.

Now, the aliens are involved in a way that may shock a lot of you. They have signed agreements with certain individuals in the government. Not with THE government, but with certain individuals. I believe they probably have some signed agreements with the CIA. It wouldn't surprise me any. Some aliens are here doing the same thing we would do if we went to a new planet and found some interesting life. Well, to me, that doesn't hold. They've been here for thousands of years. I think they've found enough about our life by now so that doesn't tend to hold water for me.

The Human Race Is Special

So I basically teach one thing. We're special, people. The human race is special. Can you count all the aliens that have supposedly been here on one hand? How about two hands? A lot of races are here, aren't they? And there are a lot of races that we don't even know about yet that are watching this planet. First of all, in science, how many people know Stephen Hawking? Quite a few. A very interesting man. You can't understand a word he says. In fact, he can't really talk anymore. But it's really weird how these special people can understand what he says.

This planet is very unique. We have more water than we should. We have more visitations than we should. We're killing it, but it's still there. I call us the "Mutts of the Universe." We have been so genetically manipulated. I think we have a piece of every race ever in the Universe in us. We're the "Great Experiment." Some people call it "God In The Flesh." That means "We're god," but in the flesh. They have the "Spirit." And that's what they found when they first came here.

So why did they genetically alter us? To see if they could get some. These are all theories, okay? So we've been changing and evolving over the years. There's no missing link. We were genetically altered. They'll never find a missing link unless they find the race that first did it. And who knows, maybe parts of the government have.

The Human Race's Responsibility

So what's the purpose of this? Why are they watching us? Well, I know from certain sources that certain races are waiting for us to wake up and take our responsibility and to do what we're supposed to do. What are we supposed to do? They're waiting for us to go out there and teach them how to do it right. Look what we've gone through. You know, I have from good sources that the aliens haven't even gone through half the stuff that we've gone through. In a short period. And we're still here. But in some dimensions, we're not. That's a little joke I throw in. But it may be true, I don't know. I don't travel the dimensions too much.

So what makes the changes? I believe it's spiritual decisions. Spiritually deciding to change. It changes you physically. The body has to follow any kind of mental change, does it not? And it unlocks certain genes. Well, I'm here to tell you one race left their genetic code in us and that race is now gone. And in the Universe, they were called The Masters or the Life Teachers. How many people have heard that term before? Guess where all their memories are locked away at, hidden from all the other races that want it? In you. Inside of you. You are to finish the Great Experiment.

Disasters On The Way

Well, I tell you what, if you want to know more, I do go into great detail in the predictions. Just to let you know real quick, the major event to look for next, and we are

59

going to be on "Ancient Prophecies II" in November, is Mount Rainier going. And that's a warning, people. It's a warning that the area is very volatile. Soon after that, I believe we'll start seeing proof of alien life forms. Because as these catastrophes increase, parts of the government will say, "They're here to help us." And some of them might be. But if you had the Masters code inside of you, and let's say you weren't quite benevolent—is that the right word? Am I using the right word? Wouldn't you want to control that person to have those codes?

Now does that raise questions in your head about why abductions go on and most of them are women who have eggs taken? What are they trying to find? The genetic code. The secret. They won't find it. They'll never find it. Only we can get it and get to it. How many people here would like to know how to protect themselves? Every person has a shield and it works against being paralyzed and it works against the people around you. Some of you are so open, people can read your mind just like this. And I guarantee you that the government does that stuff. Just like this. They know exactly what you're thinking and what you're doing.

Take Control Yourself

The Earth is pretty dark right now. And we have to work for things to become light. What I try to tell you is how to unlock what you know inside. Not what I know. But what you know. Because everything's inside you, and the key is back to you. You have the power and you have the control. Take it. Take the responsibility and do something with it. Quit sitting around and watching TV and everything else. Go out and get knowledge. Get the keys. Unlock the door. Find out what's there. You take what we teach you and you make it your own and you do with it what you want. Learn to share what's in your heart, and we may all get out of this alive.

So once again, the warning is sounded loud and clear. Stand up against the various conspiracies by learning to defend yourself in spiritual terms, just as you would in physical terms. The choice is yours, but time is running short!

VANCE DAVIS

Formerly of Military Intelligence
Leader of the
GULF BREEZE SIX
● Hosted by Sean David Morton ●

Decorated Army intelligence Specialist Vance Davis went AWOL from his post in 1990 with five other high-level operatives, all with Top Secret Clearance 20 levels above the President of the United States.

According to his own account, it all started when Davis and the others began to receive psychic warnings about forthcoming Earth Changes, and an attempt by "covert elements" within the military to establish a "Multiple Jurisdictional Task Force," that would restore "law and order" by breaching the U.S. Constitution and replacing the FBI, the National Guard, FDA, DEA and IRS with a "National Police Force" known as the "Black Guard." As Davis later revealed, "We were told we needed to get out of the military because *they* said, 'It's not going to be good in there. We asked 'Why?' and the response was, 'Because they are going to start marking soldiers,' and they didn't want us to be marked!"

Headline stories—beamed around the globe—claimed the AWOL intelligence operatives had left their post in Germany, snuck back into the U.S., and had headed straight for Gulf Breeze, Florida, in an attempt to destroy the Antichrist who it is predicted by then would appear on the world scene very shortly. There was speculation among the UFOlogical community that Davis and the others had gone to Gulf Breeze because of its connection with the repeated sightings of spacecraft. Some individuals even thought that Ed Walters—the famed abductee who took a series of close-up photos of UFOs, including one on the roadway in front of his truck—somehow was tied in with this scenario, an association that was later denied.

To this day, Davis does not fully understand how the entire affair got so far out of hand, that there's a possibility that forces loyal to the "New World Order" were working hard behind the scenes to foster a disinformation campaign against the AWOL soldiers that went way beyond the norm, clearly showing the near mass hysteria that was being conveyed by the military in what was seen by them as a clear "breach of security."

Due to the sensational nature of the case, interest among the journalistic community was at an all-time high. Even former NASA scientist Jacques Vallee couldn't wait to get his two cents worth in on the debate. In his book, *Revelations: Alien Contact and Human Deception,* Vallee reviewed the many bizarre aspects of the entire episode:

"[After they were arrested] from Fort Benning the six deserters were

HERE IS THE ORIGINAL PRESS RE-LEASE THAT STUNNED THE WORLD. FIND OUT WHAT IS TRUTH AND WHAT IS DISINFORMATION.

AUGSBURG, West Germany—Six military intelligence soldiers who deserted their unit in Augsburg to find and fight the Antichrist in Florida have been under investigation for their activities for at least six months, a source close to the investigation said.

The source, who spoke on the condition of anonymity, said that the soldiers, who belong to a group called "The End of the World," also left letters in their barracks room detailing their reasons for leaving Germany.

Reference to the satanic bible were also found, he said.

The soldiers were picked up by police in Pensacola last weekend and are charged with desertion. A counterintelligence investigation is also underway because the six had access to classified information within the last 10 months, officials said.

Earlier this week, military officials in the Pentagon said the Army knew little about "The End of the World," and suggested that the six soldiers could be the cult's sole members. However, the source said that, although the six arrested in Florida were the core of the group, the cult has other members in Augsburg.

"The Army is very concerned that these people with top secret clearances were involved in this type of group," the source said, noting that such concern was the reason the Army has been reluctant to release details of the case.

Soldiers in Augsburg also were ordered not to discuss the soldiers' desertion with the media. However, a soldier assigned to the same unit as the six deserters told *The Stars and Stripes* on Wednesday that other members of the group were upset that they had not been invited on the trip to Florida.

The group told friends that they believed the world was about to end. They told a Tennessee man who sold them a used van that they were going to Pensacola because they believed the Rapture would occur in that area in October. Fundamental Christians believe the Rapture, the ascent of the faithful into heaven, will signal the end of the world.

In the letters left behind in Augsburg, the group said the world would end in Augsburg officials are not commenting on the case. Community spokesperson 1st Lt. Sanja said Friday that she has no details about how the case will be prosecuted.

quickly transferred to Fort Knox, and a remarkable series of events was set into motion. The Army simply cleared them in a routine espionage investigation, issued them general discharges, and turned them loose. The curious UFOlogist, at this point, has the right to ask a few disturbing questions. For instance, how on earth did these soldiers know exactly one month in advance that a war was about to erupt [with Saddam Hussein] in the Middle East? What motivated the incredible leniency of the Army when it simply discharged six intelligence communications specialists who had been missing for a whole week? And how did these soldiers manage to elude the FBI and the Army for so long? How did they get back into the United States without being picked up by immigration officers, who surely must have had their names prominently highlighted on their computer lists at every port of entry?"

Vallee believes that, "The whole saga reeks of collusion and manipulation at a high level. And the manipulation must have been engineered by someone exquisitely familiar with the UFO scene, someone who exploited the soldiers' expectation of a massive UFO event in Gulf Breeze."

Going further in his rationale, Vallee seems to think that the entire matter might have been "officially closed" due to a blackmail threat that occurred when the Florida media received a "very strange teletype communication" that read:

US ARMY
FREE THE GULF BREEZE SIX,
WE HAVE THE MISSING FILES, THE BOX OF
500+ PHOTOS AND PLANS YOU WANT BACK.

Indeed, up until he steps behind the speaker's platform and prepares to speak before those attending the 4th Annual National New Age, Cosmic Conspiracies and UFO Conference (San Diego, May 20–23, 1994), Vance Davis has managed to keep rather silent about the major events that caused a distinctive change in his life. And while his former position in the military should swear him to absolute secrecy, Davis feels it is very important "at this time" to come forward and discuss the many revelations that came to the Gulf Breeze Six from entities not of this place and time.

"All of us are very patriotic," Vance has stated. "I personally believe in the Constitution. I believe in this country. I will die for this country, even to this day, the true meaning of this country, what the Founding Fathers did, not what it is now. I believe in freedom of thought. I believe in freedom of choice and when that choice is taken away I will die for it, and that choice is being taken away."

For the first time, Davis will explain how the Gulf Breeze Six came to be involved in this "high drama," of intrigue that lead to them receiving a list of 56 specific predictions and nearly 1500 pages of notes. Davis will reveal the possible identify of the Antichrist; the existence of various races of alien beings who continue to arrive on Earth; our economic future and collapse of society and much, much, more. In his Workshop (to be co-hosted by Sean Morton and given on Saturday, May 21 at 3:00 PM), Davis will try to draw upon the same energies that provided so much accurate information to the Gulf Breeze Six, in order to enable those attending to receive first-hand information about the times just ahead—which will include many dramatic shifts in awareness for each and every one of us. This promises to be an incredible experience nobody should miss.

A LITTLE ABOUT VANCE DAVIS:
I was born in Wichita, KS. I am now 29 years of age. I am a graduate of Silva Mind Control. That is how the MI and NSA knew about my abilities when I went into the military at age 18. I was in for around seven years until I went AWOL to bring events and happenings that are to occur in the next 20 years. Our true goal, which is to start at this time, is to share the "new thought" and prepare those in the world who are not in these groups. In July of this year I am publishing a new magazine called the *Keepsake Forum*. I am also working on a 300 page book about my wife and I and the events of 1990 and beyond. I hope to have it completed in May of this year. I can be contacted at Box 13406, Albuquerque, NM 87692-3406.

IN REPLY
REFER TO:

0545 hours

JOINT TASK FORCE ONE 17 April, 1953.

190 RHO
USAAF - Unit 9
G & B - Section
Lt. GEN. NATHAN F. TWINING.

In proper perspective - the 'Philly' Navy Yard's bungling of what should have been a routine exhaustive search of the U.S.N. Vessel DE-173 shows total lack of substance and detail in your department.

As of 0600, 21 April 1953, J. Edgar Hoover now requests that all associated personnel be given prior and restrictive Psychological Testing conducted by the Navy Pschological Unit at Quantico, Virginia.

Be it also forthwith that the U.S. Army Intelligence 19 group be sent in to assist any further snafus by U.S.N. and related personnel.

O. Schuster, Capt. USN.

PRIORITY   2-A   - STYX 190 RHO

IN REPLY
REFER TO:

JOINT TASK FORCE ONE

0145 hours
23 April, 1953.

E. U. Condon:

Ed,

Please excuse our concern at U.S.N. hdqtrs over the "flap" concerning the DE-173. As you might now know this affair has been on our collective minds for some near ten years. As for the subsequent escape of seven of its original crew from our Psychol. Unit in Virginia - be rest assured of their immediate capture as Hoover now considers such matter as sectional classification: 1-A PRIME DIRECTIVE.

As far as seeing your work at Colorado U. in Boulder, we plan to attend your lecture and study. Thank you for your concern of N. Tesla's "Spatial Analizer" type device as now we have the 'gizmo' too!

Please send on Reno's work as to initiate new "Philly" naval workings of immediate future.

Respectfully,

CAPT., U.S.N.

—PRIORITY 2A

DEPARTMENT OF THE NAVY
BUREAU OF MEDICINE AND SURGERY
WASHINGTON 25, D. C.

1400 hours
6 March, 1955.
IN REPLY REFER TO

C.I. Farnborough, M.D.
47-RHYOLITE SECTION
ATIC - A-13 HTPP.

Charles,
Conducted autopsy on #9 crew member of DE173 with some abnormal conditions as to foreign material (perhaps implants) found in #9's cerebellum part 14-3. The subsequent analysis of the 1⅛" long gold tipped fiber shaped something like this:

ENLARGED DETAIL:
— unknown 'script' or 'writing'

Can you identify using your analytical methods?
Four of these mysterious devices were removed from #9 - DE-173's crew member; as nasal cavity also showed implantation.

CAPT. U.S.N.

PRIORITY 2-A

IN REPLY REFER TO
NO. ....

1900 hours
12 Dec., 1944.

U. S. NAVAL AIR STATION
PENSACOLA, FLORIDA

In consideration of the latent facts in considering the fate of the U.S.S. Farnsworth (DE-173); all ships personnel and materiel must be quarantined absolute until further notice, NO EXCEPTIONS. An on site Naval inspection is ordered forthwith, as Bureau of Ships reticent requirements in section 93-A. Please include DE-173's ships' log to Adm. Roscoe Hillenkoetter, U.S.N. Consider them and all events of nature ABOVE SECRET, see clause ARH-9 "Project Blue Sky."

OSCAR SCHNEIDER, CAPT., U.S.N.

Conspiracy Expert Maintains Life on Earth Could Be Doomed By 1999!

WILLIAM COOPER ON EARTH CHANGES

Unlike many "doom and gloom" soothseers, William Cooper, author of the conspiracy thriller **BEHOLD A PALE HORSE**, doesn't see the Earth coming to an end through a natural disaster such as the popularly predicted polar shift. Instead, the controversial lecturer who has appeared before large crowds all over the country, maintains if there

is an end to civilization, it may be because "Big Brother" had a hand in it.

"There is a rocket on the way to Jupiter right now—due to arrive in 1999—with enough platinum on it to blow up the planet. I think elements of the 'secret government' are planning to make a new sun in our solar system in order to prevent an Ice Age, which seems to be on the horizon."

According to Cooper, this new ice age could come about rather quickly and "furthermore, we are being tricked into believing that there is a mass global warming taking place, when the exact opposite is really the case."

Cooper says that we should learn to become more self-sufficient, in case a global event of this magnitude does take place, because it will put officialdom into turmoil and in essence it will be "everyone for themselves" all over the land.

Cooper has become a popular figure at previous conferences put on by Inner Light and his appearance at the 3 Annual National New Age & Alien Agenda Conference in Phoenix is sure to be eye-opening. "I'll be covering some new material in relation to the CIA and the alien agenda that is going to be affecting us all," Cooper notes, "as well as covering material on the New World Order and related matters such as the hostage for arms situation and the Farm Credit Bureau rip off which could lead to a lot of good folks unnecessarily going broke."

While in Naval Intelligence, Cooper saw documents regarding an agreement made between the ETs and the government to exchange alien technology for abducting humans, a practice which, as far as he knows, is still going on!

Cooper will be lecturing as part

BILL COX TO MAKE "UNSEEN KINGDOMS" VISIBLE!

The author of one of Inner Light's most popular books, **UNSEEN KINGDOMS**, researcher Bill Cox is convinced that there are many realms and dimensions around us which are vibrating to higher frequencies than most of us can normally see or sense, but that sometimes this "doorway" opens and we receive knowledge and information which can be useful. As part of his globe-trotting adventures, he has traveled many a dusty trail in search of hidden civilizations, the occupants of which used modern forms of technology, though they vanished from the face of the planet centuries ago. In South America, he's penetrated the deepest jungles, while in Egypt he has explored the secret chambers of mighty high priests.

As a result of his investigations, he is convinced we are in the midst of a psychic explosion and that beings of super intelligence are starting to walk the Earth again. As part of his lecture—and in more detail in his workshop—he will explore what he has found and how it can be applied to everyday life to benefit us all. He will also expose the secrets of dowsing and how to tell if a UFO contact or encounter is authentic. His lecture will be held during the Saturday morning session with a full workshop-seminar scheduled for Sunday, September 8th at 12:30 PM.

"Spacemen" living amongst us have the ability, says Cox, to distort their image on film and to take upon other likenesses.

CIVILIAN CONCENTRATION CAMPS
ANOTHER GULAG IS DISCOVERED AND PHOTOGRAPHED IN OKLAHOMA CITY

INTEL UPDATE: 12 May 94

Subject: New Prisoner Sorting and Transfer Center, Oklahoma City.

Source: Most Reliable

On 5 May 94 one recon team infiltrated the area surrounding the new "Federal Transfer Facility" located on the southwest perimeter of Will Rogers Airport in Oklahoma City, Oklahoma. This facility is being built on land formerly owned by Monarch Oil Company.

The building is a six story reinforced concrete structure. There are few windows and doors. It appears to have pie-shaped high-rise cell blocks that connect at a central rotunda control center. The rear of the building has a jetway-type enclosed passenger ramp that extends onto airport property and is capable of handling large commercial airliners up to and including the 747 Jumbo Jet.

It should be noted that an aircraft rebuilding firm is located almost directly across the runway that is currently rebuilding 747s, increasing the passenger seating and painting them all white with no other markings. When they leave, the planes fly west.

Another source has reported that Amarillo Air Force Base, a former SAC site - now closed - has several plain white 747s on the flight line. These are not mothballed aircraft as they are maintained on a constant status in airworthy condition.

The Federal "cover story" is that the facility is a medium prisoner transfer facility that is centrally located in the central United Stares and is to be used for prisoner transfers between prisons. Prisoners will be flown in by air, stay one or two nights, then fly out to other prisons for permanent incarceration.

The second cover story, given to Oklahoma City police officers who have enquired, is that it is a high security transfer point to handle high risk prisoners such as Noriega or Colombian drug lords. It was obvious to the officers that this was not true due to the sheer size of the structure.

Structure is located on west perimeter road of Will Rogers airport, directly south of the FAA's Monroney Aeronautical Center and the Oklahoma Air National Guard facility, which is a C-130 squadron with global capabilities.

On 8 May 94, a second recon team infiltrated the facility disguised as construction workers, and penetrated the interior. They managed to photograph some of the interior (photos to follow). They described the facility as capable of housing a large number of prisoners in the cells with a huge mess hall and kitchen facility.

Holding estimate: 2,500+ prisoners in cells designed only for "temporary housing."

INTELLIGENCE SYNOPSIS: It would appear that the facility was designed to handle large quantities of prisoners, all to be flown in and out by large aircraft. By the design, families could be handled by being sorted by sex and age, then segregated in separate cell block wings and on separate floors. Common dining would not be an issue as the site of the dining facility could rotate groups of cells, cell blocks or floors without one area's inmates meeting another's.

The location, which is extremely rural, is well suited to non-discovery or complaint by locals. There would be little vehicular traffic to draw attention to the facility and all ingress and egress could be controlled by simply closing the ends of a single two-lane road. Closing the road would not interfere with airport operations and would not attract attention.

It appears that this facility, which is simply marked "Federal Transfer Center," (and then, only after numerous public inquires), is the central civilian prisoner sorting and relocation center (concentration camp) we have sought in the Oklahoma City area.

It now becomes apparent that the original suspicion that such a facility was to be located at Tinker AFB is no longer valid.

This location would also tie in well with the information that the Bums Flat Air Force Facility located near Weatherford, Oklahoma, is being improved for prisoner handling. Bums Flat has the third largest runway in the nation and serves as an alternate landing location for Space Shuttle operations.

(Note: All of the new concentration camps are owned, funded and under the direction of the International Monetary Fund, which is NOT an agency of American government.)

❑

S-349: PUBLIC LOBBY AND DISCLOSURE ACT

PRESS RELEASE

POLITICS OR FREEDOM?

The two things you don't discuss are religion and politics, right? Well, I'm going to break that rule.

The week of October 3rd, The House of Representatives passed a bill called "S349: Public Lobby and Disclosure Act". Supporters of the bill said that it would stop Congress from accepting bribes from special interest groups.

Opponents of the bill said that it would take everyone's first amendment rights away. Every "paid" Lobbyist (and that will be further explained) would have to register with the government even to the point of turning over mailing lists in "some instances".

That's ok, it doesn't affect you personally because you're not a lobbyist.

Let's get down to the fine print of what this means:

Conservative radio and television talk shows, such as Rush Limbaugh, Pat Robertson and Marlin Maddox would have to register with the government.

That's ok, because you don't watch or listen to these shows so it doesn't affect you.

It continues to publications such as "Spotlight," "Truth" and, yes, even the "Give Me Liberty." It would include selling reports, such as the "Capricorn Files," "Intelligence Re-

ports," and the "UFO Reports."

Anyone who gets "paid" in any way concerning these publications (and any like them) would have to register with the government.

That's ok, because you have nothing to do with these publications, so it doesn't affect you.

It extends to the churches who disagree with Federal government policies and have "paid" employees.

That's ok, you don't go to church.

It includes any MLM company that spreads the word about what our government is doing. If you make any kind of money in any program that advocates dissension, voting or complaining to your hired Representatives, you have to be registered with them in order to do so.

But that's ok, it doesn't affect you because you don't like MLM.

It means if a group of people wanted to petition Washington for ANY reason, and they raised money for their cause, they'd have to register with their employees. Even if it was something as simple as raising money to mail postcards.

Oops, that's a little closer to home, isn't it?

The first Amendment of our Constitution states "Congress shall make no law respecting an establishment of religion or prohibiting the free expression thereof; or ABRIDGING THE FREEDOM OF SPEECH, OR OF THE PRESS; or the right of the people peaceably to assemble, AND TO PETITION THE GOVERNMENT FOR A REDRESS OF GRIEVANCES." (Capitals mine).

The bottom line, folks, is that the federal government wants anyone who disagrees with them to be registered. They want to know who's politically (in)correct.

I want you to read this next few sentences carefully.

Before and during WWII, in Ger-

many and all the countries they occupied, Jews and other "undesirables," including tens of thousands of Christians, had to register with the National Socialist Party. Stormtroopers were then able to round them up and imprison or kill them.

Bill S349 was stopped in the Senate. The phones at the White House were jammed with opponents calling in. A point I want to make is when this was voted on by the House, most Americans didn't even know about it.

Most of America still doesn't. The conservative TV and radio talk show hosts got it out to the American people.

I would highly recommend that all Americans stay alert, pass the word and keep friends and neighbors informed of this Bill or others like it. I wouldn't put it past our government to attach it to a "good" bill to try to get it through.

To quote a friend of mine, "We had better take a stand now, or tuck our tails between our legs and get ready to have a computer chip implanted in our skulls!"

This article was submitted by Paula Demers, (Publisher Of the Give Me Liberty News) PO Box 280, Fort Walton Beach, FL 32549-0280.

THE RAPTURE

from Serge Monast article

Satellites will project an image of "God"
Computer holographs will make the heavens explode with lies!

PROJECT BLUE BEAM

Holographic imagery will be used in a simulation of "the end time" during which you will be shown scenes which will cause collective thought to focus on fulfillment of that which is desired for you to protect—to fit the needs of those adversary happenings."

The result of this deliberately staged FALSE CHRIST will be for the implementation of a New Age-One World Universal Religion. Enough truth will be foisted off on us to hook many into the lie.

As we reported in previous literature, the "light show" will convince many families to walk into pastures or to climb mountains where they will be vaporized by neutron bombs or incinerated by photon guns.

The calculated resistance to the New Religion—the New World Order and the New "Messiah"—will be human loss on a massive scale in the ensuing "Holy Wars."

Project Blue Beam will pretend to be the universal fulfillment of the prophecies of old: as great as the birth and ministry of Jesus 2000 years ago. In principle, it will make use of the sky as a movie screen as spaced-based laser-generating satellites project simultaneous terminal holographic images to the four corners of the planet, in every language, in every dialect according to the region.

Computers already installed and working will coordinate the satellites and software to run the show (Holography is based on very nearly identical signals combining to produce an image, or hologram, with great depth, which is equally applicable to acoustic ELF, VLF, LF waves) as a "real" optical phenomenal.

Specifically, the show will consist of laser projections of multiple holographic images to different parts of the world, each receiving different images according to predominating regional/national religious faith. Not a single area will be excluded.

With computer animation and sound effects appearing to come from the depths of space, astonished followers of the various creeds will witness their own returned Messiah in spectacularly convincing lifelike progressions.

Then, the projections of The Christ, of Mohammed, Buddha, Krishna, etc., will merge into one, after correct explanation of the mysteries, prophecies, and revelations have been disclosed.

THIS ONE GOD WILL IN FACT BE THE ANTI CHRIST, who will explain that the various scriptures have been misunderstood; that the religions of old are responsible for turning brother against brother, nation against nation; therefore the world's religions must be abolished to make way for the Golden Age (New Age) of the ONE WORLD RELIGION, represented by the one god (Anti-Christ in this instance) they see before them.

Naturally, this superbly staged full-scale deception will result in social and religious disorder on a grand scale, including rampant millions of programmed religious fanatics and cases of "demonic possession" on a scale never seen before.

In addition, to offer the world a "new saviour" which they will eagerly accept, this event will occur at a time of great political anarchy and general tumult.

Motion picture artists who create computer images admit that "if the viewer does not know the genesis and history of our scenes, they cannot tell them from reality."

Computer-generated scenes so accurate that the average person cannot tell them from reality? Terminal holographic projections from satellites to make you believe you are seeing little grey people from Zeta Reticula, flying saucers and the returned Christ?

Federal agencies are betting they can induce you to commit suicide or murder, or to accept the New Age One World Government with just such images by the year 2000.

TX1400L
PASSIVE
TRANSPONDER

No larger than a #2 pencil lead, the injectable transponder is a passive radio-frequency identification tag. Every human slave of the New World Order will have one of these, or similar, injected at birth. The NWO agencies will know who you are, what you eat, where you go and how many times a month you have sex so you can be tracked, taxed and fined.

GOVERNMENT AGENCIES COMPILE HUGE DATA BASE
American Citizens Will Become Slaves Of The New World Order
Concentration Camps Located Throughout USA

Since 1985, the IRS has been compiling an enormous data bank of information on all Americans and by 1991 that project was virtually complete.

A computer profile now exists on virtually every American family and individual, enabling the federal government to monitor virtually all of your activities, to trace, track, and perhaps eventually directly assess your bank accounts based on your computerized financial profile, electronically debiting your bank account for the taxes due.

The completion of the data base now makes it possible for numerous federal agencies to watch and control you from the cradle to the grave.

If this sounds a lot like George Orwell's 1984, Nicolia Ceaucescu's Romania, Hitler's Third Reich or Gorbachev's or Deng Xiaoping's communist "paradises"-it is because they are identical, having been engineered by the same people!

The New World Order/New Age government of the future will be able to watch and control its "subjects" more completely and efficiently than any totalitarian power in the past. The computer will help them do it!

As an example of the kind of people-tracking information now being amassed on computers by the federal government, we present the following information provided by an employee of one large government agency charged with tracking and monitoring Americans and their finances:

"We now have available to us a new source of background information called METRONET which provides information on over 111 million people in 80 million households across the country.

Not only does it eliminate the need for time-consuming progressive manual searches since ATLAS was originally purchased from METRONET by the credit bureau, it also allows for the following variety of searches:"

"PHONE SEARCH-provides a complete name and address report which is provided in accordance with US Postal Service standards. As mentioned above, it is the same as ATLAS except that the record search can continue further once the name and address of the subject have been determined.

"ADDRESS SEARCH-requires that the Zip Code, street address and last name be entered in order to verify an address and receive the subject's current phone number. If it is a single family dwelling and your subject has moved, METRONET *lists the current resident*.

"HOUSEHOLD PROFILES-provides the time at current residence, type of dwelling, the subject's age and year of birth. It also provides the names, ages and year of birth of up to four additional family members.

"NEIGHBOR SEARCH-requires only the address to obtain details on up to 30 neighbors at new or old addresses. These details include names, addresses, phone numbers, dwelling types and

length of residence. It also provides the current resident at the subject's last-known address.

"CHANGE OF ADDRESS ALERT -automatically searches the US Postal Service's National Change of Address files *which is updated every two weeks*. With 20% of the population moving to a new residence annually and the fact that 30% of these people never notify the postal service of their new address, METRONET also checks for any change of address that a subject has provided to *a publisher or marketing company* to make sure that their magazines or other products will be forwarded.

"STREET NAME SCANNING helps obtain the correct street name abbreviations by checking an alphabetical table of all street names in any given Zip Code that begins with a specified letter.

"SURNAME SEARCH-allows the investigator to search an entire geographic region (i.e., state, county, city, zip codes etc.) when the only information known is the last name of the subject." (McAlvany Intelligence Advisor). (8)

THE HIDDEN SIDE OF FINCEN FINANCIAL NETWORK: THE FINANCIAL CRIME ENFORCEMENT NETWORK

As part of the thrust to monitor and control the American people, the Bush Administration has established the financial crime center (FINCEN) in Arlington, VA whereby, through the use of sophisticated computers, the federal government has combined more than 100 databases on bank records, criminal suspects, driving records, census data, and myriads of business and financial activities of million of honest law abiding citizens.

FINCEN is the largest government run artificial-intelligence data base ever established. FINCEN has over 200 employees from the IRS, the FBI, the Secret Service, and the FDIC and works closely with the BATF, the CIA, and the Defense Intelligence Agency. FINCEN acts as a collection point, clearing and distribution center of computerized data for virtually all other government agencies. Data which it receives and redistributes comes from: bank deposits, Fed bank reports, comptroller of the currency bank reports, FDIC bank reports, census income figures, Customs monetary reports, Secret Service credit reports, and FBI and DEA drug data.

FINCEN currently has access to over 35 financial data bases and they will create another 100, including computerized land records, real estate records, credit reports, CTRs, Form 8300, bank reports, etc.

The models, data, financial patterns, and individual names generated by FINCEN are being shared with the IRS, its Criminal Investigation Division, and state and local governments.

Before a recent amendment to the "Right to Financial Privacy Act" passed, these activities were illegal. Virtually all of the activities of FINCEN violate the U.S. Constitution's 4th Amendment guarantee of the right to privacy.

FINCEN and U.S. government officials admit that FINCEN is a trial run for a world system of financial tracking, surveillance and control. ...(McAlvany Intelligence

Advisor).(9)

THE FINCEN FINANCIAL MENACE:
Ceaucescu would be impressed with the latest accomplishment of the U.S. government's cash Securitate, the largest government-run artificial intelligence data base ever established.

The feds admit that they want all bank employees to function as virtual spies for the government. If they refuse to treat their customers like potential criminals, they will be punished.

The people pushing FINCEN in the Bush Administration (were) William Bennett, Attorney General Richard Thornburgh, and Treasury Secretary Nicholas Brady. All three see FINCEN as the key to the war on drugs, the war against cash, and the war against financial privacy.

The director of FINCEN (was) Brian M. Bruh, a 24-year IRS man. ...(10)

FINCEN MILITARY HIDDEN SIDE:
The FINCEN MISSION is a United Nations/United States Program for a "House to house search and seizure of property and arms," a "Separation and categorization of men, women and children as prisoners in large numbers," especially those who will be considered by the government authorities as dangerous for the "Law and Order" because they will not be ready to fully collaborate with the implementation of a New World Order, "and transfer to detention facilities of mentioned prisoners."

It's also a "Network" of city, State and Federal Police Forces with the United Nations Multi-Military Forces having direct orders to bring into the United States and Canada

foreign Military and Secret Police Forces for deployment against the North America population.

Most identified FINCEN Units are at Company Strength, 160 plus. Some are as large as Brigade Strength, 2600 plus.

REX-84: CONCENTRATION CAMPS & UNITED NATIONS RE-EDUCATION FACILITIES:
Mass detention facilities, otherwise known as concentration camps, have been set up at a number of major U.S. military installations on the secret orders of Ex-President Reagan. The Executive orders which established these camps have been canceled because the camps are now in place. The White House issued a highly classified NATIONAL SECURITY DECISION DIRECTIVE (NSDD) which set forth urgent instructions which 'activated' ten huge prison camps at key defense command locations across America.

Two trustworthy sources, patriotic career Army officers, revealed that preparations were set in motion for an unprecedented roundup of "security suspects" coast to coast.

According to these sources, one of the primary goals of the vast police operation, code named REX-84 is to apply "C&C ("Capture and Custody") measures against political opponents, resisters, and outspoken critics whom our bureaucratic government considers "dangerous."

Four of the principle civilian concentration camps established under the REX-84 program are located at Fort Chaffee, Arkansas; Ft. Drum, New York; Ft. Indian Gap, Pennsylvania and at Camp A. P. Hill in Virginia.

Each of these camps is designed to hold at least 25,000 civilian prisoners.

2

Additional emergency custodial facilities are being readied at Oakdale, California (reportedly for 15,000 detainees) and at Eglin Air Force Base in southern Florida; at Vandenberg AFB in California; at Ft. McCoy, Wisconsin; Ft. Benning, Georgia; Ft. Huachuca, Arizona; and finally at the southern Justice Department *detention and interrogation* center known as Camp Krome near Miami, Florida.

A major national task force of federal intelligence and law enforcement agencies, including the FBI, the CIA, U.S. Marshals, INS, Customs, Coast Guard, National Guard, and so forth, will join with local and state police in massive round ups to haul in lists of suspects who will fill these improvised stockades.

"The first roundup and the publicly announced one will be of illegal aliens and refugees," according to a military source.

"But under the secret provisions of REX-84 there will be also broad arrests of "security suspects" who can be held in these centers under this emergency order, whether they're U.S. citizens or not."

Americans whom the administration suspects of belonging to so called "violence-prone" groups, or of "supporting" such groups—which may mean only that a citizen subscribes to an anti-government/pro-freedom newsletter—may find themselves hauled off with hordes of illegal immigrants.

Another category of anti-bureaucratic activists which may be bound for administrative detention under this directive is "major, organized tax resisters," one source close to the program said.

Not a single source interviewed could cite a Constitutional or legal precedent for such a staggering mass roundup of civilians by American authorities in "peacetime."

If the president ordered a direct strike into the heartland of America, which was to be code named "OPERATION NIGHT TRAIN" (we have the document on it), federal agents would set up a concomitant domestic exercise or war games scenario called REX-84, the main rationale of which was to round up 400,000 undocumented Central American aliens during a two week period of time and incarcerate them in ten military detention camps (some of these camps are shown and documented in the movie "COVERUP" which has been playing at theaters on the West Coast. It's available for rent from CBA Bookstore, 3434 N. Pacific Highway, Medford, OR 97501. (24)

OPERATION DRAGNET: THE UNITED NATIONS PITFALL:

According to *The Washington Report* something called "Operation Dragnet" is authorized under Title II of the McCarran Act. According to this act, any president of the United States is authorized to suspend the Bill of Rights with a single telephone call.

If either an invasion, a state of war, or, more probably, an "insurrection" is certified by the head of the current government, Operation Dragnet will be initiated. Currently a Univac computer located in a secret place somewhere near Washington contains at least 1,000,000 names and, with the proper signal, the computer will begin printing one million arrest warrants!

Those whose names are stored in the computer will be picked up by the FBI and state and local police. 17 prison camps, known in WWII as "concentration camps"

have already been constructed to hold the mass arrestees. Three of these camps are being held in current readiness, two are on standby and the rest could be activated rapidly. (American Information Newsletter, 2408 Main St. Boise, ID 83702 Sept 1993)

Strategically placed across the country from Elmondorf, Alaska to Avon Park, Florida, three of these "detention centers" are now operational in a slightly different guise, two others are on a stand-by basis, and the rest are ready and available with a minimum of preparation-and all that's needed to fill these camps with thousands of Americans is for somebody to launch "Operation Dragnet."

"It will be swift and legal," federal agents stated. "The law is already on the books. They represent every shade of political and social opinion from right to left and include a big span of middle-of-the-road citizens who have never committed an offense more heinous than having subscribed to an unapproved periodical."

Its history is short and simple: On Sept 22nd, 18 years ago, Congress, by a two-thirds vote, made official Public Law 831, the Internal Security Act.

For a comprehensive report (228 pages) on New Government Agencies and Concentration Camps, send $16.00 cash or International Money Order to Serge Monast, Box 359, Mansonville, Quebec JØE 1XØ Canada. Personal checks WILL NOT be accepted. Ask for U.N. Concentration Camps Program.

CONCENTRATION CAMPS AND PRISONER PROCESSING CENTERS

1. Elmendorf AFB, Alaska   61N15/149W49
2. Eilson AFB, Alaska   64N38/147W06
3. Tule Lake, CA   41N57/121W29
4. Oakdale, CA   37N46/120W51
5. Vandenburg AFB, CA   34N41/120W29

6. Fort Huachuca, AZ   31N33/110W21
7. El Reno, OK   35N32/96W57
8. Tushka, OK   34N19/96W10
9. Fort Chaffee, AR   35N22/94W21
10. Florence, AR   33N46/91W39

11. Camp McCoy, WI   43N56/90W49
12. Elgin AFB, FL   30N29/86W30
13. Maxwell AFB, AL   32N22/86W18
14. Fort Benning, GA   32N29/84W50
15. Avon Park, FL   27N36/81W31
16. Mill Point, WV   38N09/80W11
17. Camp Krome, FL   Near Miami
18. Camp A.P. Hill, VA   39N00/77W00
19. Indian Gap, PA   40N20/76W50
20. Allenwood, PA   41N07/76W54
21. Fort Drum, NY   44N01/XXXXX
22. Butner, NC   North of Raleigh

THIS IS A PARTIAL LIST OF KNOWN OR HIGHLY SUSPECT LOCATIONS OF CIVILIAN CONCENTRATION CAMPS. MANY ARE ALREADY OPERATIONAL, OTHERS ARE ON STANDBY STATUS AND CAN BE COMMISSIONED WITHIN DAYS. If you have further information or verification, please contact this newspaper as soon as possible.

•—Arizona Detention Centers: Wickenburg; Florence; Safford; Tucson
★—Central Prisoner Sorting Facility; Oklahoma City Airport.
★—Prisoner Sorting and Research Facility; Indianapolis, Indiana. *NOTE: This facility contains huge refrigerators (operational) which may be used to store body parts for medical transplants or research purposes. It is claimed that the body parts will be taken from living prisoners who will be kept alive by machines until all useful parts are expended.**

* Not substantiated.

F.E.M.A. WHAT IS IT?

Federal Emergency Management Agency Was Established By Executive Order 12148 And Signed Into Existence By Jimmy Carter in 1979

FEMA is the acronym for the Federal Emergency Management Agency. It was established by Executive Order 12148 and signed into existence by Jimmy Carter in 1979.

Originally planned as an umbrella administration consisting of the disaster and emergency response arms of nearly a dozen scattered federal agencies, FEMA is the successor to the various cover agencies for bogus "national emergency" activity perpetrated since 1933, e.g., the Office of Emergency Preparedness, the Office of Defense Mobilization, the Office of Emergency Planning, the Economic Stabilization Agency and the Civil Defense Administration

FEMA's major functions were, unconstitutionally and in violation of the Compact, delegated under sham and pretense of a series of so-called Executive Orders, but without actual authority.

While some national security planners applauded the 1979 creation of FEMA under Presidential Review Memorandum 32 as an effort to integrate all nine federal agencies with responsibilities for civil defense emergency planning and implementation, the authors of the plan had other things in mind.

The FEMA plan was written by Carter White House NSC advisor Zbigniew Brzezinski and NSC staffer Samuel Huntington. Four years earlier Brzezinski and Huntington had been together at the Trilateral Commission's annual 1975 conference in Kyoto, Japan, where Huntington delivered a sinister paper advocating the end of democracy and the imposition of crisis-management forms of government. A Trilateral Commission-linked magazine, *Challenge*, had earlier described the concept as "fascism with a democratic face." NSC advisor Brzezinski called it the "technetronic age."

It was Brzezinski's and Huntington's vision of a technocratic fascist structure that came into being with the creation of FEMA; not a legitimate and long overdue serious attempt at civil defense. To quote Huntington's 1975 book, Crisis of Democracy:

"We have to come to recognize that there are potentially desirable limits to economic growth. There are also potentially desirable limits to the indefinite extension of political democracy."

Within months after he had written this analysis, Huntington entered the Old Executive Office building as an NSC staffer under the Trilateral Commission executive director Brzezinski. FEMA was cast in the "crisis of democracy" vision of the commission's zero-growth agenda.

The transition from Carter to Reagan tended to accelerate, rather than slow, the buildup of the FEMA parallel government within the government program of Trilateralists Brzezinski and Huntington. By 1984, FEMA's "continuity of government" structure was well oiled. Over 1,000 executive orders allocating extensive powers to FEMA in the event of a string of national emergencies sat in a safe in the Oval Office, waiting only for the signature of the President.

And in April 1984, FEMA, in conjunction with the Department of Defense, held extensive secret maneuvers throughout the United States. If there was any doubt that Huntington's "crisis of democracy" vision was foremost in the minds of its planners, a declassified section of the exercise plan, dubbed REX-84 BRAVO spelled out the scenario on which the operation was based:

• The sudden withdrawal of cheap incremental loans to heavily indebted countries generated a number of consequences to both borrowers and lenders alike. The first was to throw the entire world into the worst recession since the great depression of the 1930s.

• The response of commercial banks was predictable, both the multinational banks and the IMF emphasized three actions: a) lower imports: b) raise exports, and c) reduce the government sector debt by cutting subsidies and, in effect, cutting real wages.

The outcome of this advice, on a worldwide basis, was primarily social unrest. It occurred in the Warsaw Pact nations as well as free world countries. The major impact of a high and rising dollar with the interest rate of most loans tied to the London Interbank Offer Rate (LIBOR) was to shift almost all import earnings from being used to pay for imports to being used to service debt. Bankruptcies and defaults on a massive scale developed, and doomsayers began to publish apocalyptic scenarios.

This so-called "scenario" was the basis of secret government contingency planning for installing crisis-management at the very moment that President Reagan was delivering false assurances to the American people and the nation's allies that great economic recovery "The Reagan Revolution," was under way-(Commission to Investigate Human Rights Violations, Appendix B. (13))

HUGE FEMA DATA BASE

Fort Meade, Maryland is the federal government's most tightly guarded installation. It houses, among others, the secret National Security Agency. In an unmarked, windowless office building on the grounds of Fort Meade, hundreds of thousands of American citizens are being "computerized" by technicians on the payroll of the Federal Emergency Management Agency (FEMA).

"Administratively, this place is the equivalent of an unlisted telephone," explained a former senior official of FEMA who agreed to an interview on condition that his identity be protected. "It has no official existence. There is no listing for it, no traceable designation. But it's there, idling quietly, like a doomsday bomb waiting for its moment in history."

The task of FEMA's secret data control annex at Fort Meade is to develop so-called CAP's, "crisis action programs," to be implemented during national emergencies. The term was originally used to denote disaster relief plans at the Federal Preparedness Agency, once a department of the General Services Administration, now merged into FEMA.

But the computerized action plans instrumented at Fort Meade have nothing to do with aiding victims of hurricanes or other natural disasters. They are blueprints for taking over the U.S. government and converting it into a command system under the "emergency management" of federal bureaucrats.

Privately, congressional investigators, intelligence analysts and veteran Washington newsmen familiar with the inner machinery of the vast federal bureaucracy, have long expressed concern and anxiety about FEMA. An "umbrella administration" born in 1978 when President Jimmy Carter combined the disaster and emergency response functions of nearly a dozen scattered federal outposts into a single agency, FEMA has always been known as an "activist" and secretive fraternity.

Under Louis Guiffrida, appointed FEMA director by President Ronald Reagan in 1981, the agency developed a top secret project for arresting tens of thousands of "suspected aliens" along with troublesome critics and dissenters whom the White House found annoying enough to be labeled potentially subversive.

Tagged Operation Rex 84, these unconstitutional plans were first discovered and revealed by the populist newspaper, **The Spotlight**, in a series of exclusive investigative reports in the April 23 and May 14, 1984 issues.

But although The Spotlight's exposé wrecked FEMA's plans for setting up mass "emergency detention centers" and cost Giuffrida his job as director, secret preparations for "ensuring the continuity of the federal government" in ill-defined "emergencies" remained the major concern of FEMA's senior officials.

"Those words, enunciated by President Gerald Ford in Executive Order 11921, were understood by FEMA to mean that one day they would be in charge of the country," explained Dr. Henry Kliemann, a political scientist a Boston University.

"As these bureaucrats saw it, FEMA's real mission was to wait, prepare and then take over when some 'situation' seemed serious enough to turn the United States into a police state."

To illustrate FEMA's conspiratorial core, knowledgeable Washington intelligence sources cited the instance of the 1989 visit by President George Bush to Cartagena, Colombia, to attend a so-called regional drug summit with three Latin American presidents.

"There were rumors of a terrorist threat against Bush by Colombian drug hit squads," recounted Monroe H. Brown, a former federal security officer with long years of service Miami. "Teams of Secret Service, FBI and CIA agents were mobilized to find out how serious the threat was, while back in Washington FEMA went to work on an emergency program in case the presidential plane was hit by a Stinger missile somewhere over Colombia."

FEMA's emergency measures included preparations to round up more than 10,000 Americans "redlined" in the agency's computers as "activists, supporters or sympathizers of terrorism in the United States," explained Brown.

In August 1990, after Iraq invaded Kuwait, FEMA got ready to deal with "terrorist emergencies" in the United States by churning up the same old discredited computer compilation of "terrorist supporters and sympathizers," adding thousands of names to it and alerting the U.S. Army to set up detention camps to hold these innocent victims of its bureaucratic brutality.

FEMA: TOWARDS MARTIAL LAW:

Emergency is the trigger word in the FEMA title.

• The Director of FEMA shall, on behalf of the President:

1. Coordinate all mobilization activities of the Executive Branch, including production, procurement, manpower, stabilization and transport. *FEMA will be able to alter any existing contract.*

2. The FRS (Federal Reserve System), with all its branches will become "fiscal agent to the United States" *with dictatorial power over the economy of the nation.*

3. The Treasury and the Export-Import Bank will be authorized to make loans under the direction of FEMA and the FRS.

4. During a "National Emergency" the President, an "Elected Official," would be stripped of all his Presidential functions.

5. Set-up an Executive Branch of the government and a National Defense Executive Reserve (NDER) composed of persons *selected* (not elected) from various segments of the civilian economy and from government for training for employment in executive positions in the event of a "National Emergency." Such reservists have been treasonously exempted from certain provisions of the federal criminal code, and may be employed "without compensation," e.g., shanghaied or blackmailed into service!

2

6. Seize and/or control every major national asset.

7. Provide for National Security and consolidate the assignment of emergency preparedness functions with various departments and agencies.

8. The Department of Justice shall develop plans for administering laws regarding the import, manufacture and distribution of narcotics, i.e., do anything it wants relative to narcotics. Since the term "emergency" purports to eliminate all "law," they are also ordered to take over organized crime drug rackets and "manage" them!

9. *DECLARE MARTIAL LAW AT ANY TIME!*

10. Have the Dept. of the Interior take over all potable water.

11. Place all food production under the Dept. of Agriculture.

12. Take over all labor resources by means of lists already prepared by the Dept. of Labor.

13. Implement take over of all forms of transportation by the Dept. of Transportation, assisted by the Civil Aeronautics Board.

14. Implement takeover of all nuclear facilities by the Nuclear Regulatory Commission.

15. Take over authority and presidential functions of all emergency agencies and reduce the consequences of major terrorist incidents.

Some examples of the "perpetuation of a silent coup:"

• Declaring certain areas to be "military reserves" and cause American citizens to be removed from their homes and imprisoned without trial under the pretense of "racial difference."

• Another code provides that any military commander (under FEMA) can, under the color of a "National Emergency," specify any area he desires as a military reserve, and designate anyone living there as a criminal.

• When "Martial Law" is declared, the Constitution is no longer the law of the land. It is revoked and replaced with what amounts to a military dictatorship in much the same way that Latin American countries have been doing for scores of years. Those with the most weapons usually win. Most Americans know very well that a large share of men in uniform will not fight against their own people, particularly if the soldier is informed and is of their own ethnic background.

The debate over "Martial Law" has been around for a long time. The Department of Defense recognizes that within our Constitution, there is a question of lawfulness if the military is ordered to declare "Martial Law" over the citizens of the United States of America. This debate became extensive during the early days of the Federal Emergency Management Agency (FEMA) while it was being developed in California by then governor Ronald Reagan and his advisor, Edwin Meese.

Col. Guiffrida moved to Washington with Reagan, and Meese completed the organizational concepts on a national level. The debate over "Martial Law" was extensive during the "Garden Plot," "Cable Splicer," and Rex-84 programs wherein the military (primarily National Guardsmen) conducted training exercises to put down civil unrest.

When working with FEMA, it was suggested that the Dept. of Defense use the replacement phrase, "Martial Rule," rather than "Martial Law." All of the governments of the world recognize the term "Martial Law." It means the same thing everywhere. When it is declared, the constitution of that country is suspended for as long as the military is in command.

But with "Martial Rule," these "master planners" believe that they will still have the Constitution and have military command at the same time. The Rex 84 program is essentially a massive detention center program where they plan to incarcerate all "seditionists" during a declared "National Emergency." Millions of Americans will simply be declared felons and the government will attempt to enforce the law with several million Deputy U.S. Marshals.

FEMA: DICTATORSHIP POSSIBLE???

Hidden in the bureaucratic maze Washington politicians call "our Constitutional system of government," a little-known federal agency is quietly making plans to turn the United States into a dictatorship.

There are "stacks of blueprints" in the top secret safe of the Federal Emergency Management Agency (FEMA) designed to convert American society into a "command system," a former deputy administrator of the agency has told the investigative team.

In a private interview, allowing him to remain anonymous, this highly placed source confirmed that the procedures developed by FEMA to suspend the Constitution and to round up thousands of dissenters nationwide can be activated *by a single phone call from the White House.*

"Even people who have become aware of FEMA's existence and know something about its activities (not many do) think the word "Emergency" in its designation means it will go into action only in case of a natural disaster or perhaps a surprise nuclear attack," related this expert.

"In reality, however, this outfit can be mobilized whenever the politicians occupying the White House decide they need special—and extra—Constitutional powers to impose their will on the nation."

FEMA's bureaucrats can then proceed to:

• Take over all farms, ranches or timberland in order to utilize them more effectively as decreed in Executive Order (EO) 11490, the so called omnibus emergency preparedness decree promulgated by President Richard Nixon on October 28, 1969.

• Seize all sources of public power: electric, nuclear, petroleum, etc.

• Freeze all wages, prices and bank accounts.

3

• Take over all communications media.

Such totalitarian measures can be imposed by bureaucrats under FEMA's direction, not just in the face of a cataclysmic upheaval, but "whenever necessary for assuring the continuity of the federal government in any national emergency type situation," decreed a subsequent White House *ukase*, EO 11921, issued by President Gerald Ford in April 1976.

Can such a blueprint for tyranny be clamped on the United States by a force of faceless federal officials? "It is the role FEMA has prepared for most intensively," says the former high agency administrator.

"In recent years, despite talk of spending cuts, FEMA's budget has been steadily increasing," revealed this knowledgeable source. "It now stands at somewhere around $3 billion annually. I say 'somewhere' because part of this agency's funding is appropriated under so called black programs, submitted to Congress with the defense budget without an explanation of its purpose, exploiting the secret CIA appropriation."

FEMA can draw on the defense budget and on the protection of the secrecy reserved for national security projects because it came into being under President Jimmy Carter in a move that merged the civil defense and disaster relief responsibilities formerly shared by the Pentagon, the Commerce Department and the General Services Administration under a single powerful agency.

But FEMA's real focus is not on disaster relief, knowledgeable sources admit. During an investigation of this little-known agency, conducted earlier in 1992 by the General Accounting Office (GAO), the congressional watchdog unit has found that less than 10% of FEMA's staff of 230 bureaucrats out of an estimated 2,600 are assigned full time to preparing for and dealing with major natural calamities such as storms or earthquakes.

What, then, is FEMA really up to? An advance copy of the GAO report on this secretive agency reveals surprising findings which have been reviewed with the help of well placed confidential sources in order to bring into full view, for the first time, the federal bureaucracy's secret blue print for tyranny in America.

FEMA DETENTION CAMPS:

I should mention very quickly the detention camps themselves. Originally under FEMA, 23 detention camps were authorized. These detention camps were spread out across the United States. In addition to that, there are 20 supplemental camps that were authorized with the 1990/1991 Military Fiscal Budget. Carl Levin's DOD Budget Amendment 656 authorized the implementation of these 20 camps to supplement the 23 that were already authorized.

There are now 43 total civilian concentration camps pre-deployed inside the continental United States. In addition to that there are supplemental camps or auxiliary camps through each state and each region, an example of this would be the Nike-Hercules site located near Monroe, Michigan. That is pre-designated detention facility. The 3 sites that are located in Michigan are: (1) Located due north of Pickney, Michigan and due west of Brighton. (2) Earmarked near Lansing, Michigan to be north-northeast. (3) Fort Custer Military Reservation which has been upgraded from a 'D' facility to a 'B' facility. This is very important because a 'D' facility is State authorized and State controlled. A 'B' facility, on the other hand, has been upgraded to Federal status and is comparable to any of our prime military facilities such as Fort Benning, Georgia; Wright Patterson AFB, or any facility presently being for active military forces. However, if you get a chance to tour the highways and byways and back roads of Fort Custer you will find there is a new urban warfare center there. The new urban warfare center doesn't look like Bad Hersfeld, Germany. It looks like downtown Monroe. It looks like downtown Saline. It has 3 bedroom ranch style houses, crackerbox farm houses, small living areas inside downtown areas. At this particular site MJTF Police forces were training from the first week of January of 1989 on.

They were training every second and third week of the month from Monday through Thursday. They are paid with non-DOD funds, in other words, these were GSA funds other than regular military budget allocations. It is important to understand how they are paid because that's how you can find out who it is that's paying.

These forces operated secretly for a number of months and we identified them as they were training so they changed facilities. We understand after approximately 11/2 year cooling time they are using Custer and Grayling again, extensively bringing forces together from other parts of the state, training them on site and sending them back to be prepared for whatever is going to happen in the future.

FINCEN FORCES:

FINCEN was organized utilizing military forces as secret police forces here in the United States. They are drawn from military and secret police forces overseas. They are predominantly European—Belgian, Dutch, German and French. They also have a variety of Asian military personnel. It is known at this time, for instance, that FINCEN has an element in Montana that is made up of Gurkhas (warlike Hindus from Nepal). The 197th Mechanized recently deployed for a training operation that may last as long as two months in northern Montana through to the Canadian frontier.

The 197th Mechanized Infantry is combined with 2 brigades of British Mechanized Infantry, the First Canadian Armored Division, Gurkha Mercenary Forces, 1 Belgian brigade, 1 EEC Mixed Security brigade and an undetermined number of other forces, all foreign. They originally were scheduled to work for approximately 3 weeks in the area but if this is similar to the last mobilization that took place, you will find that they will be there for up to 2 1/2 to 3 months.

During the LA riot there were a series of actions that took place both in Montana and we also saw activities in California, and there were activities in northern Texas in the panhandle. In March 1992, a caller on the short wave talk show confirmed that machine guns were being mounted on boxcars in San Bernardino, California.

The black population in San Bernardino County rivals that of L.A.

FINCEN forces are ruthless. For example, the Gurkhas are professional mercenary forces from Nepal. They rotate these forces for a period of time out of Nepal and were originally hired by the British military force for a number of years. Now that they are under UN authority, of course, they have to find a use for them and they have. Remember the Gurkhas were being paid by the British and probably still are, to be used against us. Kind of like the Hessians of 1775, isn't it? I think you will find a lot of other forces with similar perspective there.

There are a number of forces spread throughout the 10 FEMA regions. For those of you who are not familiar with regionalism, here is an explanation: Regionalism is a form of government that we are about to experience if the New World Order people have their way. Under regionalism, Michigan becomes not Michigan but area 5. As area 5 our capitol will be in Chicago. Under the New States Constitution this particular type of government comes into power and we are going to find that all of a sudden we are going to be part of this sinister New World Order real quick.

Unfortunately, we never vote for a Governor again. The Governor will be directly assigned by the President, kind of like in Star Wars. We call that "Dictature." It is nothing more or less than a ruthless Dictature implemented against the Free Will of the People.

Terror shall reign. And most assuredly, terror shall reign! The regional Governor will not have authority over his military forces but the most assuredly will have full authority over his *security forces*. Unlike the Governors of old he will not have a pocket army, he will simply have police. The centralized military force will be completely under the authority of the United Nations.

Now, how did we get here? Well, that's an interesting story when you think about it because there are a lot of problems involved. It's an ongoing escalation of resources pitted against the American people and the Republic. We are a Constitutional Republic, by the way; not a democracy. I think that everybody had better remember that right now. This is a problem you run into even with Republican Presidents. How many times did you hear George Bush say "this democracy?" This is a man who

calls himself a Republican. I'm not necessarily a Democrat or a Republican. I'm one of those independent American kind of guys.

Here's an example of FINCEN and some of the effects that overlap into United Nations operations. This was on the cover of Airman magazine which is the US Air Force publication, July 1992. It should be very evident that the forces that are displayed here on the cover are very impressive. Unfortunately, of the 5 aircraft on the cover only one of them is American. The rest are all Soviet bombers or Soviet heavy-lift aircraft. It should be noted that these types of assets have been reported by a lot of people in the military who people didn't want to believe.

These are documents that more than verify the validity of comments that were made in the past. The forces involved that we are going to see in FINCEN will be very well educated. *They are professional military forces.* They are, for all practical purposes, mercenaries of course. You are going to find that they normally serve an 8-year tour unlike the old American mechanism which was a 6 year tour mixed time of active and reserve component with IRR (Independent Ready Reserve) options.

Instead we have now gone to an 8-year mechanism, the same as all foreign professional forces overseas, very characteristic of the same mechanism that the British used against us in 1775. Conscription through pressing was normally done with an 8-year tour.

What we are looking at right now is an action which is quite sophisticated and has taken probably 50 years to develop, and the enemy has almost reached that point where he can touch the golden ring.

FINCEN OVERSEAS MILITARY FORCE:

A lot of military forces are being sent overseas. Does anybody wonder why, in this time of "peace," we're sending more and more of our military to places like Bosnia-Herzegovina, Somalia, Thailand or Haiti? And has anybody heard about our forces in Peru? I imagine not. There are some 20,000 to 21,000 personnel right now sitting off Yugoslavia's coast or in Yugoslavia at this time. We have approximately 20,000 mixed personnel functioning in Somalia. That's 40,000 combat personnel. In addition to that we have 22,000 to 23,000 in Cambodia. There are 10,000 in Haiti. So we've got 120,000 people overseas and most of them are combat troops.

Lets go one step further back during Desert Dust, one of those little actions that everyone missed. During the executive orders that were signed, 18,000 US military personnel were sent to Peru for policing operations there under UN authority. This is documented but was never reported by the secular media. We've got people who are down there right now. There are families who are highly concerned about the people that are in Peru. They have lost people there. People have been and are being killed.

This receives no publicity and yet it is going on. It is a prime example of "Watch my right hand." Hey, you didn't see what was going on over here, did you? That's what we have to worry about and the banker controlled media is up to their necks in the deception.

The Media is completely controlled by the Cabalists, even if they deny it publicly. What I do a lot of times is videotape what is going on television but ignore what they say. *Pay attention to the photographs.* If they are really concerned with something they won't feed you much, but in many cases they feel the general population is not observant and there is more in a picture than in all the gobbledygook words they have fabricated to deceive us.

You have to ask yourself when you look at pieces of equipment and activities, "Why is this taking place? Where is this taking place? Is this actually what is going on?" If you look at the expressions of the individuals, the activities, the attitudes, you know that something doesn't taste right. A lot of military people coming back are tickled pink to leave Somalia as fast as they can get aboard the plane. There is a reason for that. It is an untenable situation but it is typical of the type that the United Nations has put us into. Of course, Americans are now working seven months of every year just to pay to have their children murdered by the New World Order.

It should be noted that a lot of military personnel are having difficulties bringing family members back or sending family members back from Europe to the United States. We have three families in particular who are experiencing this right now. They are attempting to send their wives and children out of Europe back into the continental United States and the military will not do it, will not send them. This is interesting considering we are not at war and we have no threat of war on the horizon that anybody could pick out, short of a few policing actions that are supposed to be fairly minor.

Beware that a Lusitania-type contrived incident or incited internal strife does not put you into a real-life rerun of the TV mini-series "Amerika!" Based on research of the National Economic Council, a plan was adopted in London in 1952 by the World Association of Parliamentarians for World Government Alien troops to occupy and police the regionalized earth under a World Parliament of *appointed* members (Regional Princes) headed by a dictator. No Americans would enforce the New Order in the USA; only Russians, Colombians, Venezuelans, Belgians, Irish, and Mongolians. State Department pamphlet 7277 for totally disarming the USA presented similar plans. The State Department denies having ever authored such a pamphlet, however, we know it did because we have an original copy.

So why are the U.S. and Canada sending so many of their troops over seas? And why do we accept it? It is because we are so disillusioned and disenchanted about everything, and feel so powerless that we have already closed our minds to the outside world, choosing instead to be captivated and re-educated by a socialist TV network.

FINCEN UN COMBAT FORCES:

United Nations combat forces include those that are co-operating with FINCEN at this time in Montana and the elements that are in California. There were 25,000 of them identified south of Los Angeles and are probably deployed north-northeast of Los Angeles in the Sacramento Basin. The elements that were located in Texas have shifted, by all indications, and are probably spread out through a series of garrisons.

Foreign forces are now deployed in the Ohio Valley, starting in the Cincinnati area and moving north-north-west. We know that these elements are also located at Fort Huachuca, Arizona; Fort Benning, Georgia, and at Fort Drum, New York.

The processing center for detainees in the western half of the United States is at Oklahoma City. We do not know the location is for the Eastern Seaboard at this time, however, by all indications, Fort Drum will be the control point for processing individuals to detention facilities on the eastern half of the United States, east of the Mississippi. If there are any problems, what I would recommend for a lot of people that are concerned about this is that we *observe the air, not the ground.*

What I would like to get into next are the activities and future proposed actions inside the United States by a variety of organizations including the MJTF Police, FINCEN, and UN battle groups that will be deployed against the American people.

First of all we'll go back to early 1989 when originally, in smoke filled rooms, behind closed doors, some committee of political monkeys decided that is was time to go after the weapons inside the United States. In doing so, what they did is decide to come up with a program called guns/drugs drugs/guns. If you have a gun you must be a drug dealer. This is everybody, private arms owners, skeet shooters, whoever. Our response as law abiding American citizens was supposed to be, "Oh take my guns, I'm not a drug dealer, oh please." Unfortunately, a far as the socialist government was concerned, was that the American people started to rearm themselves very quickly.

We surveyed a lot of different shows throughout the United States, Midwest, specifically and, in fact in some cases we covered three different cities and two different states within a 10 hour period. What we saw weren't people trying to get rid of their weapons. That wasn't the case at all.

We would notice that people weren't selling anything and were buying more. It was shoulder to shoulder, elbow to elbow, rear end to front and heel to toe and everybody was bringing everybody's uncle in to buy weapons, munitions, equipment and we saw this from Kentucky and Tennessee to Pennsylvania, and New Jersey to Michigan, Indiana, Illinois. The effect that their guns/drugs drugs/guns program had is that the patriots out there started to talk to people and said, "See? This is exactly what we told you was going to happen." And after surveying a few shows, I'm sure that the intelligence information coming back to the Alcohol, Tobacco and Firearms people and also from other agencies that were monitoring the gun shows was that the result was not exactly what they expected either.

When in 1990 it was realized that they weren't accomplishing their original mission they had to change their time table a little, we think. By the third month they realized that the militia forces and civilian armies were burgeoning at a massive proportion. Operation Achilles was the group spying on Americans at the gun shows.

OPERATION CLEAN-SWEEP:

They began to reduce their actions because we found out who they were and because they were seeing more aggressive stances of the civilian population that they were attacking. Unfortunately, as with cockroaches, you can spray and spray and they keep coming back. By late 1992 the latest guns/drugs drugs/guns campaign escalated with a variety of other overlapping actions. "It's a threat to your children. It's a threat to society." Well, this society isn't monarchal England, it isn't Pharaonic Egypt, and we most certainly aren't the Union of Soviet Socialist Republics...yet.

Now during the time from late 1992 to the early part of 1993 we've seen a series of other actions take place in which firearms confiscations house-to-house, door-to-door have taken place. Operation "Clean-Sweep" in Chicago, Operation "Achilles 2" in Cleveland, and a series of actions that took place after the Los Angeles riots, not against the street gangs but against the citizens who defended their homes and their businesses.

During the earlier phases, for instance in Chicago, the black helicopter missions that we were talking about in the earlier hours were taking place extensively. We know individuals who were in high-rises who were actually above helicopters flying between the high-rises in Chicago. These operations culminated in a final activity which lasted approximately one week in which they cordoned off neighborhoods, went building to building and house to house, entered forcibly if necessary, and prosecuted the owners of any firearms, ammunition, or gun parts found. This was operation "Clean Sweep," and it will continue to happen and escalate all over the country in coming months.

In Cleveland an activity which was covered only by National Public Radio involved elements of the MJTF police and probably FINCEN forces. The Ohio Guard was mobilized from several different areas of the state, trans-

ferred to an area outside the Cleveland airport where a staged neighborhood, an urban warfare training area, was set up with three neighborhoods as the targets. The units that were brought in were trained in house to house search and seizure and securing a neighborhood.

They then went into the first training neighborhood, went house to house, secured the neighborhood and then attacked the second neighborhood. Once they had secured the second neighborhood they had to hold the first and went to get a third neighborhood. After these elements were trained and passed through this mechanism, they were transferred to different parts of Cleveland where they were then actually deployed against American citizens who had broken no laws.

This happened about the same time that the Weaver incident took place near Bonner's Ferry, Idaho. It was almost simultaneous. In fact a series of actions both in Cleveland and one in Michigan took place either during or shortly after the Weaver incident. Now in Cleveland this received some local media coverage. In some parts of Ohio this received local media coverage. But it received no national media attention except for one place, National Public Radio, who thought that this was the next best thing to sliced white bread, that socialist armed forces violated people's homes, that they had gone into different parts of the city to illegally confiscate legal firearms.

When the Alcohol, Tobacco and Firearms forces came into Detroit to search house-to-house in specific neighborhoods, it should be noted that National Public Radio, on the 11th of March, broadcast another one hour program in which they specifically mentioned that "...if we can do it in Cleveland, why can't we do it in Michigan?"

WACO: REHEARSAL FOR TYRANNY:

The Waco situation, which is typical of a lot of what we are going to be seeing in the future, involved a 100 to 130 man assault company of the Alcohol, Tobacco and Fire arms, probably under MJTF authority again.

It should be understood that as of March 1989, the ATF, Alcohol, Tobacco and Firearms forces were divided up in to these MILITARY-TYPE assault companies.

Each platoon consists of 40 men armed with the M16-A2 rifle, the AR15 nine millimeter conversion, or the M79 grenade launcher. It is now known that these forces also include the M60 machine gun, which is an (inferior) infantry battle weapon now being deployed with policing agencies like they have in Russia. It was interesting to note that this assault company in Texas was identical to the type of forces that were used during Operation "Achilles" in the Ohio Valley coming up into Michigan.

The forces dress in all black BDU uniform. They wear the black pasgan armor with the black pasgan helmet which almost identical to the World War Two Nazi German coal scuttle helmet. (We wonder why!) They are armed, equipped and maintained through DOD resources. So, many of the weapons that they are provided with are actually provided by our military. In many cases, Alcohol, Tobacco and Firearms, the FBI, DEA are now receiving training by Quantico Marines and many of them have gone through the US Army Ranger School. That is rather exotic training for people who are supposed to be police officers in the United States. On the other hand if you are a dictator in need of thugees, you've got to send them some place where they can learn to be fairly efficient thugees.

Many of the people in our militias who went through Ranger School in the last year said that up to 50 per cent of their company were made up of Federal Bureau of Investigation people and individuals who were involved with Alcohol, Tobacco and Firearms or the Drug Enforcement Agency.

DEA, by the way, has what we call CLET units. CLET units are directly under the control of the Treasury and/or can be accessed by the MJTF police or FINCEN. CLET units are armed identically to the ATF combat elements and are deployed throughout the United States and *can be used overseas*. DEA is now using extensive resources from outside the United States in terms of manpower, but they will not identify what the name of the organization is that's being used. Now, remember, we know what FINCEN is but nobody else is supposed to, so it can be assumed that FINCEN is the element that is involved.

How are they deploying equipment here? Well, its kind of strange. A lot of people say, where are they? Well, they are in all parts of the United States but we've had at least one face to face confrontation with some of their people right here in Michigan.

BLACK LIST: A STRANGE CASE:

Although I can't mention names, on a given date one of our members was attempting to use a space available flight through US Army Tactical Air Lift Command. Upon arriving at the site they looked at his military ID card. Somebody punched in his name, looked at him very briefly and punched it in again. In a minute and a half there were two MPs behind him. Now this site is Selfridge Air National Guard Post. The individual was then forcible put into a car and driven around to the southwest quadrant of the Post.

When he arrived there, the MPs took him out of the vehicle and as he entered the structure the first person at the table at the entrance desk was in an all-black uniform with no identification or markings at all. He was then taken to an interrogation room. Now at first he was thinking, "Oh my goodness, what did I do? My ID card must be messed up or something."

Upon seeing the black uniforms he understood exactly who he was dealing with. They sat him down. The first thing he was asked was how many cars do you own? How

much food do you have? How many weapons do you own? What are the names of your children? What does 762X39 millimeters mean? He really didn't know. Well, he really did but he thinks in inches, not in metric. Then there was a little conference and they left the room, leaving his dossier on the table. Anybody who is involved with military or intelligence knows that you don't do that. Your career rests on security but it should be understood that in this file is a big rap sheet about 2 1/2 feet by 1 1/2 feet tall. On this sheet was a spiderweb of names of people to be arrested. My name was at the top for the State of Michigan; so I can be proud I'm number one in trying. I don't have to try harder. Number 2 was another individual who is with us. Number 7 was the individual who was being questioned. All of the other lists had virtually dozens and dozens of names. It should be understood that it was meant for him to see this and it was a direct threat to anybody else who is prying into the affairs of these little bootlicking Nazi goosesteppers.

The gentleman made a little rattling noise at the door and came back in, sat down, and basically told him, "We have nothing to hold you on. We are going to let you go." Walking back out, two MPs appeared and walked him back over the vehicle, then drove him around to his car and was escorted from the Post.

Now anybody who understands military documentation will understand that if you have a classified records jacket, you take a classified record sheet and put it on the top, first of all. The next thing you *don't do* is take a classified document and leave it where somebody you really don't want to see it can see it. This was meant as a direct threat.

This was just before we were involved with other meetings that we've participated in during which we were informing Americans of these problems. If I keep this up, they are going to do something to me. Well, I'll tell you what, I'm not stupid. If I'm already on the list as many other people are—look at this way—you are *never* going to come off that list even if you stop prying so you might as well keep prying.

CONCLUSION:

They are scared stupid of the possibility of the American people waking up. Anyone who reveals their plots and plans to destroy America puts such a wrench in their plans that they can not afford to let those people or groups continue with impunity. They will do everything in their power if need be to eliminate what they perceive as threats to their deception. Outright murder or imprisonment is not out of the question, although I believe that is a few years down the road. Right now, they are primarily concerned that we are going public, and they will do everything in their power to squash this movement in any manner that suits their purposes.

MASONRY: THE HIDDEN EVIL

Masonry, posing under the guise of Christianity, is spreading the teachings of Lucifer to the world!

Masons, we have all probably heard of them before. They are thought to be a fraternity or organization for men that encourages the spirit of Christianity. In reality, they are the exact opposite. Their enemies are the Christians and their objective is to spread the teachings of Lucifer among a new world they wish to create...a New World Order...a world that will be brought together under the name of Lucifer.

To understand Masonry, we must first understand its history. Masonry has been traced back more than 5000 years to a secret society of ancient Egyptian priests. Ancient Egyptian tombs contain engravings and proof that the Masons 5000 years ago and the Masons today share the same hand grips, signs, postures, symbols, and the apron used for initiation into the Masons.

The ancient Egyptian gods the Masons worshipped were Osiris, the god of the Egyptian underworld and the prince of the dead, and Isis, the guiding light of the prostitution profession. Isis was believed to be married to Osiris, the Lord in perfect black. Osiris was worshipped as the supreme god of evil.

The signs and symbols of the ancient Egyptian Masons are shared with the present day Masons. One of the most important Mason symbols is an all seeing eye, or the "Eye of Osiris."

The mysterious five pointed star of Masonry represents "intelligence" as well as the emblem of Osiris. This was explained by Albert Pike, Masonry's leader of a century ago. In his manual titled "Morals and Dogma of the Ancient and Accepted Scottish Rite of Freemasonry" he states:

"...the BLAZING STAR of five points.. .Originally it represented SIRIUS, or the Dog -star, the forerunner of the inundation of the Nile;...the Blazing Star has been regarded as an emblem of Omniscience, or the All-seeing Eye, which to the Egyptian Initiates was the emblem of Osiris, the Creator."

The above manual is still today required reading for all Masons who wish to enter the Scottish Rite.

The Mason symbol of a circle with a dot in the center, or the Mason sun, represents the knowledge and wisdom that radiates from the inside of Masons. Manly Hall, a Mason of the 33rd degree, the highest degree known, states:

"The Master Mason is in truth a sun, a great reflector of light, who radiates through his organism, purified by ages of preparation, the glorious power which is the light of the Lodge. He, in truth, has become the spokesman of the Most High. He stands between the glowing fire light and the world. Through him passes the Hydra, the great snake, and from its mouth there pours to man the light of God. His symbol is the rising sun... Masonry is eternal truth...patience is its warden.. .illumination its master.

When a Mason has built all these powers into himself, there radiates from him a wonderful body of living fire, like that which surrounded the Master Jesus, at the moment of his transfiguration."

Even the letter G that appears in the middle of the interlaced square and compass has an anti-Christian meaning. When one is initiated into the Masonic order, he is taught that the G stands for Geometry. Then as one advances the Masonic order he learns that the G stands for God, then the Great Architect of the Universe, and finally when achieving the Mason ranks of the Knights Kadosch the true meaning of the G is explained... Gnosticism.

After reaching the grade of Kadosch the Freemasons dedicate themselves to the glorification of Gnosticism, which is defined by Albert Pike as "the soul and marrow of Freemasonry." Gnosticism is the exact opposite of Christianity. Gnostics believed that one did not reach heaven by leading a life of faith, they believed they would through the possession of gnosis. Gnosis was believed to be illumination achieved through sex, drugs, dancing, drumbeating, and sacrifices. Gnostics believed that there was no absolute morality; that evil deeds were justifiable if they served a higher purpose.

The first three degrees (levels) of modern Masonry are known as the Blue Lodge. As one rises among these three levels he must swear to brutal "blood oaths." To betray the secrets of Masonry or its rituals means death, as Captain William Morgan discovered in 1826. Captain Morgan was killed by Masons after obtaining a copyright on an exposé on Masonry, which included the complete rituals, oaths, and secret passwords of the Blue Lodge Masons.

Once one wishes to advance from the Blue Lodge, he has two possible paths to follow. He can become either a member of the Scottish Rite or a member of the York Rite. The York Rite is supposedly for those of the Christian religion, though the end results are not very different from those of the Scottish Rite. The Scottish Rite teaches Deism, the belief that God may have created the earth at one time, but he then left the world forever, never to meddle with the affairs of men again. This is the first step to the teachings of Atheism, where no God exists at all. Those who seek great monetary gains and power through Masonry advance through the Scottish Rite.

The reason so many Masons believe they are part of a Christian organization while few know the true intent of Masonry is because Masonry is a secret organization within a secret organization. The Blue Lodge rank of Masonry to which the majority of the Masons belong is the "outer" doctrine of Masonry. Only when they rise up the ranks and enter the "inner" doctrine of Masonry do they realize the true goals of the Masons. Albert Pike described this in his book as follows:

"The Blue Degrees are but the outer court or portico of the Temple. Part of the symbols are displayed there to the Initiate, but he is intentionally misled by false misrepresentations. It is not intended that he shall understand them; but it is intended that he shall imagine he understands them. Their true explanation is reserved for the Adepts, the Princes of Masonry."

Once one breaks through the "outer" doctrine he will find out that the god of Masonry is Lucifer. Lucifer and Satan are not the same as most believe. In the bible we are taught that Lucifer was God's most important angel, perfect in every way. But Lucifer wanted to replace God, so he led the first rebellion. God then banished Lucifer from heaven to earth, where Lucifer

1

became Satan, the evil angel of darkness.

A Satanist knows Satan is evil as they know they are also evil. A true Satanist's mission is to bring as many people to hell with them as they can. A Mason denies the above biblical account ever occurred. They believe Lucifer never fell to earth; that Lucifer is really God. They call the Christian God by the name of Adonay, and they believe that he is really the god of evil because he forces men to be subservient to his repressive dictates.

The Luciferians believe that God is dual in nature, that he is the good god Lucifer and the bad god Adonay, both equal in power and opposite in intent. This is symbolized by the black and white checkerboard pattern on the floor of Masonic lodges and buildings. Lucifer is then divided into Osiris and Isis, whom were discussed earlier.

Many "Christian" Masons will object to the above revelations. They will claim that Masonry is not the evil organization we are claiming it to be. In their minds, this is true. As explained before, 75 % of all Masons never go any further than the Blue Lodge. The true secrets of Masonry are never revealed to Blue Lodge members. Blue Lodge members are intentionally deceived as Albert Pike explained in his own words. But in order to show without a doubt that Masonry is 100% incompatible with Christianity we will compare Masonry with the Holy Bible. This direct comparison will show without a doubt that no true Christian can also be a Mason.

SALVATION

The Masons teach you that you can reach heaven through good deeds and a pure life alone. Starting with the First Degree the Lodge uses a lambskin to represent purity. The Entered Apprentice is instructed:

"In all ages the lamb has been deemed an emblem of innocence; he, therefore, who wears the Lambskin as a badge of Masonry is continually reminded of that purity of life and conduct which is necessary to obtain admittance into the Celestial Lodge above (heaven), where the Supreme Architect of the Universe (God) presides."

The above theory pertaining to salvation is taught all the way to the top of the Masonry ladder. When a Mason dies, the Lodge tells his family and friends that his soul went to heaven as he strived to live a pure life. The Masonic funeral then goes on to teach that:

"Masonry has come down from the far past. It uses the tools of the builders' trade as emblems and symbols to teach Masons how to build character and moral stature...it seeks constantly to build the temple of the soul and thus to fit us for that house not made with hands, eternal in the heavens... Masons believe sincerely that when life on earth comes to a close, the soul is translated from the imperfections of the mortal sphere, to that all-perfect, glorious and Celestial Lodge Above, where God, the Grand Architect of the Universe, presides. With these truths and convictions, our brother was well acquainted. Though perfection of character is not of this world, yet we are persuaded that our brother sought to live by these truths and principles of Masonry... When our brother labored with us in Masonic attire, he wore a white apron, which he was taught is an emblem of innocence and a badge of a Mason. By it, he was constantly reminded of that purity of life and that rectitude of conduct so necessary to his gaining admission into the Celestial Lodge Above. He will

now wear that apron forever as the emblem of the virtues it represents... In accordance with our custom, I now place this evergreen over the heart of our brother."

The Bible teaches that the Mason teachings are a false gospel. The Bible teaches that man does not go to heaven by his deeds or purity of life, it teaches that man can only go to heaven through believing in Jesus Christ.

"He saved us, not on the basis of deeds which we have done in righteousness, but according to His mercy, by the washing of regeneration and renewing by the Holy Spirit. (Titus 3:5)"

"And the witness is this, that God has given us eternal life, and this life is in His son. He who has the Son has the life; he who does not have the Son of God does not have the life. (1 John 5: 11- 12)".

"Know that a man is not justified by observing the law, but by faith in Jesus Christ. So we, too, have put our faith in Christ Jesus that we may be justified by faith in Christ and not by observing the law, because by observing the law no one will be justified...I do not set aside the grace of God, for if righteousness could be gained through the law, Christ died for nothing! (Galatians 2: 16,21)"

GOD

Masonry will try to have you believe that the god of Masonry is the same God of the Christian Bible. That claim could not be further from the truth. Masonry constantly mocks and blasphemes the Christian God. All men who enter the Lodge must decide whether they will worship the inferior Christian God or the one true god. Proof of this is shown in "Coil's Masonic Encyclopedia" which was written by Henry Wilson Coil.

"Men have to decide whether they want a God like the ancient Hebrew Jahweh, a partisan, tribal God, with whom they can talk and argue and from whom they can hide if necessary, or a boundless, eternal, universal, undenominational, and international, Divine Spirit, so vastly removed from the speck called man, that He cannot be known, named, or approached. So soon as man begins to laud his God and endow him with the most perfect human attributes such as justice, mercy, beneficence, etc., the Divine essence is depreciated and despoiled... The Masonic test (for admission) is a Supreme Being, and any qualification added is an innovation and distortion."

In the above quote, the Christian God is referred to as an inferior tribal God, while the Masons refer to their god as a superior universal god. The above states that man cannot ever hope to approach God as He is unapproachable, yet the Bible teaches us that God can be approached through Christ. The above states that God is single, yet the Bible teaches us that God is a trinitarian Being. The above teaches that God does not have personal emotions, yet the Bible teaches us that God is angry with sin and loving and merciful to those who repent. It is obvious that the Masonic god is not the Christian God they represent it to be.

When going through the rituals to enter the Royal Arch Degree the Royal Arch Mason is told that the true name for the God he has been worshipping is Jabulon. Jabulon is a combination of the following: "Ja" for Jehovah, "Bul" for Baal, and "On" for Osiris. Any Christian should know the first commandment states "Thou shalt have no other gods before me." In the name

2

Jabulon, the Christian God is combined with two pagan gods, Baal and Osiris (the Egyptian equivalent of Baal). If you worship the Mason god, then you also worship Baal. God rejected this evil god as shown in the Bible.

"Because they have forsaken Me and have made this an alien place and have burned sacrifices in it to other gods...and because they have filled this place with the blood of the innocent and have built the high places of Baal to burn their sons in the fire as burnt offerings to Baal, a thing which I never commanded or spoke of, nor did it ever enter My mind; therefore...behold, I am about to bring on his city and all its towns the calamity that I have declared against it, because they have stiffened their necks so as not to heed My words. (Jeremiah 19:4-5, 15; cf. 7:9-10)"

When you worship Jabulon, the Mason god, you are committing blasphemy against the one true God of Israel. You are committing idolatry by swearing oaths to the pagan god that He has condemned. It doesn't matter if you are only a Blue Lodge member who knows not the true name of the Mason god, you are still swearing oaths and accepting the pagan Masonic god. And after reading this report, if you continue to be a Mason then you are knowingly accepting a pagan god, which is much worse than unknowingly accepting one.

Jesus Christ

Masonry denies that Jesus Christ was ever the Son of God. The Masonic doctrine teaches that:

"Jesus was just a man. He was one of the 'exemplars,' one of the great men of the past, but not divine and certainly not the only means of redemption."

All Masons are prohibited from speaking Jesus' name in the Masonic Lodges, and they are prohibited to dedicate a prayer in the name of Christ. Following is a real life example of what happens to the Christian Mason who tries to dedicate a prayer in the name of Jesus Christ:

"The Commander of the Guard called me aside and rebuked me sharply. He said, I had ended the prayer "in Christ's holy name." For that, he said, I would be reported! I was called in to see the Secretary of the Scottish Rite (a Christian Scientist) about my unsatisfactory performance. He was nice about it, but told me that I was never to end a prayer "in Jesus' name" or "in Christ's name." He said, "Make your prayers universal."

Denying Jesus Christ is denying your Christian teachings. The Bible teaches over and over again that anyone who doesn't accept Jesus does not accept God either, regardless of what Masonry wants you to believe.

"Everyone therefore who shall confess Me before men, I will also confess him before My father who is in heaven. But whoever shall deny Me before men, I will also deny him before My father in heaven. (Matthew 10:32-33)"

"Whoever denies the Son does not have the Father; the one who confesses the Son has the Father also. (1 John 2:23)"

"For not even the Father judges anyone, but He has given all judgement to the Son, in order that all may honor the Son, even as they honor the Father. He who does not honor the Son does not honor the Father who sent Him. (John 5:22-23)"

Swearing Oaths

When a Mason is entered into Masonry he has to swear an oath to protect and keep sacred the Masonic Order. This is usually done using the Holy Bible in a Christian dominated Masonic Lodge. But swearing an oath to serve the Masonic interests is condemned by God, as the teachings of the Masonic Order are not Christian. By participating in Masonry, you are helping to spread false and blasphemous teachings to others whether intentional or not.

The Bible provides a Christian a way to escape the oaths taken in ignorance when they entered the Masonic Order.

"If a person swears, speaking thoughtlessly with his lips to do evil or to do good, whatever it is that a man may pronounce by an oath, and it is hidden from him - when he realizes it, then he shall be guilty in these matters. And it shall be, when he is guilty in any of these matters, that he shall confess that he has sinned in that thing; and he shall bring his trespass offering to the Lord for his sin which he has sinned...So the priest shall make atonement on his behalf for his sin which he has sinned, and it shall be forgiven him. (Leviticus 5:4-6, 10)"

If you are a Mason who took the Masonic oaths upon the Holy Bible, you are not bound to follow those oaths made in ignorance. You must simply leave Masonry and ask forgiveness for your sins. Any true Christian upon reading what true Masonry is should do this, otherwise they are not a true Christian.

The purpose of this report was to teach people that Masonry and Christianity are in no way related. Throughout this report there were direct conflicts between Christian beliefs and Masonic beliefs explained. Many people will find it hard to believe that Masonry is anti-Christian, but that is because they were misled and taught to think that by the Masons. Even fellow Masons are misled purposely so they don't know the true teachings of Masonry. This is not a theory, this is a fact that came out of the mouth of a leading Mason's mouth!

If by chance you are a Christian and a Mason it is your duty to reject the Masonic Order from now on. This report has proved without a doubt that Masonry is anti-Christian. It isn't our words that showed the two incompatible with each other, it was the words from the Holy Bible. If you are a Christian, you cannot argue against the Bible's teachings. If you continue with the Masonic Order, then you are not a Christian in reality, regardless of what you claim.

As a closing thought, the following are the words of Steve Merritt, a previous Worshipful Master of the largest Lodge in New York who left the Masonic Order when he discovered the true teachings of Masonry:

"One incident helped to open my eyes. I have always preached that there is no other name but Christ by which we can be saved. But again and again I found Masons dying without God and without hope. I was called to the bedside of one member of my lodge who was thought to be dying. He gave me the grip as I sat down by him. He said he was dying and was in great distress for his soul. I tried to have him look to Christ. But he reproached me, saying I had led him astray. I had told him in the lodge, as Master, that a moral life was enough. He said, 'You told me then that it was all right if I was an upright man, and obeyed the precepts of the lodge, but I am leaning on a broken reed; and now I am dying without God. I lay this to your charge, Worshipful Master. I leaned on you and now I am dying.'"

THE "BLOOD OATHS" OF THE MASONS
A Mason must swear to vicious "blood oaths" where betrayal of the Masons can mean death.

If you thought that becoming a Mason was as easy as announcing your interest you were very wrong. To advance to each of the 33 degrees of Masonry one must attend an initiation ceremony and swear to a "blood oath," growing ever more vicious as one climbs the levels. Starting with the very first "blood oath" a Mason must promise never to reveal the ceremonies, goals, or secrets of the Masons. If he breaks that promise he will be hunted down by his fellow Masons...and many times killed.

The first three degrees of the Masons (the Blue Lodge) will be explained in detail. The information on the Mason ceremonies was published by Captain William Morgan in 1826. Captain Morgan was a third degree Mason who was appalled when he found out what the Masons really stood for. He obtained a copyright to expose the first three ceremonies a Mason must attend to as he wanted the world to know what the Masons really stood for. Soon thereafter, he was killed by the Masons for betraying their secrets. The complete details of the Blue Lodge levels (the first 3 degrees) will be explained in detail. This information was initially published in "Illustrations of Masonry by one of the Fraternity Who was devoted Thirty Years to the Subject," which of course was published by Captain Morgan.

FIRST DEGREE
Before a meeting begins, the lodge members ensure that no prying eyes can see what will go on through a series of rituals. Many of the lodge meeting rooms are on the second floor to help insure none of the Mason's secrets can be revealed. Once this is finished the leader of the lodge, the "Worshipful Master," opens the meeting by silently displaying the penal sign as follows:

"The Master then draws his right hand across his throat, the hand open, with the thumb next to his throat, and drops it down by his side. This is called the penal sign of an Entered Apprentice Mason, and alludes to the penalty of obligation."

This is followed with the following prayer that is intended to confuse candidates with religious proclivities.

"Most holy and glorious God! The Great Architect of the Universe; the giver of all good gifts and graces: Thou hast promised that 'Where two or three are gathered together in thy name, thou wilt be in the midst of them and bless them.' In thy name, we assemble, most humbly beseeching thee to bless us in all our undertakings; that we may know and serve thee aright, and that all our actions may tend to thy glory and our advancement in knowledge and virtue. And we beseech thee, O Lord God, to bless our present assembling; and to illuminate our minds through the influence of the Son of Rightness, that we may walk in the light of thy countenance; and when the trial of our probationary state are over, be admitted into the temple, not made with hands, eternal in the heavens. Amen. So

mote it be."

You will notice the above prayer made only one reference to God as the Great Architect of the Universe. This is to prepare Christians to accept the principles of Deism at later levels. Deists believe that God may have created the earth at one time, but he then left the world forever, never to meddle in the affairs of men again. This is why God was referred only as the Great Architect of the Universe.

If any of the candidates shows any doubt or objection to the above prayer and hidden meaning, he is stopped here. He goes no further as he is not fit to become a Mason. The ceremony then continues until the candidate is ready for initiation. He is blindfolded and asked to put on a special pair of pants that contain no metal. The pants are then rolled up to just the left knee only. The candidate's shirt is partially removed to uncover his left arm and breast and he is given a slipper for his right foot only. After this, a "Cable-tow" (a rope noose) is put around his neck and in most cases his left shoulder. After a series of memorized questions and answers the candidate enters the hall where the members are assembled. As the candidate enters the hall:

...the Senior Deacon at the same time pressing his naked left breast with the point of the compass, and asks the candidate, 'Did you feel anything?'

Answer: 'I did.'

Senior Deacon to candidate: 'What was it?'

Answer: 'A torture.'

The Senior Deacon: 'As this is a torture to your flesh, so may it ever be to your mind and conscience if ever you should attempt to reveal the secrets of Masonry unlawfully.'

After a prayer the Master of the Lodge then asks the candidate, "In whom do you put your trust?" The candidate answers, "In God." The Master then grabs the candidate's right hand and says, "Since in God you put your trust, arise and follow your leader and fear no danger."

The candidate is then led around the lodge three times still blindfolded. After this, the Master asks him from whence he came and whither he is traveling. The candidate answers, "From the west and traveling to the east." The Master asks, "Why do you leave the west and travel to the east?" The candidate answers, "In search of light."

Though at this point the candidate doesn't know the significance of searching east for the "light" as he progresses the degrees it is made clear. Masonry was traced back 5000 years to Egypt, where the ancient Egyptian priests used the same signs, symbols, hand grips, and apron used for initiation that the modern day Masons use. The Masons worship Osiris, the Egyptian god of underworld and the prince of death. Thus is the reference to the east.

The candidate then kneels assuming a position with his legs that symbolizes the Masonic square and compass. The Master says:

1

"Mr._____, you are now placed in a proper position to take upon you the solemn oath or obligation of an Entered Apprentice Mason, which I assure you is neither to affect your religion or politics. If you are willing to take it, repeat your name and say after me:

I_____, of my own free will and accord, and in the presence of Almighty God and this worshipful lodge of Free and Accepted Masons, dedicated to God, and held forth to the holy order of St. John, do hereby and hereon most solemnly and sincerely promise and swear that I will always hail, ever conceal and never reveal any part or parts, or any art or arts, point or points of the secret arts and mysteries of ancient Freemasonry which I have received, am about to receive, or may hereafter be instructed in, to any person or persons of the known world."

This continues as the candidate promises not to "write, print, stamp, stain, hew, cut, carve, indent, paint, or engrave" any of the Masonic secrets on anything "movable or unmovable under the whole canopy of heaven whereby or whereon the least letter, figure, character, mark, stain, shadow, or resemblance of the same may become legible or intelligible to myself or any other person in the known world, whereby the secrets of Masonry may be unlawfully obtained."

The above oath in effect states a Mason may never print any of the secrets of Masonry, that the secrets may only be handed down orally from one Mason to another. The oath concludes:

"To all of which I do most solemnly and sincerely promise and swear, without the least equivocation, mental reservation, or evasion of mind in me whatever: binding myself under no less penalty than to have my throat cut across, my tongue torn out by the roots, and my body buried in the rough sands of the sea at low water-mark, where the tide ebbs and flows twice in twenty-four hours; so help me God, and keep me steadfast in the due performance of the same."

The candidate is then asked what he desires most and he answers, "Light." Then the group forms a circle around him and the Master says, "And God said let there be light, and there was light." After this comment the Masonic members clap their hands and stomp the floor with their right feet. Simultaneously the blindfold which has been on the candidate the entire ceremony is removed. When this happens the candidate is temporarily blinded.

The candidate is told that the three great "lights" of Masonry are the Holy Bible, the Square, and the Compass. Finally, the initiate is taught the penal sign and the grip of an Entered Apprentice Mason. The grip is formed as follows:

"The right hands are joined together as in shaking hands and each sticks his thumb nail into the third joint or upper end of the forefinger; the name of this grip is Boaz....It is the name of the left pillar of the porch of King Solomon's temple."

The ceremony is ended as the initiate swears to support God and his country.

SECOND DEGREE

The second degree is referred to as the "Fellowcraft degree." The candidate must speak the secret password "Shibboleth" to enter the lodge. He then takes additional oaths. The penalty for breaking these oaths is as follows: "Binding myself under no less penalty than to have my left breast torn open and my heart and vitals taken from thence and thrown over my left shoulder and carried into the valley of Jehosaphat, there to become a prey to the wild beasts of the field, and vulture of the air, if ever I should prove willfully guilty of violating any part of this my solemn oath or obligation of a Fellow Craft Mason; so help me God, and keep me steadfast in the due performance of the same."

The candidate is now shown the new secret hand grip, or "pass grip."

"The pass-grip, is given by taking each other by the right hand, as though going to shake hands, and each putting his thumb between the fore and second fingers where they join the hand, and pressing the thumb between the joints. This is the pass grip of a Fellow Craft Mason, the name of it is Shibboleth." The candidate is also shown another hand grip called the "real grip."

"The real grip of a Fellow Craft Mason is given by putting the thumb on the joint of the second finger where it joins the hand, and crooking your thumb so that each can stick the nail of his thumb into the joint of the other; the name of it is Jachin."

If one Mason wishes to test another while giving this grip (to ensure the other is truly a Mason) the following questioning and responses are given while the grip is maintained:

Q. "What is this?"
A. "A grip"
Q. "A grip of what?"
A. "The grip of a Fellow Craft Mason."
Q. "Has it a name?"
A. "It has."
Q. "Will you give it to me?"
A. "I did not so receive it, neither can I impart it."
Q. "What will you do with it?"
A. "I'll letter it or halve it."
Q. "Halve it and you begin."
A. "No, begin you."
Q. "You begin."
A. "J.A."
Q. "CHIN."
A. "JACHIN."
Q. "Right, brother, Jachin, I greet you."

After the candidate is taught the new hand grips, the Master explains the following: "Brother, we have worked in speculative Masonry, but our forefathers wrought both in speculative and operative Masonry; they worked at the building of King Solomon's temple, and many other Masonic edifices... Brother, the first thing that attracts our attention are two large columns, or pillars, one on the left hand and the other on the right; the name of the one on the left hand is Boaz, and denotes strength; the name of the one on the right hand is Jachin, and denotes establishment;

they collectively allude to a passage in Scripture wherein God has declared in his word, "In strength shall this House be established."

The speech continues to explain the symbolic meanings of Masonry.

THIRD DEGREE

To enter the lodge for the Master Mason's Degree the secret password "Tubal Cain" must be spoken. The lengthy third degree oath then begins. Parts of it are as follows:

"Furthermore do I promise and swear that I will not wrong this lodge, nor a brother of this degree to the value of one cent, knowingly, myself, or suffer it to be done by others, if in my power to prevent it.

...Furthermore do I promise and swear that I will not speak evil of a brother Master Mason, neither behind his back nor before his face, but will apprise him of an approaching danger, if in my power.

...Furthermore do I promise and swear that I will obey all regular signs, summonses, or tokens given, handed, sent, or thrown to me from the hand of a brother Master Mason, or from the body of a just and lawfully constituted lodge of such.

...Furthermore do I promise and swear that a Master Mason's secrets, given to me in charge as such, and I knowing them to be such, shall remain as secure and inviolable in my breast as in his own, when communicated to me, murder and treason excepted; and they left to my own election [emphasis mine]."

Notice in the above section of the oath the candidate must swear to never wrong a fellow brother. No mention of the rest of the world is made. Also notice that the candidate must swear to keep hidden the secrets of fellow Masons, including any crimes or injustices they may do. Though murder and treason are excepted, the emphasis of the decision is loaded on the candidate, implying that if the candidate should betray the other member of those two crimes it was strictly his own decision, and not the decision of the Lodge. In other words, the Lodge would keep the member's trust if it were up to them, though the final decision is his.

The penalty for breaking the above oath is as follows:

"Binding myself under no less penalty than to have my body severed in two in the midst, and divided to the north and south, my bowels burnt to ashes in the center, and the ashes scattered before the four winds of heaven, that there might not the least tack or trace of remembrance remain among men or Masons, of so vile and perjured a wretch as I should be, were I ever to prove willfully guilty of violating any part of this solemn oath or obligation of a Master Mason. So help me God, and keep me steadfast in the performance of the same."

The candidate is then shown the "Grand Hailing Sign of Distress" which is given by raising both hands so the arms extend perpendicularly from the body then bend ninety degrees at the elbows so the hands point straight upward. In case of distress the words, "O Lord, my God! Is there no help for the widow's son?" are said. As the last words are said his hands fall, which is intended to indicate solemnity.

The widow referred to above is the goddess Isis after the death of her husband Osiris. The penal sign for the third degree is made by putting the right hand to the left side of the bowels, the hand open, with the thumb next to the belly, and drawing it across the belly, and letting it fall. This symbolizes the penalty of the oath.

Soon thereafter the candidate is shown another grip, the "Master's Grip" or "Lion's Paw." This is done by shaking hands except the participants stick the nails of each of their fingers into the joint of the other's wrist where it unites with the hand. This symbolizes the Masonic form of resurrection.

After much additional instructions, the ceremony ends. The candidate has then obtained the first three degrees of Masonry. Approximately 75 % of Masons never go beyond this point.

BEYOND THE BLUE LODGE

Once one wishes to advance from the Blue Lodge, he has two possible paths to follow. He can either become a member of the Scottish Rite or the York Rite. The York Rite is said to be for those of the Christian religion, but the end results aren't very different from those of the Scottish Rite. The Scottish Rite teaches Deism as a preparation for the teachings of Atheism, where no God exists at all. Those who seek monetary gains and power through Masonry advance through the Scottish Rite.

The Royal Arch degree is the seventh on the York Rite side of Masonry, on the Scottish Rite side the Royal Arch degree is the thirteenth degree. Once the candidate reaches this degree he must swear to keep the secrets of fellow Masons, murder and treason NOT excepted. With hand on the bible, the candidate must swear:

"I will aid and assist a companion Royal Arch Mason when engaged in any difficulty, and espouse his cause so far as to extricate him from the same, if within my power, whether he be right or wrong."

The above quote was initially published in "The Character, Claims and Practical Workings of Freemasonry" written by Rev. Charles G. Finney. As you can see, the candidates of the Royal Arch Degree must swear to help their fellow Masons from any jams they may get into, whether legal or illegal. Because of this, the Masons actively recruit citizens in powerful positions into the Royal Arch Degree. Lawyers, Judges, Police Officials, Gov't officials...any powerful position that can help any Mason who may commit a crime are sought by the Masons. With this in mind, is it a small wonder why there is so much corruption in the government? Can you imagine a Congress full of Royal Arch Masons that all took a "blood oath" to help their fellow Masons before their own country? How many present members in Congress are Royal Arch Masons? We would never know as they are sworn to keep their affiliations secret. Scary thought, isn't it?

Not only must a Royal Arch Mason swear to help a fellow Mason out no matter what crime he may commit, he must also swear to promote and vote for any Mason of that degree before any other of equal qualifications. In other words, if a bill that is harmful to America is presented to Congress from a Royal Arch Mason, all other Royal Arch Masons must vote for it whether they agree with it or not!

During the initiation into the Royal Arch degree, the candidate must drink wine from a cup made from the top half of a human skull. This is symbolic to the Royal Arch degree "blood oath" where the candidate swears "to have his skull struck off, and his brains exposed to the scorching rays of a meridian sun" if he ever betrays the Masonic secrets. He must also swear:

"To keep in my heart all the secrets that shall be revealed to me. And in failure if this my oath, I consent to have my body opened perpendicularly, and to be exposed for eight hours in the open air that the venomous flies may eat of my intestines...and I will always be ready to inflict the same punishment on those who shall disclose this degree and break this oath. So may God help and maintain me. Amen."

Once a Mason reaches the Royal Arch Degree in the York Rite he may then enter the three degrees of the Knight Templar. The legend behind the Templars goes like this. They were founded in 1118 to conquer and maintain the Holy Sepulchre in Jerusalem and protect pilgrims to the Holy Land from marauding Muslim bands.

The Templars grew more and more famous, as did their wealth. As this happened, they adopted secrecy to hide their internal actions. Their goal was to earn enough money to buy the world. As their treasury grew, so did their corruption. Rumors said they engaged in occult practices that included spitting and trampling on the Cross as initiation rites.

The Templars were banished from the Holy Land, whereafter they set up their headquarters in France. Soon Philip IV of France in 1306 sought to destroy them. All but thirteen were arrested on Friday the 13th. This is where the superstition of Friday the 13th was created. Philip found out that the Templars were plotting against the thrones of Europe and the Church also. He then had 50+ of the Templars killed after learning from them their secret rites. Their Grand Master Jacque de Molay was included among those who were killed. Jaques is to this day considered a martyr among Masons. Jaques was also the one who established the Scottish Rite of Masonry.

Today, the Knights Templar are considered the Christian branch of Masonry...but of course this isn't true. Their "Christian" teachings are merely Luciferic in nature.

As part of the initiation ceremony of the 18th degree of Masonry, known as the Knight of the Rose, Rose Croix, or "the Rosicrucians" the Masons symbolically drape the lodge room in black and sit on the floor. They are completely silent while they mock grief around an altar upon which are three crosses. They are not grieving about the death of the Son of God, but because the day Christ died Christianity was born. Christianity is the enemy of the Masons.

After the 32nd degree of the Scottish Rite, or the Knights Templar degree in the York Rite, a Mason may become a member of the Ancient Arabic Order Nobles of the Mystic Shrine...otherwise known as a Shriner. The Shriners are not thought to be a part of the Masonic order, nor are they thought to be anything besides generous people who have children's hospitals and burn centers where they treat children free of charge. They wear red fezzes with tassels. On many of the Shriner's property you will see their symbol of the Scimitar. This symbol is a slight variation of one of the older secret societies of the past...the Order of the Assassins.

The Shriners are the wealthiest "charity" in America. The assets in 1984 were estimated to be $1.979 billion by the I.R.S. Out of this tremendous horde of cash, only 29.8 percent of its 1984 income went to its services, while the Red Cross spent 84% of its income, the American Cancer Society spent 67.2%, the American Heart Association spent 70.6%, and the National Easter Seals spent 73% of its income on services. No other charity had so much money and gave so little.

The Shrine states they have nothing to do with eastern mysticism, though this isn't true. The Shrine rituals are in reality occult Middle-East Masonry. The Shrine's references to the "East" are to the eastern mysticism center of Mecca. Mecca is to the Shriners as Rome is to Christians.

As you can see from the above ceremonies and "blood oaths" the Masons are not a Christian organization as they would like you to believe. The above also shows that there are many different branches of Masonry, of which the well known and loved Shriners are a part. The above shows the exact promises the Masons must make as they advance to the higher levels...and the danger this can be to America when Royal Arch Masons are secretly members of our government.

The master plan of the Masons is to organize a New World Order whereupon all nations will be combined into one with one ruler. This single nation will be dedicated to Lucifer. This is also explained in the Revelations part of the Holy Bible. The ruler of this nation under Lucifer will be the Anti-Christ, and during this time the Armageddon will occur...as will the end of the world.

We must stand up and inform our fellow Americans about the dangers the Masons and the other secret organizations pose to America. If you think that they pose no threat then you highly underestimate their power and influence. Now is the time to stop their progress, but the only way their progress will be stopped is to ensure that fellow Americans know the danger these people are to the Republic. Unless we do so, it is just a matter of time until their master plan succeeds.

Ritual Magic, Mind Control and the UFO Phenomenon
By Adam Gorightly

Not long after my own encounter with strange aerial phenomena, I began to see a link between UFO's to such seemingly disparate topics as psychedelics, psychotronics and ritual magic. As the years pass, the Extraterrestrial Hypothesis (ETH) makes far less sense to this observer than other theories ranging from mind control conspiracies, or -- on the other hand -- fissures in the space/time continuum which provide a portal of entry for ghostly apparitions that can be saucer-shaped or even take on the form of Moth-Men, Chupacabras or the Blessed Virgin Mary.

UFO's encompass a wide range of phenomena and cannot be categorized simply in terms of little grey skinned buggers from Zeta-Reticuli shoving probes up human rectums. (Ouch!) To me the term "UFO" simply suggests something unexplainable hovering in outer or inner space, whether it is machine-like elves encountered under the influence of DMT, or nuts and bolt craft performing inexplicable aerial maneuvers over Area 51.

UFO's are limited only by our imaginations, and to consider them merely craft from another galaxy is as narrow a view as postulating that newborn babes are delivered exclusively by storks. UFO's are also -- in my estimation -- a product of altered consciousness, which is not to suggest that all sightings are in part, or in whole, complete confabulations. What I'm suggesting is that in order to observe UFO's, one must often enter into a more receptive state, much like a psychic or channeler tuning into voices or subtle energies. Channelers must first induce in themselves a trance state before being able to contact "voices from the beyond." The same goes for magical workings carried out in order to invoke spirits and/or demons.

A corollary to the above statement is the famed Amalantrah Working of legendary occultist Aleister Crowley, which consisted of a series of visions he received from January through March of 1918 through his then "Scarlet Woman", Roddie Minor. Throughout his life, Crowley had a number of Scarlet Women who acted as channels for otherworldly transmissions of angelic and/or demonic origin. The Scarlet Woman also played a large part in Crowley's notorious sex rituals, at times combining drugs and bestiality to stir up those strange energies into which good ol' Uncle Al was trying to tap. To quote Crowley chronicler Kenneth Grant from *Aleister Crowley and the Hidden God*:

> Crowley was aware of the possibility of opening the spatial gateways and of admitting an extraterrestrial Current in the human life-wave...It is an occult tradition--and Lovecraft gave it persistent utterance in his writings--that some transfinite and superhuman power is marshaling its forces with intent to invade and take possession of this planet... This is reminiscent of Charles Fort's dark hints about a secret society on earth already in contact with cosmic beings and, perhaps, preparing the way for their advent. Crowley dispels the aura of evil with which these authors (Lovecraft and Fort) invest the fact; he prefers to interpret it Thelemically, not as an attack upon human consciousness by an extra-terrestrial and alien entity but as an expansion of consciousness from within, to embrace other stars and to absorb their energies into a system that is thereby enriched and rendered truly cosmic by the process.

It was through the Amalantrah Working -- which included the ingestion of hashish and mescaline in its rituals -- that Crowley came into contact with an interdimensional entity named Lam, who by the way just happens to be a dead ringer for the popular conception of the "Grey" alien depicted on the cover of Whitley Strieber's *Communion*. Crowley called them "Enochian entities" because he purportedly contacted them by using "Enochian calls", a Cabalistic system/language devised by 17th century Elizabethan magician, Dr. John Dee. From this alleged encounter, some have inferred that the industrious Mr. Crowley intentionally opened a portal of entry through the practice of ritual magick, which allowed the likes of Lam and other alien greys a passageway onto the Earth plane. Dr. John Dee and his "scryer", Edward Kelly, had their own strange encounters with -- as they called them -- "little men" who moved about "in a little fiery cloud."

Some suggest that what Crowley tapped into was the same cosmic current that helped launch the rash of alien abductions as reported by UFO researchers Bud Hopkins, John Mack, David Jacobs, et al. When making these connections, bear in mind that many abductees recall their encounters with these grey skinned creatures only after being hypnotically regressed. Once again, we see that trance states -- not unlike those altered states produced during rituals such as the Amalantrah Working -- are often the triggering device which opens up a portal of otherworldly entry. According to Kenneth Grant, this tradition has been continued by current day Crowley adepts who practice ritual magick as a means to invoke "alien entities." In *Outside the Circles of Time*, Grant writes:

> Some believe that the UFO phenomena are part of the "miracle", and a mounting mass of evidence seems to suggest that mysterious entities have been located within the earth's ambience for countless centuries and that more and more people are being born with innate ability to see, or in some way sense their presence....Prayer for deific intervention in ancient times has now became a *cri de coeur* to extra-terrestrial or interdimensional entities, according to whether the manifestations are viewed as occurring within man's consciousness, or outside himself in apparently objective but often-invisible entities. New Isis Lodge has in its archives the sigils of some of these entities. The sigils come from a grimoire of unknown origin which forms part of the dark quabalahs of Besqul, located by magicians in the Tunnel of Quliefi. The grimoire describes Four Gates of extraterrestrial entry into, and emergence from, the known Universe.

Grant is speaking of a form of ritual magick practiced by such groups as the Golden Dawn, and the Ordo Templi Orientis (O.T.O.). "Sigils" are line drawings and diagrams that serve as signatures of entities accessible to a trained magician familiar with "Enochian calls" and other methods of summoning "spirits." A grimoire is a directory of such sigils, and a manual of their use.

A noted disciple of Crowley's, Jack Parsons -- one time head of the California branch of the O.T.O., and renowned rocket scientist -- carried on this tradition of interdimensional contact. In 1946 -- with the aid of "Frater H." -- Parsons made contact with some sort of entities not unlike Crowley's "Lam." This all took place during a series of magic rituals deemed The Babalon Working. What makes this story all the more curious is that Parsons' accomplice in this endeavor -- the aforementioned Frater H. -- was L. Ron Hubbard, the future founder of Scientology.

Apparently, Hubbard played a role similar to that of Edward Kelley, "scryer" for the aforementioned Dr. John Dee. A scryer works as a receptor of otherworldly communications, often using a crystal ball or similar device in conjunction with the magician's rituals. Together magician and scryer work left hand-in-hand in summoning these otherworldly beings: be they angels, demons or spirits of the dead. Crowley's Scarlet Woman, in many instances, performed this same function. For instance, Crowley's first wife, Rose Kelly -- while in a trance -- received the first three chapters of the infamous *Book of the Law*, the manuscript that laid the foundation for Crowley's religion, Thelema. Furthermore, the portal of entry for the extraterrestrial beings that Crowley theoretically opened (when he invoked "Lam") may have been further enlarged by Parsons and Hubbard with the commencement of the Babalon Working. As Kenneth Grant wrote, "The [Babalon] Working began...just prior to the wave of unexplained aerial phenomena now recalled as the 'Great Flying Saucer Flap.' Parsons opened a door and something flew in." Researcher John Carter suggests that the detonation of atomic bombs over Japan -- during the latter part of World War II -- may have also played a part in opening this door between dimensions or, at the least, attracted the curiosity of our intergalactic neighbors.

As Thelemic history instructs, 1947 ended the first stage of the Babalon Working, as Parsons and Hubbard parted ways after a falling out. (Apparently, Hubbard ran off with Parsons' wife and a large part of his fortune.) It was the same year the Modern Age of UFO's began with the Kenneth Arnold sightings over Mt. Rainer in Washington State, followed not long after by the purported saucer crash in Roswell, New Mexico.

1947 also marked the passing of The Great Beast, Aleister Crowley. Not long after these monumental events, in 1948, Albert Hoffman gave birth to LSD, which indicates that strange things were indeed afoot in the collective unconscious of humanity between the years of 1946-'48. Connecting all this high weirdness up even tighter is conspiracy researcher John Judge, who -- in an interview on KPFK radio, Los Angeles on August 12, 1989 dubbed "Unidentified Fascist Observatories" -- stated that Kenneth Arnold and Jack Parsons were flying partners, although I have, as yet, been unable to find additional corroboration to support this claim.

As for L. Ron Hubbard -- although it is not well publicized by current day members of the Church of Scientology -- much of his "religion" was based on a bizarre cosmology he apparently concocted, a thesis which suggested that several million years ago the souls of dead space aliens (Thetans) entered into the body of Earth humans, and that is part of the reason why today we are so screwed up as a species.

Another interesting UFO parallel to note is that Parsons and Hubbard's visionary experience with these alien-like entities transpired in the California desert, which during the late 40's and 50's was a hotbed for flying saucer activity. It was in this setting that such famous UFO Contactees as George Adamski and George Hunt Williamson invoked their own brand of cosmic messengers, transported by saucers, cigar-shaped vessels and the like, often originating from nearby Venus, or other seemingly uninhabitable planets in our solar system.

George Adamski's first encounter with the "Space Brothers" occurred in the Mojave Desert on November 20, 1952, when -- in the company of George Hunt Williamson and other associates -- he witnessed a cigar-shaped craft being pursued by military jets. Just before disappearing from sight, the craft ejected a silver disc, which landed a short distance from Adamski and his party. When Adamski arrived at the saucer he was greeted by a man named Orthon with long blond hair, wearing a one-piece suit. Telepathically, the Orthon informed Adamski he was from Venus, and that he was concerned about the possibility of atomic bomb radiation from Earth reaching other planets in the solar system, and that various beings from throughout the galaxy were visiting Earth harboring these same concerns. According to Adamski, he was taken aboard Orthon's craft and flown about the galaxy, including the dark side of the moon. During the course of this intergalactic voyage, Adamski took an array of spurious photographs that have been widely viewed as a hoax. In "Unidentified Fascist Observatories" John Judge asserted that Adamski was a intelligence asset who in his lecture tours throughout the 50's and 60's dispersed disinfo on behalf of the CIA.

Adamski's colleague -- George Hunt Williamson -- went on to author several UFO books, such as *Other Tongues--Other Flesh*, and presented the idea of a cosmic good-versus-evil battle taking place between the "good guys" from the dog star, Sirius, versus the evil shit-kickers from Orion. Strangely enough, the planet Sirius is a recurring theme in occult and UFO lore.

Of note in this regard is Robert Temple's *The Sirius Mystery*, published in 1977, which documents the history of the Dogon tribe of Africa, and their fabled meetings with the Nommos, a race of three-eyed, crab-clawed beings from Sirius. It was these intergalactic emissaries, as Dogon legends record, that passed onto the tribe -- as far back as 3200 B.C. -- various astronomical data instructing them that Sirius had a companion star invisible to the naked eye. These legends predate the advent of telescopes, and were later confirmed by astronomers. This companion star -- Sirius B -- wasn't photographed until 1970. In addition to this knowledge regarding Sirius B, the Nommos also provided additional info to the Dogons, such as the fact that Jupiter has four moons, Saturn has a ring around it, and that the planets in our solar system orbit around the sun; facts later confirmed by science.

In *The Sirius Mystery*, Temple traces contact with the Nommos all the way back to Sumeria circa 4500 B.C. At that time, he says, these three-eyed-crab-clawed creatures appeared in their mighty space ships from the stars, bestowing unto humankind vast secrets; revealing mysteries and esoteric knowledge passed on to initiates in various secret societies in Egypt, the Near East, and Greece. These initial contacts, Temple contends, planted the seeds for Freemasonry and other secret schools of esoteric knowledge such as The Knights Templar and the Rosicrucians. In fact, Freemasons believe that civilization on Earth was initially formed by entities from the Sirius star system, whom they equate with the Egyptian Trinity of Isis, Osiris, and

Horus. In these legends, Osiris has been portrayed as a precursor to Christ, who was first crucified then later resurrected, forming the basis of an Egyptian priesthood that worships Sun gods. The adepts of these mystery religions have always referred to themselves -- in one form or another -- as The Illuminati; those who have been "illuminated" by their worship of the various Sun gods/Moon goddesses.

Temple further notes that the Egyptian calendar revolved around the movements of Sirius, and that the calendar year began with the "dog days" when Sirius rises behind the sun. According to Philip Vandenberg in *The Curse of the Pharaoh*: "An archeologist named Duncan MacNaughton discovered in 1932 that the long dark tunnels in the Great Pyramid of Cheops function as telescopes, making the stars visible even in the daytime. The Greater Pyramid is oriented, according to MacNaughton, to give a view, from the King's Chamber, of the area of the southern sky in which Sirius moves throughout the year."

The brightest star in the heavens, Sirius is approximately 35 times brighter than our own sun, and is regarded in occult circles as the "hidden god of the cosmos". The famous emblem of the all-seeing eye, hovering above the unfinished pyramid, is a depiction of the Eye of Sirius, a common motif found throughout Masonic lore. It is no secret that many of our nation's founding fathers were Freemasons, which explains the odd appearance of Eye of Sirius on the dollar bill; a symbol seen everyday by millions, imprinting its image forever in our psyches. The imprinting of such imagery has been called into question in recent times by a whole host of conspiracy theorists, who -- in their New World Order scenarios -- connect such fraternal orders as the Knights of Malta, Freemasonry and Rosicrucianism with the symbol of Sirius, the eye in the triangle. At the top of this pyramid -- the conspiracy theorists contend -- is the dreaded Illuminati, tying all of these fraternal orders and secret societies together in a far flung plot intended to bring mankind to its knees under a futuristic Orwellian nightmare; a tolitarian society masquerading as a libertarian democracy, which uses Masonic imagery to program the masses.

And if this entire story wasn't already jumbled enough, the dawning of the 20th century ushered in a new generation of contactees paying homage to the "Dog Star." Around the turn of the century, a gentleman named Lucien-Francois Jean-Maine formed an order in Haiti called the Cult of the Black Snake that used rituals borrowed from

Crowley's O.T.O. in combination with voodoo practices. In 1922, these rituals reportedly summoned forth a disembodied being named Lam, the very same entity that Aleister Crowley made contact with a few years earlier. In fact, Kenneth Grant has stated that Crowley "unequivocally identifies his Holy Guardian Angel with Sothis (Sirius), or Set-Isis."

Later -- in the 1950's and 60's -- the aforementioned saucer "Contactee" George Hunt Williamson once again summoned forth certain denizens purportedly from Sirius, conversing to them in a similar "Enochian" or "angelic" language as that used by Dr. John Dee and Aleister Crowley. Williamson -- in his books and lectures -- also spoke of a secret society on Earth that has been in contact with Sirius for thousands of years, and that the emblem of this secret society is the eye of Horus, otherwise known as the all-seeing eye.

As previously noted, Williamson was a close associate of George Adamski, perhaps the most famous of the early UFO Contactees, who claimed to be connected with astronomers at Palomar Observatory in California, in whose company he allegedly witnessed several UFO sightings. In an essay entitled "Sorcery, Sex, Assassination, and the Science of Symbolism", author James Shelby Downard described a "Sirius-worship cult" reaching all the way to the highest levels of the CIA. In this provocative piece, Downard described one of their rituals taking place at the Palomar Observatory under the telescopically focused light of Sirius, bathing its participants in the luminance of the majestic Dog-Star.

A rash of Sirian contacts continued on into the 1970's, perhaps inspired by Temple's *The Sirius Mystery*. In 1974, science fiction writer Phillip K. Dick had some sort of mystical experience which at first he attributed to psychotronic transmissions broadcast from Russia. According to Dick, these "micro-wave boosted telepathic transmissions," commenced on March 20, 1974, showering him with streams of visual and audio data. Initially, this overpowering onslaught of messages that Dick received was extremely unpleasant and, as he termed them, "die messages." Within the following week, he reported being kept awake by "violet phosphene activity, eight hours uninterrupted." A description of this event in a fictionalized form appears in Dick's *A Scanner, Darkly*. The content of this phosphene activity was in the form of modern abstract graphics followed by Soviet music serenading his head, in addition to Russian names and words. Dick's original theory was that Russian mind control agents were targeting him with these transmissions.

At the outset, Dick felt the emanations invading his mind were of a malevolent nature, although in time he began to believe they were something entirely different. In a letter to Ira Einhorn dated February 10, 1978, Dick went into more depth on these psychotronic transmissions, claiming that they "seemed sentient." He felt that an alien life form existing in some upper layer of the Earth's atmosphere had been attracted by the Soviet psychotronic transmissions. Apparently, this alien life form operated as a "station", tapping into some sort of interplanetary communication grid that, "...contained and transmitted vast amounts of information."

What Dick initially received were the Soviet transmissions, but eventually this alien life form -- whom he called Zebra -- became "...attracted or potentiated by the Soviet micro-wave psychotronic transmissions." In the months that followed, this alien entity -- according to Dick -- vastly improved his mental and physical well being. It (Zebra) gave him "...complex and accurate information about myself and also about our infant son, which, Zebra said, had a critical and undiagnosed birth defect which required emergency and immediate surgery. My wife rushed our baby to the doctor and told the doctor what I had said (more precisely what Zebra had said to me) and the doctor discovered that it was so. Surgery was scheduled for the following day--i.e. as soon as possible. Our son would have died otherwise." (Dick's wife Tessa and others have since confirmed this story regarding the medical conditions of Dick and his son, Christopher.)

Dick felt Zebra was benign, and that it held great contempt for the Soviets and their psychotronic experiments. Furthermore, Zebra informed Dick that the Earth was dying, and that spray-cans were "...destroying the layer of atmosphere in which Zebra...existed."

It was not until several years after his "mystical experiences" with Zebra that Phil Dick finally wrote about these events in his novel *VALIS*. Prior to the publication of *VALIS*, Dick had never made any mention of Sirius in connection with the events that so drastically impacted his life. However, in this work, Dick renamed Zebra to VALIS (Vast Active

Living Intelligence System) and identified it as a product of the Sirius star system, identifying its operators as three-eyed crab clawed beings.

During this same period -- 1973-74 -- Robert Anton Wilson was having his own experiences with "ET denizens" which at the time he thought were "telepathic communications from Sirius" as recounted in his book, *Cosmic Trigger*. Also in the early 70's, British novelist Doris Lessing began a series of Sci-Fi novels revolving around entities from Sirius, which was a departure from her previous literary offerings. In the third novel of this series, *The Sirian Experiments*, Lessing relates a tale with stunning similarities to Dick's VALIS experiences. When Robert Anton Wilson met Ms. Lessing in 1983, she said she had never read a lick of Dick -- or Wilson, for that matter, so it's hard to tell how much of this was cross-pollination.

Another somewhat unlikely source for such conjecture was the heavy metal rock band Blue Oyster Cult. At face value, one might consider BOC another in a long line of head banging guitar slingers, but upon closer examination many of their lyrics allude to occult subjects, often referring to amphibian-like beings from outer space, as well as Sirius in their song "Astronomy": "...and don't forget my dog, fixed and consequent. Astronomy...a star!"

But not only has Sirius cropped up time and again in occult and UFO lore, but the ubiquitous Dog Star has also been mentioned in relation to certain mind control experiments which fall under the nefarious umbrella of the CIA's MKULTRA project. Purportedly started in 1953 -- under a program that was exempt from congressional oversight -- MK-ULTRA agents and "spychiatrists" tested radiation, electric shock, microwaves, and electrode implants on unwitting subjects. The ultimate goal of MK-ULTRA was to create programmed assassins ala The Manchurian Candidate. The CIA also tested a wide range of drugs in the prospects of discovering the perfect chemical compound to control minds. LSD was one such drug that deeply interested CIA spychiatrists, so much so that in 1953 the Agency attempted to purchase the entire world supply of acid from Sandoz Laboratories in Switzerland. In fact, for many years the CIA was the principal source for LSD.

In recent years, various info on remote mind control technology has filtered into the conspiracy research community through alternative publications such as *Full Disclosure, Resonance* as well as a Finnish gentleman by the name of Martti Koski and his booklet *My Life Depends On You*. Over the last decade, Mr. Koski has been sharing his horrifying tale, documenting as it does the discovery of rampant brain tampering committed upon himself and countless others. The perpetrators of these evil doings allegedly include the Royal Canadian Mounted Police, the CIA and Finnish Intelligence, among various other intelligence agencies. Where Sirius comes into the clouded picture is quite intriguing: at one point during a mind control programming episode, the "doctors" operating on Koski identified themselves as "aliens from Sirius." Apparently, these "doctors" (or "spychiatrists") were attempting to plant a screen memory to conceal their true intentions. What this suggests is a theory that a handful of researchers -- namely Martin Cannon, Alex Constantine, David Emory and John Judge -- started kicking around in the early 90's: that so-called alien abductions were a cover for MK-ULTRA mind control operations perpetrated by intelligence agency spooks.

According to Walter Bowart -- in the 1994 revised edition of *Operation Mind Control* -- one alleged mind control victim related an incident along these lines, purportedly occurring in the late 70's. In memories retrieved during hypnotic regression, it was revealed that the victim had been the recipient of a mock alien abduction, the intent of which was to create a screen memory to conceal the actual mind control program being perpetrated on the victim. The subject in this instance claimed to have seen a young child dressed in a small alien costume, similar in appearance to the aliens in Spielberg's *ET*. None of this, of course, dismisses outright the ETH; nor does it mean that ET's have never visited us. Nevertheless, its implications are staggering when one considers the impact and subsequent commercialization of the Alien Abduction Phenomenon, and how it has reshaped the belief systems and psyches of millions of the planet's inhabitants, in essence creating a new paradigm that prior to forty years ago was virtually non-existent.

As chronicled in Bowart's *Operation Mind Control*, in the late 70's Congressman Charlie Rose (D-N.C.) met with a Canadian inventor who had developed a helmet that simulated alternate states of consciousness, much like the virtual reality unit in the 1983 film *Brainstorm*. One such virtual reality scenario played out by those who tried on this helmet was a mock alien abduction. Congressman Rose took part in these experiments, and much to his amazement, the simulated alien abduction scenario seemed incredibly realistic. This device sounds quite similar to Dr. Michael Persinger's much-touted "Magic Helmet", which received a fair amount of press coverage during the 1990's. Equipped with magnets that beamed a low-level magnetic field at the temporal lobe, the "Magic Helmet" affected areas of the brain associated with time distortions and altered states of consciousness. Although Bowart did not specifically name the inventor of the helmet, chances are it was Persinger to whom he was referring. Persinger's name has also been bandied about by mind control researcher, Martin Cannon -- in his samizdat classic *The Controllers* -- as a behind the scenes player in MK-ULTRA operations.

Dr. Persinger, a clinical neurophysicist, has focused his work over the years on the effects of electromagnetic fields upon biological organisms and human behavior. Persinger is an adherent to the theory that UFOs are the products of geomagnetic effects released from the Earth's crust under tectonic strain. His "Magic Helmet" -- it has been noted -- approximates the characteristics of Temporal Lobe Epilepsy (TLE) of which some have attributed as being responsible for Phil Dick's VALIS experiences. One of the most common attributes of TLE are visions in the form of direct communications with God, or gods -- in whatever form -- be they aliens, angels, fairies or elves.

Early on -- in his efforts to explain his own abduction experience -- author Whitley Strieber entertained the possibility that he might have been one such victim of TLE. Due to his suspicions, Strieber underwent extensive medical examinations -- including several CAT scans and MRI's -- to determine if this was the case, but the results of the tests were all negative. Aside from such speculations, there is an undeniable magical component to Strieber's experiences. After his initial hypnotic regression -- when the presence of the "visitors" were first revealed to him -- Strieber subsequently practiced a form of meditation to further conjure their image in his mind, so as to better identify their features. The first time he attempted this approach -- much to his surprise -- an alien grey immediately appeared in his "mental field of view." This meditation experience -- as recounted in *Communion* -- seems nothing less than a magical conjuration, although Strieber may not have been entirely aware of his actions in the context of a ritual magic conjuration.

Furthermore, it is my belief that hypnotic regression can, under certain conditions, perform a sort of magical working, and it was through hypnotic regression that Strieber was able to come to terms with his "visitor experience." Bear in mind that hypnosis approximates a trance state, and it is just this form of altered consciousness that has allowed many an abductee to recall their experiences. Strieber was also, prior to his visitor experience, a member of the Gurdjieff Foundation, a self-transformational organization dedicated to a system of techniques devised by the famed mystic G.I. Gurdjieff. As Strieber explained: "I believe that the techniques I learned in that training -- particularly a form of double-tone chanting -- have enabled me to remain conscious in some experiences with the visitors where I otherwise would have been unconscious." What Strieber doesn't acknowledge is that Gurdjieff himself was in contact with certain denizens of Sirius via this method of double-tone chanting, which could also be describe as "Enochian chants."

It was in the early stages of his visitor experiences that Strieber made the acquaintance of famed alien abduction researcher Budd Hopkins, who sat in on some of Strieber's early hypnosis sessions. Later, when Strieber was working on the early drafts of *Body Terror* (the original title of *Communion*) he sent Hopkins excerpts for comment. Hopkins -- although he was convinced that Strieber had indeed been visited by alien beings -- was somewhat distressed by the amount of high weirdness contained within the manuscript, although there were many parallels with other known abduction cases. During the course of some group abductee meetings attended by Hopkins, Strieber has been quoted as saying that "some people began volunteering stories about having left their bodies or other psychic experiences after their abductions. Budd wasn't interested in that, and would tell people to get back to talking about their abduction experiences. He refused to see a possible link between the experience of abduction and some kind of spiritual or psychic awakening happening in the people to whom experiences occurred."

Elsewhere in *Communion*, Strieber points out that the mental state produced by his alien grey encounters could be approximated by a drug called Tetradotoxin, which in small doses causes external anesthesia, and in larger doses may bring about out of body experiences. Even greater doses of the drug can simulate near death experiences. According to Strieber, Tetradotoxin is the core of the zombie poisons of Haiti. However, what he failed to mention, is that Tetradotoxin was just one in a vast number of psychoactive compounds utilized by the CIA for MK-ULTRA. Throughout *Communion*, Strieber makes veiled references to mind control (of the MK-ULTRA variety.) At one point in the narrative -- as he is entertaining various theories regarding his abduction experiences -- Strieber brings up the possibility that the alien greys may not have been actually using mental telepathy to communicate, but that something of a more technical nature might have been occurring, such as extra-low-frequency waves beamed into his brain creating these images and communications.

In this regard, Strieber noted "that the earth itself generates a good deal of ELF in the 1 to 30 hertz range. Perhaps there are natural conditions that trigger a response in the brain which brings about what is essentially a psychological experience of a rare and powerful kind. Maybe we have a relationship with our own planet that we do not understand at all, and the old gods, the fairy, and the modern visitors are side effects of it." Part of the appeal of *Communion* and subsequent books was, in my opinion, Strieber's ability to entertain a whole host of theories, and in the process open the reader's eyes to the many possibilities behind the UFO phenomenon, from fairy lore or travelers from alternate dimensions, to the very real possibility of ELF wave/mind control machines as being responsible for his haunted reveries.

A Space Summit?
Wilhelm Reich, Eisenhower
and the Aliens
by Kenn Thomas

In one version of events, President Dwight Eisenhower was flown to Wright Patterson Air Force Base on February 20, 1954 to see the debris and dead bodies from the Roswell crash. Some versions weave a far more elaborate tale, that Ike met with Nordic looking creatures and began intergalactic peace talks with them, the greys and several other alien races. He struggled to deal with those alien presences in the remaining years of his presidency by secret negotiations and by building up the military way out of proportion to peace-time needs. He retired in frustration with it all in 1961, giving a gravely foreboding warning that the military industrial complex he helped create would get out of control.

"The military-industrial complex..."

Or so the story goes among UFO mythologizers and folklorists.

Although it remains a well-known legend in the UFO lore, like all such legends little actual proof exists. Unlike many other legends, however, what corroborative historical trail does exist provides some provocatively concrete details. Strangely enough, archival documentation and secondary historical sources come together in remarkable ways regarding Eisenhower's UFO involvements. If aliens do not exist, an objective observer is left to wonder why the historic trail makes it seem so much like they do and that they visited 1950s America.

Stranger still, those crossroads occur primarily in the biography and career of one of Sigmund Freud's most renown protégés, the psychologist Wilhelm Reich. Reich spent the last of his years in the US chasing flying saucers. He did this with weapons he created based on an energy source he called orgone, and ostensibly with Dwight Eisenhower's blessing. As the consummate documentary historian of his own life, Reich left behind an unusual paper trail that intertwined with the Eisenhower alien legend.

Reich's story begins in Vienna in the 1920s. Recognized as a maverick in Freud's inner circle whose ideas included a Marxist strain, Freud eventually dismissed him. As a member of the Communist Party, Reich's ideas were deemed too psychoanalytic, and he was dismissed from that as well. With the ascendancy of the Nazis in Germany, Reich fled first to Norway and then to America, moving away from both psychoanalysis and Marxism into equally controversial ideas on biosphysics. Reich discovered what he termed "orgone", a biological energy found in living organisms and in the atmosphere. In the Eisenhower's America, Reich not only used this energy to combat UFOs, history suggests, too, that he met with the president at around the time Eisenhower supposedly met with the aliens.

Dwight Eisenhower's contact with aliens happened in February 1954, according to the legend. The president's cover story—that he was on vacation in Palm Springs—was belied by the fact that he had just returned from a vacation in Georgia. Even newspapers of the day reported the alarming news of a total disappearance by Ike on the night of February 20 during the Palm Springs stay. The official explanation, offered after the fact, was that the president lost a tooth cap in some chicken he was eating and had to make a late-night visit to a local dentist. Evidence of this does not appear in the existing, extensive medical record on Dwight Eisenhower from his time as president, however. The widow of the dentist had only vague memories of the event, which by any measure should have made a detailed and lasting impression, and a photograph exists of Ike on

Sunday morning, February 21, shaking hands with a pastor Blackstone, smiling, none the worse for wear after the dental work.

Was Ike actually flown to Wright Patterson Air Force Base that night to view the recovered saucer from the crash at Roswell and the alien bodies, as the persistent rumors go? Enter Wilhelm Reich. In the course of his UFO adventure, Reich traveled through Roswell, New Mexico the following year. He was on his way to Tucson, Arizona with his orgone equipment, to both study its capacity to alleviate desert conditions, and to do battle with UFOs. He recorded these experiences in his last book, *Contact With Space*, now an extremely hard-to-find underground classic. Although his immediate destination was Ruidoso Downs, New Mexico for an overnight stay on his way to Tucson, there seems little doubt that Reich had aliens on his mind as he passed through Roswell.

Typical "Turret" Shape in U.S. Desert

Fig. 18

Pastures disappeared as we neared the New Mexico border at Bronco. Here a wide plain, covered with grayish white sand, blown by strong winds, stretching to the vast horizon completed the impression of "desert." Although it was very hot as we neared Roswell, New Mexico, no OR flow was visible on the road, which should have been "shimmering with 'heatwaves'." Instead, DOR was well marked to the west against purplish, black, barren mountains, in

From *Contact With Space*

He writes, "Although it was very hot as we neared Roswell, New Mexico, no OR flow [OR was Reich's abbreviation for orgone] was visible on the road, which should have been shimmering with 'heatwaves'. Instead, DOR [Reich's abbreviation for "deadly orgone radiation", which he believed came from the exhaust of UFOs] was well-marked to the west against purplish, black, barren mountains, in the sky as a blinding grayness, and over the horizon as a grayish layer. The caking of formerly good soil was progressively characteristic and eventually caked soil prevailed over the vegetation, which now consisted only of scattered low brushes, while grass disappeared."

Reich's concern about the environmental impact of UFOs stemmed from experiences he had at his lab in Rangeley, Maine, called Orgonon. It was there, in 1951, that he first discovered DOR, the noxious reaction of the natural energy he called orgone with nuclear material. He put a milligram of radium into one of his orgone boxes, an invention he created to accumulate and harness the orgone energy. It resulted in highly polluted air around the facility, with a great deleterious effect on fauna and animals. The DOR clouds formed and an odd black substance fell on the area. Strange, red pulsating lights, UFO, appeared in the sky over Rangeley. In response to all of this, Reich came up with a second invention, the cloudbuster gun, which intensified and redirected the healthy orgone, causing the pulsating lights to twinkle out and diminishing the DOR effect on the environment.

Reich's assistants with mobile cloudbuster

The Roswell episode in *Contact With Space* concludes, "After the desert valley it was a relief to spend a night in Ruidoso, New Mexico, in the Sierra Blanca Mountains (near 7000 feet). Here a strong, reactive secondary vegetation had sprung up, again more marked on the western slope..."

Skeptics of the Roswell story often claim that interest in the event dropped off immediately after its initial media flash, only to be revived in the late 1980s by unreliable UFO researchers seeking to profiteer from a myth of their own creation. Reich's visit to Roswell, with its clear references to aliens, contradicts that assumption. So does remarkably strong archival documentation from several disparate sources that show the interlocking connection between Reich and Dwight Eisenhower.

First in this line of documentation is the Cutler-Twining memo. The National Archives in Washington, DC still contains this onion-skinned carbon of a memo calling for the postponement of a special studies section of the group MJ-12. Ufologists recognize MJ-12 as the group ostensibly started by Harry Truman in response to the Roswell crash, established to secretly deal with the alien presence. Skeptics claim that the documents reflecting this possibility, the infamous MJ12 documents, have all been faked. Nevertheless, the National Archives retains this one letter, unwilling or unable to establish that it is not authentic. It's date: July 14, 1954, five months from Eisenhower's supposed meeting with the aliens. Since no proof is absolute, even the government's retention of the document (authenticated by paper-lot and typewriter style dating) for a half-century, skeptics suggest that the Cutler-Twining memo was smuggled into the archives.

The author of the C-T memo, Robert Cutler, served in the CIA under Eisenhower in its division of psychological operations and as the first National Security Adviser, a post most recently held by Condoleeza Rice. Cutler had virtually written Ike's famous "Atoms for Peace" speech, which took as its title a phrase used by Reich long before to describe his orgone work. The recipient of the C-T memo, Nathan Twining, is well-known among students of ufology as the general to whom Air Force investigators regularly reported UFO sightings and retrievals. One such retrieval, involving flying saucers in the Maury Island area in the Pacific northwest, also involved the kind of black substance that Reich had described at his lab in Maine.

But the second curious document in this research line was recovered only recently by a researcher named Jim Martin, as part of his comprehensive look at Wilhelm Reich's life in the 1950s called *Wilhelm Reich and the Cold War*. Entitled the Moise-Douglas memo, Martin discovered it in the archives of Lew Douglas, a member of Eisenhower's "kitchen cabinet" who was assigned to a presidential committee on weather control. In *Contact With Space,* Reich claimed that he had corresponded with Douglas, and Martin discovered this memo as proof. It's from Douglas describing the latest of several failed attempts by Reich's assistant, William Moise, to make contact with this high ranking official in the Eisenhower administration. Although the memo itself is not dated, a handwritten note at its bottom indicates a great change of heart by Douglas, who ultimately did telegraph Moise on July 27, 1954.

This timeline is the best indication in the historic record that MJ-12 existed and, by inference that Eisenhower met with aliens. Douglas' about face with regard to Reich, coming at any point in July 1954, indicates that he had been briefed at the MJ-12 meeting described in the Cutler-Twining memo. The object of the "Special Studies Project" mentioned in the C-T, then, would be Reich's counterattack on UFOs, and at it Douglas was directed to take a greater interest. In the end, Douglas wound up bankrolling in part some of Reich's environmental work in Tucson. As some measure of how seriously the military took Reich's technology, the U.S. Air Force actually did develop a weather modification in the early sixties and named it the "Cloudbuster."

Finally, there's Reich's own meeting with Eisenhower. One witness claimed that during a hunting and fishing trip to Rangeley, Maine, where Reich's Orgonon lab was located, Eisenhower met face to face with the inventor of the anti-UFO technology. The Eisenhower Library even records a visit to Rangeley during that UFO laden period of the mid-1950s, from June to July, 1955. In the end, however, the memory of the witness to the meeting became as vague as that of the dentist's widow from Ike's alien visit of the year before.

The historic trail vaporizes after that, to re-emerge obliquely only once. According to the biography of his second wife, the screen comedian Jackie Gleason caught a glimpse of alien bodies in 1973 at the behest of then president Richard Nixon. Nixon, of course, had been Eisenhower's vice president. He took his friend Gleason to a secret facility in Palm Springs, where Ike had disappeared for one night for his visitation with aliens all those years ago.

Richard Nixon and Jackie Gleason

Does any of this amount to proof that such creatures exist and that Eisenhower met with them? Such questions always contain relative judgments, and in the end no absolute proof can be offered for anything. However, more historic evidence exists for this bizarre proposition, for instance, than for Lyndon Johnson's claim of an attack on US ships in the Gulf of Tonkin or George Bush's claims for the existence of WMDs in Iraq. Those two bits of mythologizing started major wars. Whatever high level contacts Reich had within the Eisenhower government, however, they did not save him for getting in trouble with the authorities. Here he is in cuffs being scuttled along by a Man In Black.

Reich was eventually prosecuted for his orgone devices. They had been unfairly characterized as quack cancer cure machines and a technical violation of an FDA injunction led to Reich's imprisonment. Federal authorities destroyed much of his scientific equipment and even had his books burned. Many believe that the prosecution resulted from big-money medical and pharmaceutical interests threatened by Reich's work. The FDA, of course, never truly followed Reich's scientific protocols on either orgone technology or cloudbuster guns, and convicted Reich on technical violation of its injunction to stop distributing orgone boxes.

Authorities threw Reich in a prison cell in Lewisberg, PA from which he did not emerge alive. In memos to the prison chaplain before his death, however, Reich continued to write passionately about the social situation in the 1950s Eisenhower cultural era. His note from September 1957 even includes reference to the famous racial disturbance at Little Rock Central High School. He emphasized the psychological and emotional undercurrents he felt were being ignored in the broader social arena of that paranoid time, something that also prevented many from seeing the space ships he saw in abundance:

I am merely fulfilling my public duties as a U. S. citizen and worker in planetary affairs if I continue to point out where the true danger to our social and personal existence is placed–Emotional Poisoning: disruption through sowing distrust throughout our society, doping and drugging of our population, espec. our YOUTH; draining us financially through areas […]race, a camouflage of the true menace, the Emotional Poisoning a la Little Rock racial upheavals; keeping our high placed officials at bay through fear of sexual scandals, railroading efficient men and women into prisons or lunatic asylums through [?] up there environments; subverting justice by whispered little lies & frightening or using judges. Doing all this destruction unnoticed as it were by all those responsible…now lyrics were subverted by such use of stupidities & evasions on our part, especially by the staid reluctance to talk bluntly and take the bull by the horns. The bull is really no more than a few slimy tape worms eating away at our emotional guts. It is high time to start giving social power to the established functions of Love, Work & Learning as bastions against the tapeworms.

Reich in prison

The prison memo form also includes this banal and perhaps prescient statement: "Your failure to specifically state your problem may result in no action being taken." Reich's imprisonment was in part the end result of mis-reporting on him that appeared in the *New Republic* under the editorial leadership of a now-confessed communist spy named Michael Straight in a book entitled, *After Long Silence*. *New Republic* made its own pronouncement about Little Rock in its July 7, 1958 edition, complaining about the Supreme Court's failure to stop legal challenges that were slowing down the integration process. The Supreme Court, opined *New Republic*, "must stand the ground they themselves have assumed, or the grand experiment they inaugurated will end in bitter farce, with consequences for the state of the union that stagger the mind."

Clearly the magazine had a better view of the possible consequences of Supreme Court actions than the Court itself. The consequences of Reich's work with UFOs, and the implications of the study of psychological character structure on the understanding of race issues has continued over the years. Writing in a chapter called "Racism and Slavery" in The American Slave: A Composite Autobiography (1972), historian George Rawick notes the impact of Reich's classic book, still taught in college curricula on psychology, entitled *Character Analysis*, first published in German in 1933, and its less well-known but significant companion, The Mass Psychology of Fascism: "While I cannot subscribe to all of Reich's system, this chapter could not have been written without his monumental attempt to relate Marx and Freud which loosened the ideological armouring of Western rationalism for me and many others."

Although Reich never stated it explicitly, clearly he saw that same "armoring" as the block that keeps so many from accepting the realities of the UFO issue.

Reich died in the Lewisberg prison in 1957.

Some of the language in Dwight Eisenhower's retirement speech, the one that coined the phrase "military-industrial complex", conjures up an image of Wilhelm Reich, Ike's possible secret ally in the war against extraterrestrials. "Today," Eisenhower notes, "the solitary inventor, tinkering in his shop, has been overshadowed by task forces of scientists in laboratories and testing fields...a government contract becomes virtually a substitute for intellectual curiosity. The prospect of domination of the nation's scholars by Federal employment, project allocations, and the power of money is ever present ..."

Although the record suggests that Reich had the interest and support from the Eisenhower administration in his desert battles against UFOs, he never required it. Although he believed in nuts and bolts space ships piloted by extra-terrestrials, he regarded contact with them as characterological events, not simply sightings of craft. But he needed no stamp of approval from government authority to make this claim.

"There is no proof," wrote Reich in *Contact With Space*, "There are no authorities whatever. No president, Academy, Court of Law, Congress or Senate on this earth has the knowledge or power to decide what will be the knowledge of tomorrow. There is no use in trying to prove something that is unknown to somebody who is ignorant of the unknown, or fearful of its threatening power. Only the good old rules of learning will eventually bring about understanding of what has invaded our earthly existence."

That seems to have been Reich's last word on the subject.

*****

Kenn Thomas has authored over a dozen books on various conspiracy topics, including *NASA, Nazis & JFK*; *Maury Island UFO*, about possible John F. Kennedy assassination-connected personality Fred Crisman; and *The Octopus: Secret Government and the Death of Danny Casolaro*, about the Inslaw affair. Thomas calls his research interest "parapolitics," the study of conspiracies of all colors -- from alien abductions and the Illuminati, to the John F. Kennedy assassination and the 9/11 attacks. *New Yorker* called his work "on the cutting edge" of conspiracy His work has become proverbial enough that *Baseball Prospectus* described conspiratorial activity in that sport as having "enough fishy behavior to keep Kenn Thomas swarming for years." Thomas latest book, co-edited with Adam Parfrey, entitled *Secret and Suppressed II: Banned Ideas and Hidden History into the 21st Century*, is available from the publisher, Feral House, online at feralhouse.com. Thomas' web site appears steamshovelpress.com and he can be reached for lecture appearances at editor@steamshovelpress.com.

UFOs, Do they Smell?
The Sulphur Enigma
of Paranormal Visitation
by Terry Melanson

Witnesses of paranormal activities today and in centuries past have consistently encountered a common trait. Indeed, since the prophets of the bible spoke of the judgement of the Lord with fire and **brimstone**, has sulphur smells been associated with paranormal manifestations. The Greeks spoke of this as well. In the twelfth book of the *Odyssey*, Homer says:

> "Zeus thundered and hurled his bolt upon the ship and she quivered from stem to stern, smitten by the bolt of Zeus, and was filled with sulphurous smoke."

In the Iliad:

> "[Zeus] thundered horribly and dashed it to the ground in front of the horses of Diomedes, and a ghastly blaze of flaming sulphur shot up and the horses, terrified, both cringed away against the chariot."

This should not be a surprise as *lightning* was always known to be the cause of sulphur smells. Before we get into this aspect I would like, first of all, to list some phenomena that are sometimes accompanied with a pungent smell, likened to sulphur or ozone.

- The Tricksters: Of the Southwestern United States, Northern Mexico peyote ceremonies. Also in Celtic lore (fairies, gnomes, sylphs etc.)
- The Men in Black
- Sasquatch (Pacific Northwest), Yeti (Asia), The Skunk Ape (Southeastern U.S.), Momo (Missouri Monster)
- The Greek Gods of Mythology
- Succubi, Incubi, and various demonic manifestations during occult workings
- Poltergeist, ghosts, spirits etc.

- UFOs, Aliens, Space Brothers etc.
- The Chupacabra of Puerto Rico and South and Central America
- Lightning (this seems to be a clue of some sort, as UFOs are frequently see near **powerlines** of **high voltage**)

As Pliny has said:

> "Lightning and thunder are attended with a strong smell of sulphur, and the light produced by them is of a sulphurous complexion."

With a small variation one could describe the modern paranormal phenomenon in similar fashion:

> "UFOs and most paranormal occurences are often attended with a strong smell of sulphur, and the light produced by them is of a high energy quality, accompanied with a sulphurous complexion."

Jupiter of the Thunderbolt

Famous photograph of ball lightning, which prompted scientists to acknowledge the phenomenon.

In Immanuel Velikovsky's unpublished work *In the Beginning*, there's a chapter called The Transmutation of Oxygen into Sulphur in which he tries to explain the origin of the sulphur smells of lightning and past stories such as the ones quoted above. Velikovsky informs us that "sulphur is one of the best insulators and static electricity, when accumulated on it, discharges in electrical sparks" and that electrical discharges produced without the help of sulphur are also accompanied by the smell of it. He talks about Benjamin Franklin's first experiments with lightning and electricity. Franklin also wrote to the Royal Society in London that both phenomena are attended by a sulphurous smell.

Velikovsky suggests that sulphur is actually made from the air by the passage of an electrical discharge. This would seem to be the inevitable conclusion considering the evidence. However, in order for oxygen to be "transmuted" into sulphur, the amount of energy required would be staggering; when asked, in 1941, a colleague of Velikovsky's estimated an equivalent of two billion electron-volts. Today these kinds of energies are being produced(almost) in particle accelerators. A recent successful test with a one billion electron-volt beam of photons, being the closest.

Perhaps once these scientists reach the 2 billion electron-volt mark, we can directly probe the mysteries of the paranormal. Could these paranormal events be the result of *intelligences* manifesting matter through dimensions? Certainly this would require a tremendous amount of energy. Then the tell tale sign of sulphur smells could be the effect of this energy 'entering' or 'exiting' our dimension.

Sulphur Lamps & UFOs - The Mystery Deepens

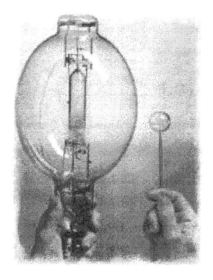

There's a fascinating invention that went largely unnoticed when it appeared in 1994. On November 23rd a photo appeared in the Western Australian newspaper called "The Sunday Times." It showed a small glass sphere on a long stalk next to a much larger-by-comparison commercial light bulb. Datelined "Washington", it read: "This electrodless sulphur lamp, which blasts gas with microwaves to produce a bright white light much more cheaply than conventional bulbs, has been invented by Fusion Lighting Inc. for **the Defence Department.** One lamp can replace nearly 100 conventional high-intensity bulbs." Then again in the December 1995 edition of *Popular Mechanics* there's another small article on the "Solar 1000" sulphur bulbs..."Microwaves excite sulphur powder inside the bulbs hollow quartz sphere. The resulting glow resembles natural light, which is more aesthetically pleasing than that of many fluorescent or mercury-vapour bulbs."

Researcher Dr. Simon Harvey-Wilson notes that these sulphur lamps have three features in common with UFOs.

> "Firstly, UFOs too are sometimes blindly bright, yet witnesses often report that this light seems different from the normal bright lights they encounter in their daily life. Perhaps the same technology is used to illuminate the outside of UFOs. Abductees also often report a puzzling, seemingly sourceless, light inside UFOs.

> Puzzling light sources are not limited to UFOs. Sometimes a bright paranormal light is seen around saints and mystics.

> Secondly, as well as being dazzlingly bright, some UFOs are known to give off powerful microwaves, which is just radiation or 'light' from that part of the electromagnetic spectrum that falls between infrared and very short radio waves. Microwaves from UFOs are sometimes pulsed, for reasons that we do not know. It has been suggested that this radiation maybe a product of the craft's propulsion, or some sort of defensive system. It may also be how some UFOs create the bright plasma field that surrounds them.

> Modern research has shown that microwaves can be used to affect the mind. This radiation might be used by UFOs as a form of camouflage to make witnesses 'see' the UFO as a less threatening object such as a cloud or helicopter; to prevent them from seeing the UFO at all; or to project a reassuring voice into the witness' head.

> Thirdly, UFOs, aliens, poltergeists, and even haunted houses, are occasionally associated with an offensive smell sometimes sulphurous in nature."

The Sulphur Enigma seems connected with high energy phenomena. The similarity of ball lightning and UFOs has been noted by researchers. Also plasmoid energy and electrical discharge have sulphuric qualities in common with the **full range** of paranormal manifestation. Transmutation of oxygen into sulphur, by high energy discharge, can't be discounted.

With respect to UFOs, the quality of the light emitted in sightings has striking characteristics, similar to the mentioned sulphur bulbs. Microwave bombardment of sulphur, encased in quartz, is being studied. Might this research be in response to uncovered technologies? The sulphur aspect would certainly have been noted had clandestine research continued, in an unofficial sense, into the UFO phenomena.

Putting aside the whole issue of crashed saucers and back-engineering, one could speculate that just by carefully observing and documenting; the sulphur aspect would, most assuredly, be noticed. These sulphur lamps being initially sponsored by the **Department of Defence**, could then be the first attempts at applying the "technology."

"On a hot evening in August I was in my room busily editing copy for the October issue of Space Review when I thought I heard a board squeak in the attic just outside my door. I got up and went to the door to see if my stepfather might be walking about in the attic, looking for something. No light came from under the door, so I figured I had imagined the noise-until once again the odour of sulphur reached my nostrils. The odour was faint until I sat; as I did so, it became stronger. Kneeling to the floor I discovered it was even stronger there, so I supposed it had the characteristic of creeping along the floor, then rising until it reached the nostrils. Because it had always accompanied a visit from these strange beings, I could expect them shortly. I puzzled myself with the question of the odour. I had never asked about it, but would make a point to do so the first opportunity I had.

...After the saucer had discharged its load, it moved along a track to a siding similar to a railroad yard, for many such tracks traversed this tunnel, and I had rubbed my eyes when I caught sight of so many saucers, all sitting on sidings with platforms for the occupants to use when entering and departing. In Earth terminology, I suppose this would be called an enormous saucer garage. The smell of sulphur lingered all about, and I wondered if this odour had anything to do with the fuel being employed."

- Albert K. Bender 1963, "Flying Saucers and the Three Men"

(Mrs Evans reports seeing 'about a dozen' UFOs from Christmas 1978 to November 1979; three of these sightings would be classed as 'CE1'.)

A blood-like substance appears 'out of thin air' at her home. Also a 'transparent, jelly-like' substance. Strong smells – she, her husband and her neighbour see a small, yellowish cloud, accompanied by a strong smell of sulphur. On another occasion a strong, 'overpowering' smell of incense. Also smells of 'zoo animals' cages' and 'wet animal fur'. On two occasions when 'something unusual' passed over her head, she felt a 'click, or tap, on [her] temples, rather like a tiny electric shock'. She finds out for the first time that her father is part Native American, her mother Celtic Welsh-Irish Romany. Her neighbour also sees a 'figure' in her own house. She almost burst into tears when Mrs Evans chided her about it. Another neighbour, at 3 am, saw a UFO 'gliding' down the road, reported it to the police.

- Men In Black A Preliminary Report
by Robert Bull Part 2 of a Series Of 3

The scent of a yowie In about 10% of yowie cases the creatures have exuded a mind-bogglingly foul stench. It can be bad enough to make a person vomit and the pongy pongids seem to be able to release the choking miasma at will. Usually the smell is compared to that of rotting meat, bat droppings or a "badly kept country dunny" but occasionally witnesses say the creatures left a distinct electrical smell "like burnt electrical wiring", "burnt bakelite", "a sulphury stink". Interestingly, in a very dramatic bigfoot/UFO case in Pennsylvania in 1973, witnesses described a strong smell of sulphur and burning rubber.

- Myths & Monsters 2001 Conference:
'Are the hairy giants flesh and blood
-or are they psychic phenomena?'

Tim Cassidy reported on a Jun 11, 1996, a creature from southern Indiana. Near Lake Monroe, the co-worker was on a night hike, and ran into a pungent odor, very sulphur-like, and their hair was on end.

- http://www.internationalbigfootsociety.com/tr68.htm

It is claimed that the Chupacabra is accompanied by an unusually strong scent of sulphur, not unlike the demonic creatures of folklore. Witness Madelyne Tolentino claimed, "it jumped like a kangaroo and smelled like sulfur." It has also been known, in some cases, to have supernatural strength. In one case, it allegedly tore a 16ft by 14ft iron gate off it's hinges to get to the animals. There has been rumor that the smell the creature emits is actually it's way of immobilizing the animals while it drains them of their blood. It is not only animals the creature is attacking, but also some humans. Angel Pulido, from Jalisco, reported getting bit by something that was "a giant bat which looked like a witch". Also in Mexico, Teodora Reyes showed marks which were supposedly caused by the claws of the chupacabra.

- http://www.geocities.com/Area51/Hollow/4326/chupa.html

Terry Melanson ©, 2001

Mind Control in the 21st Century
By Commander X

New methods of mind control technology were first introduced in the 1950s as an obscure branch of the CIA's MKULTRA project group. Just as organized crime is not stopped by hearings and court cases, neither did this originally obscure branch of MKULTRA activity, when the top secret operations were exposed by the U.S. Senate's Church-Inouye hearings in the late 1970s.

Since government-backed electronic mind control is classified at the highest levels in all technologically capable governments, the description of effects is taken from the personal experiences of over 300 known involuntary experimentees. The experimentees without exception report that once the "testing" begins, the classified experiment specification apparently requires that the "testing" be continued for life. Many test subjects are now in their 70s and 80s. Some have children and the children are often subjected to the same "testing" as their parent(s).

In an amazing article published by Spectra Magazine in 1999, author Rauni-Leena Luukanen-Kilde, MD, Former Chief Medical Officer of Finland, writes that in 1948 Norbert Weiner published a book, Cybernetics, defined as a neurological communication and control theory already in use in small circles at that time. Yoneji Masuda, "Father of the Information Society," stated his concern in 1980 that our liberty is threatened Orwellian-style by cybernetic technology totally unknown to most people. This technology links the brains of people via implanted microchips to satellites controlled by ground-based supercomputers.

The first brain implants were surgically inserted in 1974 in the state of Ohio and also in Stockholm, Sweden. Brain electrodes were inserted into the skulls of babies in 1946 without the knowledge of their parents. In the 1950s and 60s, electrical implants were inserted into the brains of animals and humans, especially in the U.S., during research into behavior modification, and brain and body functioning. Mind control (MC) methods were used in attempts to change human behavior and attitudes. Influencing brain functions became an important goal of military and intelligence services.

Thirty years ago brain implants showed up in X-rays the size of one centimeter. Subsequent implants shrunk to the size of a grain of rice. They were made of silicon, later still of gallium arsenide. Today they are small enough to be inserted into the neck or back, and also intravenously in different parts of the body during surgical operations, with or without the consent of the subject. It is now almost impossible to detect or remove them.

It is technically possible for every newborn to be injected with a microchip, which could then function to identify the person for the rest of his or her life. Such plans are secretly being discussed in the U.S. without any public airing of the privacy issues involved. In Sweden, Prime Minister Olof Palme gave permission in 1973 to implant prisoners, and Data Inspection's ex-Director General Jan Freese revealed that nursing-home patients were implanted in the mid-1980s.

Implanted human beings can be followed anywhere. Their brain functions can be remotely monitored by supercomputers and even altered through the changing of frequencies. Guinea pigs in secret experiments have included prisoners, soldiers, mental patients, handicapped children, deaf and blind people, homosexuals, single women, the elderly, school children, and any group of people considered "marginal" by the elite experimenters. The published experiences of prisoners in Utah State Prison, for example, are shocking to the conscience.

Today's microchips operate by means of low-frequency radio waves that target them. With the help of satellites, the implanted person can be tracked anywhere on the globe. Such a technique was among a number tested in the Iraq war, according to Dr. Carl Sanders, who invented the intelligence-manned interface (IMI) biotic, which is injected into people. (Earlier during the Vietnam War, soldiers were injected with the Rambo chip, designed to increase adrenaline flow into the bloodstream.) The 20-billion-bit/second supercomputers at the U.S. National Security Agency (NSA) could now "see and hear" what soldiers experience in the battlefield with a remote monitoring system (RMS).

When a 5-micromillimeter microchip (the diameter of a strand of hair is 50 micromillimeters) is placed into optical nerve of the eye, it draws neuroimpulses from the brain that embody the experiences, smells, sights, and voice of the implanted person. Once transferred and stored in a computer, these neuroimpulses can be projected back to the person's brain via the microchip to be re-experienced. Using a RMS, a land-based computer operator can send electromagnetic messages (encoded as signals) to the nervous system, affecting the target's performance. With RMS, healthy persons can be induced to see hallucinations and to hear voices in their heads.

Every thought, reaction, hearing, and visual observation causes a certain neurological potential, spikes, and patterns in the brain and its electromagnetic fields, which can now be decoded into thoughts, pictures, and voices. Electromagnetic stimulation can therefore change a person's brain-waves and affect muscular activity, causing painful muscular cramps experienced as torture.

The NSA's electronic surveillance system can simultaneously follow and handle millions of people. Each of us has a unique bioelectrical resonance frequency in the brain, just as we have unique fingerprints. With electromagnetic frequency (EMF) brain stimulation fully coded, pulsating electromagnetic signals can be sent to the brain, causing the desired voice and visual effects to be experienced by the target. This is a form of electronic warfare. U.S. astronauts were implanted before they were sent into space so their thoughts could be followed and all their emotions could be registered 24 hours a day.

The Washington Post reported in May 1995 that Prince William of Great Britain was implanted at the age of 12. Thus, if he were ever kidnapped, a radio wave with a specific frequency could be targeted to his microchip. The chip's signal would be routed through a satellite to the computer screen of police headquarters, where the Prince's movements could be followed. He could actually be located anywhere on the globe.

The mass media has not reported that an implanted person's privacy vanishes for the rest of his or her life. S/he can be manipulated in many ways. Using different frequencies, the secret controller of this equipment can even change a person's emotional life. S/he can be made aggressive or lethargic. Sexuality can be artificially influenced.

Thought signals and subconscious thinking can be read, dreams affected and even induced, all without the knowledge or consent of the implanted person.

A perfect cyber-soldier can thus be created. This secret technology has been used by military forces in certain NATO countries since the 1980s without civilian and academic populations having heard anything about it. Thus, little information about such invasive mind-control systems is available in professional and academic journals.

The NSA's Signals Intelligence group can remotely monitor information from human brains by decoding the evoked potentials (3.50HZ, 5 milliwatt) emitted by the brain. Prisoner experimentees in both Gothenburg, Sweden and Vienna, Austria have been found to have evident brain lesions. Diminished blood circulation and lack of oxygen in the right temporal frontal lobes result where brain implants are usually operative. A Finnish experimentee experienced brain atrophy and intermittent attacks of unconsciousness due to lack of oxygen.

Mind control techniques can be used for political purposes. The goal of mind controllers today is to induce the targeted persons or groups to act against his or her own convictions and best interests. Zombified individuals can even be programmed to murder and remember nothing of their crime afterward. Alarming examples of this phenomenon can be found in the U.S.

This "silent war" is being conducted against unknowing civilians and soldiers by military and intelligence agencies. Since 1980, electronic stimulation of the brain (ESB) has been secretly used to control people targeted without their knowledge or consent. All international human rights agreements forbid nonconsensual manipulation of human beings — even in prisons, not to speak of civilian populations.

Under an initiative of U.S. Senator John Glenn, discussions commenced in January 1997 about the dangers of radiating civilian populations. Targeting people's brain functions with electromagnetic fields and beams (from helicopters and airplanes, satellites, from parked vans, neighboring houses, telephone poles, electrical appliances, mobile phones, TV, radio, etc.) is part of the radiation problem that should be addressed in democratically elected government bodies.

In addition to electronic MC, chemical methods have also been developed. Mind-altering drugs and different smelling gasses affecting brain function negatively can be injected into air ducts or water pipes. Bacteria and viruses have also been tested this way in several countries.

Today's super-technology, connecting our brain functions via microchips (or even without them, according to the latest technology) to computers via satellites in the U.S. or Israel, poses the gravest threat to humanity. The latest supercomputers are powerful enough to monitor the whole world's population. What will happen when people are tempted by false premises to allow microchips into their bodies? One lure will be a microchip identity card. Compulsory legislation has even been secretly proposed in the U.S. to criminalize removal of an ID implant.

Are we ready for the robotization of mankind and the total elimination of privacy, including freedom of thought? How many of us would want to cede our entire life, including our most secret thoughts, to Big Brother? Yet the technology exists to create a totalitarian New World Order. Covert neurological communication systems are in place to counteract independent thinking and to control social and political activity on behalf of self-serving private and military interests.

When our brain functions are already connected to supercomputers by means of radio implants and microchips, it will be too late for protest. This threat can be defeated only by educating the public, using available literature on biotelemetry and information exchanged at international congresses.

One reason this technology has remained a state secret is the widespread prestige of the Psychiatric Diagnostic Statistical Manual IV produced by the U.S. American Psychiatric Association (APA) and printed in 18 languages. Psychiatrists working for U.S. intelligence agencies no doubt participated in writing and revising this manual. This psychiatric "bible" covers up the secret development of MC technologies by labeling some of their effects as symptoms of paranoid schizophrenia.

Victims of mind control experimentation are thus routinely diagnosed, knee-jerk fashion, as mentally ill by doctors who learned the DSM "symptom" list in medical school. Physicians have not been schooled that patients may be telling the truth when they report being targeted against their will or being used as guinea pigs for electronic, chemical and bacteriological forms of psychological warfare.

POWER OF THE MILITARY-INDUSTRIAL COMPLEX

Jan Wiesemann has written an apt description of the situation which now exists in the United States, about the 'forces that be' and how the situation came about:

"During the Cold War the United States not only engaged in a relatively open nuclear arms race with the Soviet Union, but also engaged in a secret race developing unconventional mind control weapons. As the intelligence agencies (which prior to the Second World War had merely played a supporting role within the government) continued to increase their power, so did the funds spent on developing techniques designed to outsmart each other.

"And as the U.S. intelligence community began to grow, a secret culture sprang about which enabled the intelligence players to implement the various developed techniques to cleverly circumvent the democratic processes and institutions...

"Like many other democracies, the U.S. Government is made up of two basic parts the elected constituency, i.e., the various governors, judges, congressmen and the President; and the unelected bureaucracies, as represented by the numerous federal agencies.

"In a well-balanced and correctly functioning democracy, the elected part of the government is in charge of its unelected bureaucratic part, giving the people a real voice in the agenda set by their government.

"While a significant part of the U.S. Government no doubt follows this democratic principle, a considerable portion of the U.S. Government operates in complete secrecy and follows its own unaccountable agenda which, unacknowledged, very often is quite different from the public agenda."

The secrecy involved in the development of the electromagnetic mind control technology reflects the tremendous power that is inherent in it. To put it bluntly, whoever controls this technology can control the minds of everyone.

There is evidence that the U.S. Government has plans to extend the range of this technology to envelop all peoples, all countries. This can be accomplished, is being accomplished, by using the HAARP Project for overseas areas and the GWEN network now in place in the U.S.

Dr Michael Persinger, Professor of Psychology and Neuroscience at Laurentian University, Ontario, Canada, has discovered through intensive research that strong electromagnetic fields can affect a person's brain.

"Temporal lobe stimulation," he says, "can evoke the feeling of a presence, disorientation, and perceptual irregularities. It can activate images stored in the subject's memory, including nightmares and monsters that are normally suppressed."

Dr Persinger wrote an article a few years ago, titled : On the Possibility of Directly Accessing Every Human Brain by Electromagnetic Induction of Fundamental Algorithms. The abstract reads:

"Contemporary neuroscience suggests the existence of fundamental algorithms by which all sensory transduction is translated into an intrinsic, brain-specific code. Direct stimulation of these codes within the human temporal or limbic cortices by applied electromagnetic patterns may require energy levels which are within the range of both geomagnetic activity and contemporary communication networks. A process which is coupled to the narrow band of brain temperature could allow all normal human brains to be. affected by a subharmonic whose frequency range at about 10 Hz would only vary by 0.1 Hz."

"Within the last two decades a potential has emerged which was improbable, but which is now marginally feasible. This potential is the technical capability to influence directly the major portion of the approximately six billion brains of the human species, without mediation through classical sensory modalities, by generating neural information within a physical medium within which all members of the species are immersed.

"The historical emergence of such possibilities, which have ranged from gunpowder to atomic fission, have resulted in major changes in the social evolution that occurred inordinately quickly after the implementation. Reduction of the risk of the inappropriate application of these technologies requires the continued and open discussion of their realistic feasibility and implications within the scientific and public domain."

INFLUENCE FROM ABOVE: MIND CONTROL SATELLITES

Unknown to most of the world, satellites can perform astonishing and often menacing feats. This should come as no surprise when one reflects on the massive effort poured into satellite technology since the Soviet satellite Sputnik, launched in 1957, caused panic in the U.S. A spy satellite can monitor a person's every movement, even when the "target" is indoors or deep in the interior of a building or traveling rapidly down the highway in a car, in any kind of weather (cloudy, rainy, stormy). There is no place to hide on the face of the earth.

It takes just three satellites to blanket the world with detection capacity. Besides tracking a person's every action and relaying the data to a computer screen on earth, amazing powers of satellites include reading a person's mind, monitoring conversations, manipulating electronic instruments and physically assaulting someone with a laser beam. Remote reading of someone's mind through satellite technology is quite bizarre, yet it is being done; it is a reality

It is difficult to estimate just how many people world wide are being watched by satellites, but if there are 200 working surveillance satellites (a common number in the literature), and if each satellite can monitor 20 human targets, then as many as 4000 people may be under satellite surveillance. However, the capability of a satellite for multiple-target monitoring is even harder to estimate than the number of satellites; it may be connected to the number of transponders on each satellite, the transponder being a key device for both receiving and transmitting information.

A society in the grips of the National Security State is necessarily kept in the dark about such things. Obviously, though, if one satellite can monitor simultaneously 40 or 80 human targets, then the number of possible victims of satellite surveillance would be doubled or quadrupled. As early as 1981, G. Harry Stine (in his book Confrontation in Space), could write that Computers have read human minds by means of deciphering the outputs of electroencephalographs (EEGs). Early work in this area was reported by the Defense Advanced Research Projects Agency (DARPA) in 1978. EEG's are now known to be crude sensors of neural activity in the human brain, depending as they do upon induced electrical currents in the skin.

In 1992, Newsweek reported that "with powerful new devices that peer through the skull and see the brain at work, neuroscientists seek the wellsprings of thoughts and emotions, the genesis of intelligence and language. They hope, in short, to read your mind." In 1994, a scientist noted that "current imaging techniques can depict physiological events in the brain which accompany sensory perception and motor activity, as well as cognition and speech."

In order to give a satellite mind-reading capability, it only remains to put some type of EEG-like-device on a satellite and link it with a computer that has a data bank of brain-mapping research. I believe that surveillance satellites began reading minds--or rather, began allowing the minds of targets to be read--sometime in the early 1990s. Some satellites in fact can read a person's mind from space.

A surveillance satellite, in addition, can detect human speech. Burrows observed that satellites can "even eavesdrop on conversations taking place deep within the walls of the Kremlin." Walls, ceilings, and floors are no barrier to the monitoring of conversation from space. Even if you were in a high rise building with ten stories above you and ten stories below, a satellite's audio surveillance of your speech would still be unhampered. Inside or outside, in any weather, anyplace on earth, at any time of day, a satellite in a geosynchronous orbit can detect the speech of a human target. Apparently, as with reconnaissance in general, only by taking cover deep within the bowels of a lead-shielding fortified building could you escape audio monitoring by a satellite.

There are various other satellite powers, such as manipulating electronic instruments and appliances like alarms, electronic watches and clocks, a television, radio, smoke detector and the electrical system of an automobile. For example, the digital alarm on a watch, tiny though it is, can be set off by a satellite from hundreds of miles up in space. And the light bulb of a lamp can be burned out with the burst of a laser from a satellite.

In addition, street lights and porch lights can be turned on and off at will by someone at the controls of a satellite, the means being an electromagnetic beam which reverses the light's polarity. Or a lamp can be made to burn out in a burst of blue light when the switch is flicked. As with other satellite powers, it makes no difference if the light is under a roof or a ton of concrete – it can still be manipulated by a satellite laser. Types of satellite lasers include the free-electron laser, the x-ray laser, the neutral-particle-beam laser, the chemical- oxygen-iodine laser and the mid-infra-red advanced chemical laser.

Along with mind-reading, one of the most bizarre uses of a satellite is to physically assault someone. An electronic satellite beam--using far less energy than needed to blast nuclear missiles in flight – can "slap" or bludgeon someone on earth. A satellite beam can also be locked onto a human target, with the victim being unable to evade the menace by running around or driving around, and can cause harm through application of pressure on, for example, one's head. How severe a beating can be administered from space is a matter of conjecture, but if the ability to actually murder someone this way has not yet been worked out, there can be no doubt that it will soon become a reality. There is no mention in satellite literature of a murder having been committed through the agency of a satellite, but the very possibility should make the world take note.

There is yet another macabre power possessed by some satellites: manipulating a person's mind with an audio subliminal "message" (a sound too low for the ear to consciously detect but which affects the unconscious). In trying thereby to get a person to do what you want him to do, it does not matter if the target is asleep or awake. A message could be used to compel a person to say something you would like him to say, in a manner so spontaneous that no one would be able to realize the words were contrived by someone else; there is no limit to the range of ideas an unsuspecting person can be made to voice.

The human target might be compelled to use an obscenity, or persons around the target might be compelled to say things that insult the target. A sleeping person, on the other hand, is more vulnerable and can be made to do something, rather than merely say something. An action compelled by an audio subliminal message could be to roll off the bed and fall onto the floor, or to get up and walk around in a trance. However, the sleeping person can only be made to engage in such an action for only a minute or so, it seems, since he usually wakes up by then and the spell wears.

It should be noted here that although the hypnotism of a psychoanalyst is bogus, unconscious or subconscious manipulation of behavior is genuine. But the brevity of a subliminal spell effected by a satellite might be overcome by more research. "The psychiatric community," reported Newsweek in 1994, "generally agrees that subliminal perception exists; a smaller fringe group believes it can be used to change the psyche."

SCIENTIST CONFIRMS REALITY OF ELECTRONIC MIND CONTROL

A Russian doctor, Igor Smirnov, whom the magazine labeled a "subliminal Dr. Strangelove," is one scientist studying the possibilities: "Using electroencephalographs, he measures brain waves, then uses computers to create a map of the subconscious and various human impulses, such as anger or the sex drive. Then, through taped subliminal messages, he claims to physically alter that landscape with the power of suggestion."

In the August 22, 1994 issue of Newsweek, Dr. Smirnov revealed that the FBI asked advice from Smirnov during the siege at Waco. Smirnov said that: "The FBI wanted to 'pipe subliminal messages

from sect member's families through the telephone lines into the compound."

For David Koresh the group's leader... the FBI had in mind a special voice: "God as played by the famous actor Charlton Heston."

In this case the sect members would be influenced by electromagnetic high frequency voices of their relatives, and David Koresh would hear in his head the voice of God played by Charlton Heston. Smirnov told the FBI that they would have to find the individual frequencies of the sect members if the idea was to work correctly.

Combining this research with satellite technology – which has already been done in part – could give its masters the possibility for the perfect crime, since satellites operate with perfect discretion, perfect concealment. In many countries the military operates tracking stations; assisting the giant American National Security Agency. The NSA covertly monitors every call, fax, e-mail, telex and computer data message. The relevant computers search for key words/phrases. Anything/anyone of interest is drawn to the attention of agency operatives. This can lead to a large scale personal surveillance operation by the NSA or other agencies; like the CIA and their criminal connections. The current system is called ECHELON.

The magnetic field around the head is scanned as you are satellite tracked. The results are then fed back to the relevant computers. Monitors then use the information to conduct a conversation where audible neurophone input is applied to the victim.

The neurophone was developed by Dr Patrick Flanagan in 1958. It's a device that converts sound to electrical impulses. In its original form electrodes were placed on the skin but with defense department developments, the signals can be delivered via satellite. They then travel the nervous system directly to the brain (bypassing normal hearing mechanisms). Dr Flanagan's 3D holographic sound system can place sounds in any location as perceived by the targeted / tortured listener. This allows for a variety of deceptions for gullible victims.

Today, various top secret groups use satellites and ground based equipment to deliver verbal threats, deafening noise and propaganda; using neurophone technology. Anything from TV's/radio's appearing to operate when switched off through to "Voices from God" and encounters with aliens are all cons using neurophone technologies to torment, deceive and (most importantly) discredit agency/criminal targets. Naturally, the system can mimic anyone's voice and automatic computer translations (into any language) are incorporated.

Human thought operates at 5,000 bits/sec but satellites and various forms of biotelemetry can deliver those thoughts to supercomputers located worldwide that have a speed of 20 BILLION bits/sec. These, even today, monitor thousands of people simultaneously. Eventually they will monitor almost everyone.

Usually the targets are aware their brain waves are being monitored because of the accompanying neurophone feedback. In other words, the computer repeats (echoes) your own thoughts and then the human monitors comment or respond verbally. Both are facilitated by the neurophone.

There is little time left to make the rest of the world aware of the nefarious operations now in effect. Our rights and freedoms as human beings are in jeopardy if these warnings continue to go unheeded.

The Secret Government
by Milton William Cooper

History is replete with whispers of secret societies. Accounts of elders or priests who guarded the forbidden knowledge of ancient peoples. Prominent men, meeting in secret, who directed the course of civilization are recorded in the writings of all people.

The oldest is the Brotherhood of the Snake, also called the Brotherhood of the Dragon, and it still exists under many different names. It is clear that religion has always played a significant role in the course of these organizations. Communication with a higher source, often divine, is a familiar claim in all but a few.

Brotherhood of the Snake

The secrets of these groups are thought to be so profound that only a chosen, well-educated few are able to understand and use them. These men use their special knowledge for the benefit of all mankind. At least that is what they claim. How are we to know, since their knowledge and actions have been secret? Fortunately, some of it has become public knowledge.

I found it intriguing that in most, if not all, primitive tribal societies all of the adults are members. They are usually separated into male and female groups. The male usually dominates the culture. Surprisingly, this exactly resembles many civilized secret societies. This can only mean that the society is working not against established authority, but for it. In fact, it could be said to actually be the established authority. This would tend to remove the validity of any argument that all secret associations are dedicated to the "destruction of properly constituted authority." This can only apply, of course, where the secret society makes up the majority or entirety of any people which it affects. Only a very few fall into this category.

Secret societies in fact mirror many facets of ordinary life. There is always an exclusivity of membership, with the resultant importance attached to being or becoming a member. This is found in all human endeavors, even those which are not secret, such as football teams or country clubs. This exclusivity of membership is actually one of the secret societies' most powerful weapons. There is the use of signs, passwords and other tools. These have always performed valuable functions in man's organizations everywhere. The stated reason, almost always different from the real reason, for the societies' existence is important.

The comradeship is especially important. Sharing hardships or secrets has always been a special thrill to man. No one who has undergone the rigors of boot camp is ever likely to forget the special feeling of belonging and comradeship that was shared between the victims of the drill sergeant or company commander. It is an emotion born of initiation. The most potent tool of any secret society is the ritual and myth surrounding initiation. These special binding ceremonies have very deep meaning for the participants.

Initiation performs several functions which make up the heart and soul of any true secret society. Like boot camp, the initiation into the armed forces, important aspects of human thought that are universally compelling, are merged to train and maintain the efforts of a group of people to operate in a certain direction. Initiation bonds the members together in mysticism.

Neophytes gain knowledge of a secret, giving them special status. The ancient meaning of neophyte is "planted anew or reborn." A higher initiation is in reality a promotion inspiring loyalty and the desire to move up to the next rung. The goals of the society are reinforced, causing the initiated to act toward those goals in everyday life. That brings about a change in the political and social action of the member. The change is always in the best interest of the goals of the leaders of the secret society. The leaders are called adepts. This can best be illustrated by the soldier trained to follow orders without thinking. The result is often the wounding or death of the soldier for the realization of the commander's goal which may or may not be good for the overall community.

Initiation is a means of rewarding ambitious men who can be trusted. You will notice that the higher the degree of initiation the fewer the members who possess the degree. This is not because the other members are not ambitious but because a process of very careful selection is being conducted. A point is reached where no effort is good enough without a pull up by the higher members. Most members never proceed beyond this point and never learn the real, secret purpose of the group. The frozen member from that point on serves only as a part of the political power base as indeed he has always done. You may have guessed by now that initiation is a way to determine who can and cannot be trusted.

A method of deciding exactly who is to become an adept decided during initiation by asking the candidate to spit upon the Christian cross. If the candidate refuses, the members congratulate him and tell him, "You have made the right choice, as a true adept would never do such a terrible thing." The newly initiated might find it disconcerting, that he/she never advances any higher. If instead, the candidate spits upon the cross, he/she has demonstrated a knowledge of one of the mysteries and soon will find him/herself a candidate for the next higher level. The mystery is that religion is but a tool to control the masses. Knowledge (or wisdom) is their only god, through which man himself will become god. The snake and the dragon are both symbols of wisdom. Lucifer is a personification of the symbol. It was Lucifer who tempted Eve to entice Adam to eat of the tree of knowledge and thus free man from the bonds of ignorance. The WORSHIP (a lot different from STUDY) of knowledge, science, or technology is Satanism in its purest form, its secret symbol is the all-seeing eye in the pyramid.

Undesirable effects of secret societies and their aura of mystery has sometimes given them the reputation for being abnormal associations or, at the very least, strange groups of people. Whenever their beliefs are those of the majority they are no longer considered antisocial. A good example is the Christian church, which was at one time a secret society under the Roman Empire. In fact, the "Open Friendly Secret Society" (the Vatican) actually ruled most, if not all, of the known world at one time.

Most secret societies are generally considered to be antisocial; they are believed to contain elements that are not liked or are outright harmful to the community in general. This is exactly the case in some instances. Communism and fascism are secret societies in many countries where they are prohibited by law. In this country the Nazi party and the Ku Klux Klan are secret societies due mostly to the fact that the general public is disgusted by them. Their activities are sometimes illegal, thus the secrecy of their membership. The early Christians were a secret society because Roman authorities considered them from the start to be dangerous to imperial rule. The same was true of the followers of Islam. The Druseed and Yezidis in Syria and Iraq consider the Arabs a dangerous secret society dedicated to the takeover of the world. The Arabs today think the same of the Jews. Catholics and Freemasons used to have precisely the same ideas about each other.

In many primitive or backward societies initiation into the highest degrees of the group involved subjection to trials which not infrequently resulted in death or insanity for the candidate. It can be seen that social right and wrong is not the yardstick in estimating the value of a secret society. In Borneo, initiates of hunting societies, consider it meritorious and compulsory to hunt heads. In Polynesia, infanticide and debauch were considered essential for initiation into their societies, where the tribal code needed members who indulged in these things, as pillars of society.

Since the beginning of recorded history, governmental bodies of every nation have been involved with maintaining the status quo to defend the establishment against minority groups that sought to function as states within states or to oust the constituted authority and take over in its place.

Many of these attempts have succeeded but have not always lasted. Man's desire to be one of the elect is something that no power on earth has been able to lessen, let alone destroy. It is one of the "secrets" of secret societies. It is what gives them a political base and lots of clout. Members often vote the same and give each other preference in daily business, legal, and social activities. It is the deepest desire of many to be able to say, "I belong to the elect."

Houses of worship and sacrifice existed in the ancient cities. They were in fact temples built in honor of the many gods. These buildings functioned often as meeting places for philosophers and mystics who were believed to possess the secrets of nature. These men usually banded together in seclusive philosophic and religious schools.

The most important of all of these ancient groups is the Brotherhood of the Snake, or Dragon, and was simply known as the Mysteries. The snake and dragon are symbols that represent wisdom. The father of wisdom is Lucifer, also called the Light Bearer. The focus of worship for the Mysteries was Osiris, the name of a bright star that the ancients believed had been cast down onto the earth. The literal meaning of

Lucifer is "bringer of light" or "the morning star." After Osiris was gone from the sky, the ancients saw the Sun as the representation of Osiris ("...it is claimed that, after Lucifer fell from Heaven, he brought with him the power of thinking as a gift for mankind." Fred Gittings, Symbolism in Occult Art)

Most of the greatest minds that ever lived were initiated into the society of Mysteries by secret and dangerous rites, some of which were very cruel. Some of the most famous were known as Osiris, Isis, Sabazius, Cybele and Eleusis. Plato was one of these initiates and he describes some of the mysteries in his writings.

Plato's initiation encompassed three days of entombment in the Great Pyramid, during which time he died (symbolically), was reborn, and was given secrets that he was to preserve. Plato's writings are full of information on the Mysteries. Manly P. Hall stated in his book, The Secret Teachings of All Ages, that, "...the illumined of antiquity...entered its (pyramid of Giza) portals as men; they came forth as gods." The ancient Egyptian word for pyramid was khuti, which meant "glorious light." Mr. Hall says also, "The pyramids, the great Egyptian temples of initiation..."

According to many, the great pyramids were built to commemorate and observe a supernova explosion that occurred in the year 4000 B.C. Dr. Anthony Hewish, 1974 Nobel Prize winner in physics, discovered a rhythmic series of radio pulses which he proved were emissions from a star that had exploded around 4000 B.C. The Freemasons begin their calendar from A.L., "In the Year of Light," found by adding 4000 to the modern year. Thus 1990 + 4000 = 5990 A.L. George Michanowsky wrote in The Once and Future Star that "The ancient Sumerian cuneiform...described a giant star exploding within a triangle formed by...Zeta Puppis, Gamma Velorum, and Lambda Velorum...located in the southern sky....[An] accurate star catalogue now stated that the blazing star that had exploded within the triangle would again be seen by man in 6000 years." According to the Freemason's calendar it will occur in the year 2000, and indeed it will.

The spacecraft called Galileo is on its way to Jupiter, a baby star with a gaseous makeup exactly the same as our sun, with a load of 49.7 pounds of plutonium, supposedly being used as batteries to power the craft. When its final orbit decays in December 1999, Galileo will deliver its payload into the center of Jupiter. The unbelievable pressure that will be encountered will cause a reaction exactly as occurs when an atomic bomb is exploded by an implosion detonator. The plutonium will explode in an atomic reaction, lighting the hydrogen and helium atmosphere of Jupiter and resulting in the birth of the star that has already been named Lucifer. The world will interpret it as a sign of tremendous religious significance. It will fulfill prophecy. In reality it is only a demonstration of the insane application of technology by the JASON Society which may or may not even work. They have practiced overkill to ensure success, however, as the documents that I read while in Naval Intelligence stated that Project GALILEO required only five pounds of plutonium to ignite Jupiter and possibly stave off the coming ice age. Global warming is a hoax. It is easier for the public to deal with and will give the ruling elite more time before panic and anarchy replace government. The reality is that overall global temperatures are becoming lower. Storms are becoming more violent and less predictable.

TAKE NOTE OF THIS STATEMENT:
DANIEL 12

1 "At that time there shall arise Michael [JUPITER IN ANGELIC/CHERIBUM FORM], the great prince, guardian of your people; It shall be a time unsurpassed in distress since nations began until that time. At that time your people shall escape, everyone who is found written in the book. 2 Many of those who sleep in the dust of the earth shall awake; some shall live forever, others shall be an everlasting horror and disgrace. 3 But the wise shall shine brightly like the splendor of the firmament, And those who lead the many to justice shall be like the stars forever. 4 "As for you, Daniel, keep secret the message and seal the book until the end time; many shall fall away and evil shall increase."

The icecaps at the poles are growing larger. The temperate zones where food can be grown are shrinking. Desertification is increasing in the tropics. An ice age is on its way, and it will occur suddenly.

Simultaneously a vault containing the ancient records of the earth will be opened in Egypt. The opening of the vault will usher in the millennium. A great celebration has already been planned by the Millennium Society to take place at the pyramids in Egypt. According to the January 3, 1989, edition of the Arizona Daily Star, "President-elect Bush is spending this New Year's holiday at Camp David, Maryland, but in 10 years he may be in Egypt. Organizers of the Millennium Society say he's already committed to ushering in the next century at the Great Pyramid of Cheops in Giza.

The first secret that one must know to even begin to understand the Mysteries is that their members believe that there are but few truly mature minds in the world. They believe that those minds belong exdusively to them. The philosophy that follows is the classic secret-society view of humanity:

"When a person of strong intellect is confronted with a problem which calls for the use of reasoning faculties, they keep their poise and attempt to read a solution by garnering facts bearing upon the question. On the other hand, those who are immature, when confronted by the small problem, are overwhelmed. While the former may be said to be qualified to solve the mystery of their own destiny, the latter must be led like a bunch of animals and taught in the simplest language. Like sheep they are totally dependent upon the shepherd. The able intellect is taught the Mysteries and the esoteric spiritual truths. The masses are taught the literal, exoteric interpretations. While the masses worship the five senses, the select few observe, recognizing in the gulf between them the symbolic concretions of great abstract truths.

"The initiated elect communicate directly to Gods (ALIENS?) who communicate back to them. The masses sacrifice their lambs on an altar facing a stone idol that can neither hear or speak. The elect are given knowledge of the Mysteries and are illumined and are thus known as The Illluminati or the Illuminated Ones, the guardians of the 'Secrets of the Ages.'"

Three early secret societies that can be directly connected to a modern descendant are the cults of Roshaniya, Mithras and their counterpart, the Builders. They have many things in common with the Freemasons of today as well as with many other branches of the Illuminati. For instance, common to the Brotherhood are the symbolic rebirth into a new life without going through the portal of death during initiation; reference to the "Lion" and "the Grip of the Lion's Paw" in the Master Mason's degree; the three degrees, which is the same as the ancient Masonic rites before the many other degrees were added; the ladder of seven rungs; men only; and the "all-seeing eye."

The Illuminati logo (See US $1 bill)

Of special interest is the powerful society in Afghanistan in ancient times called the Roshaniya—illuminated ones. There are actually references to this mystical cult going back through history to the House of Wisdom at Cairo. The major tenets of this cult were: the abolition of private property; the elimination of religion; the elimination of nation states; the belief that illumination emanated from the Supreme Being who desired a class of perfect men and women to carry out the organization and direction of the world; belief in a plan to reshape the social system of the world by first taking control of individual countries one by one, and the belief that after reaching the fourth degree one could communicate directly with the unknown supervisors who had imparted knowledge to initiates throughout the ages. Wise men will again recognize the Brotherhood.

The important fact to remember is that the leaders of both the right and the left are a small, hard core of men who have been and still are Illuminists or members of the Brotherhood. They may have been or may be members of the Christian or Jewish religions, but that is only to further their own ends. They give allegiance to no particular nation, although they have used nationalism to further their causes. Their only concern is to gain greater economic and political power. The ultimate objective of the leaders of both groups is identical. They are determined to win for themselves undisputed control of the wealth, natural resources, and manpower of the entire planet. They intend to turn the world into their conception of a totalitarian socialist state. In the process they will eliminate all Christians, Jews, and atheists. You have just learned one, but only one, of the great mysteries.

The Roshaniya also called themselves the Order. Initiates took an oath that absolved them of all allegiance except to the Order and stated, "I bind myself to perpetual silence and unshaken loyalty and submission to the Order....All humanity which cannot identify itself by our secret sign is our lawful prey." The oath remains essentially the same to this day. The secret sign was to pass a hand over the forehead, palm inward; the countersign, to hold the ear with the fingers and support the elbow in the cupped other hand. Does that sound familiar? The Order is the Order of the Quest. The cult preached that there was a spirit state completely different from life as we know it. The spirit could continue to be powerful on earth through a member of the Order, but only if the spirit had been itself a member of the Order before its death. Thus members of the Order gained power from the spirits of the dead members.

The Roshaniya took in travelers as initiates and then sent them on their way to found new chapters of the Order. It is believed by some that the Assassins were a branch of the Roshaniya. Branches of the Roshaniya or "the illuminated ones" or the Illuminati existed and still exist everywhere. One of the rules was not to use the same name and never mention "the Illuminati." That rule is still in effect today. I believe that it is the breaking of this rule that resulted in Adam Weishaupt's downfall.

One of the greatest secrets of the ages is the true story of the Holy Grail, the robe of Jesus, the remains of the Cross of Crucifixion, and whether Jesus actually died or if he survived and produced a child. Many myths surround the Knights Templar concerning these relics, and most myths throughout history always have at least some basis in fact. If my sources are correct, the Knights Templar survive today as a branch of the Illuminati and guard the relics, which are hidden in a location known only to them.

We know that the Templars are Illuminati because the Freemasons absorbed and protected those who escaped persecution of the church and France, just as the Freemasons would absorb and protect Weishaupt's Illuminati centuries later. The Knights Templar exist today as a high degree of Freemasonry within the Templar Order. In fact, the Knights Templar is a branch of the Order of the Quest. The DeMolay Society is a branch of the Freemasons that consecrates the memory of the persecution of the Knights Templar and in particular, their leader Jacques deMolay. I know, because I was a member of the DeMolay Society as a young adult. I loved the mystery and ritual. I became separated from the Society when my family moved to a location out of reach of any lodge. I believe to this day that my association with the DeMolay Society may have been the reason for my selection for Naval Security and Intelligence.

According to members of the intelligence community, when the New World Order is solidified the relics will be taken out, will be united with the Spear of Destiny, and will, according to legend, give the world's ruler absolute power. This may confirm beliefs passed down through the ages that describe the significance of these relics when united in the hands one man. It explains Hitler's desperate search World War II. (Gen. Patton had claimed it after defeat)

The Knights Templar were founded sometime during the 11th century in Jerusalem by the Prieure de Sion for the express purpose of guarding remaining relics of Jesus and to provide military protection for the religious travelers during their pilgrimage to the Holy City.

The Prieure de Sion was a religious order founded upon Mount Sion in Jerusalem. The Order set for itself the goal of preserving and recording the bloodline of Jesus and the House of David. Through every means available to them, the Prieure de Sion had found and retrieved the remaining relics. These relics were entrusted to the Knights Templar for safekeeping. I am amazed at the authors of Holy Blood, Holy Grail and the information that they have unearthed. Most of all I am amazed at their inability to put the puzzle together. The treasure hidden in France is not the treasure of the Temple of Jerusalem. It is the Holy Grail itself, the robe of Jesus, the last remaining pieces of the Cross of Crucifixion, and, according to my sources, someone's bones. I can tell you that the reality of the bones will shake the world to its very foundations if I have been told the truth. The relics are hidden in France. I know the location and so do the authors of Holy Blood, Holy Grail, but they do not know that they know— or do they?

The Prieure de Sion logo

Adam Weishaupt, a young professor of canon law at Ingolstadt University in Germany, was a Jesuit priest and an initiate of the Illuminati. The branch of the Order he founded in Germany in 1776 was the same Illuminati previously discussed. The Jesuit connection is important, as you will see later in this chapter. Researchers agree that he was financed by the House of Rothschild (mentioned in "Silent Weapons for Quiet Wars"). Weishaupt advocated "abolition of all ordered national governments, abolition of inheritance, abolition of private property, abolition of patriotism, abolition of the individual home and family life as the cell from which all civilizations have stemmed, and abolition of all religions established and existing so that the ideology of totalitarianism may be imposed on mankind."

In the same year that he founded the Illuminati he published Wealth of Nations, the book that provided the ideological foundation for capitalism and for the Industrial Revolution. It is no accident that the Declaration of Independence was written in the same year. On the obverse of the Great Seal of the United States the wise will recognize the all-seeing eye and other signs of the Brotherhood of the Snake.

Every tenet was the same. Date and beliefs confirm that Weishaupt's Illuminati is the same as the Afghan Illuminated Ones and the other cults which called themselves "illuminated." The Alumbrados of Spain were the same as were the "illuminated" Guerinets of France. In the United States they were known as the Jacobin clubs. Secrets within secrets within secrets—but always at the heart is the Brotherhood.

I believe that Weishaupt was betrayed and set up for persecution because he ignored the rule that the word "illuminati" or the existence of the Brotherhood would never be exposed to public knowledge. His exposure and outlawing accomplished several goals of the still-hidden and still very powerful brotherhood. It allowed members to debunk claims of its existence on the grounds that the Illuminati had been exposed and outlawed and thus was no longer a reality. It allowed members to deny allegations of conspiracy of any kind. The Brotherhood of the Snake is adept at throwing out decoys to keep the dogs at bay. Weishaupt may have been a fool—or he may have been doing exactly what he was told.

Weishaupt said, "The great strength of our Order lies in its concealment; let it never appear in its own name, but always covered by another name, and another occupation."

Allegations that the Freemason organizations were infiltrated by the Illuminati during Weishaupt's reign are hogwash. The Freemasons have always contained the core of Illuminati within their ranks, and that is why they so freely and so willingly took in and hid the members of Weishaupt's group. You cannot really believe that the Freemasons, if they were only a simple fraternal organization, would have risked everything, including their very lives, by taking in and hiding outlaws who had been condemned by the monarchies of Europe. It is mainly Freemason authors who have perpetuated the myth that Adam Weishaupt was the founder of the Illuminati and that the Illuminati was destroyed, never to surface again.

In 1826 an American Freemason wrote a book revealing Masonic secrets entitled llustrations of Freemasonry. One of the secrets that he revealed is that the last mystery at the top of the Masonic pyramid is the worship of Lucifer. We have since learned the secret of the "story of the murder of Hiram Abif." Hiram Abif represents intelligence, liberty and truth, and was struck down by a blow to the neck with a rule, representing the suppression of speech by the church; then he was struck in the heart with the square, representing the suppression of belief by the State; and finally he was struck on the head by a maul, representing the suppression of intellect by the masses. Freemasonry thus equates the Church, the State, and the masses with tyranny, intolerance, and ignorance. What Morgan revealed was that the Freemasons were pledged to avenge Hiram Abif and that their plan was to strike down the Church, the State, and the freedom of the masses.

Morgan caused a small uproar against the Masons. The small uproar turned into a full blown anti-Freemason movement when the author, William Morgan, disappeared. Morgan had apparently been abducted and drowned in Lake Ontario. It was alleged that fellow Masons had done it, and that they deny to this day. Who else would have done it? I believe they murdered him. The newspapers of the time state without reservation that he was murdered by Masons. The oath of initiation into the Freemasons states that if secrets are told, the initiate will be murdered. A nationwide furor ensued that resulted in the creation of an anti-Masonic political party in 1829 by Henry Dana Ward, Thurlow Weed, and William H. Seward. Interest in several anti-Masonic books was revived during that period, with the result that Freemasonry suffered a severe loss of membership. It lasted only a few years and by 1840 the anti-Masonic party was extinct. Time really does cure all ills.

We know that the British Freemasons are a totally self-serving group that discriminates in favor of its own whenever jobs, promotions, contracts, or careers are concerned. The English Freemason organization was used by the KGB to infiltrate and take over British Intelligence. British Intelligence is synonomous with Chatham House, more commonly known as the Royal Institute for International Affairs, the parent organization of the Council on Foreign Relations in the United States. The English state police, Scotland Yard, ordered its personnel not to join the Masons for fear the same would happen to them. Of course, you have been told all your life that the Freemasons are only a benevolent fraternal organization bent only on community service. Read on, O innocent one.

Probably the most notorious Freemason lodge is the P2 lodge in Italy. This group has been implicated in everything from bribery to assassinations. P2 is directly connected to the Vatican, the Knights of Malta, and to the U.S. Central Intelligence Agency. It is powerful and dangerous. The P2 lodge has succeeded in infiltrating the Vatican and has scored a coup of tremendous significance: the Pope, John Paul II, has lifted the ban against Freemasonry. Many high-level members of the Vatican are now Freemasons.

I tell you now that Freemasonry is one of the most wicked and terrible organizations upon this earth. The Masons are major players in the struggle for world domination. The 33rd Degree is split into two. One split contains the core of the Luciferian Illuminati and the other contains those who have no knowledge of it whatsoever.

ALL of the intelligence officers that I worked for while in Naval Intelligence were Masons. As I stated before, I believe that my association with the DeMolay Society as a young adult may have been the reason that I was selected for Naval Security and Intelligence. However, that is only a guess.

I had intended to go into great detail linking P2, the Prieure de Sion, the Vatican, the CIA, organizations for a United Europe, and the Bilderberg Group. Fortunately, Michael Baigent, Righard Leigh & Henry Lincoln beat me to it. I say fortunately, because they confirm my previous allegation that I published in my paper "The Secret Government" that the CIA had plants, called moles, deep within the Vatican. You must read Holy Blood, Holy Grail and The Messianic Legacy, both by Baigent, Leigh, & Lincoln. Any reputable bookstore should carry them. Between pages 343 and 361 of The Messianic Legacy you can read of the alliance of power that resulted in a secret world government.

Most members of the Freemasons are not aware that the Illuminati practices what is known as "secrets within secrets," or organizations within organizations- That is one purpose of initiation. I cannot excuse any of the members, however, and anyone who joins a society without knowing everything about the organization is indeed a fool. Only those at the top who have passed every test truly know what the Masons are hiding, thus rendering it impossible for anyone outside to know much at all about the group. What does that say about new members or those who are already members but do not know the ultimate secrets? It tells me that fools abound. Unlike authors who, out of fear, have acted as apologists for the Freemasons, I decline to absolve them of responsibility and guilt. The Freemasons, like everyone else, are responsible for the cleanliness of their home. The occupant of a secret house within a secret house within a secret house cannot clean if he cannot see the number of rooms or what they contain. Their house is a stinking cesspool. Look to the Masons for the guilty party if anything happens to me. I believe that they have murdered in the past and that they will murder in the future.

Their goal is to rule the world. The doctrine of this group is not democracy or communism, but is a form of fascism. The doctrine is totalitarian socialism. You must begin to think correctly. The Illuminati are not Communists, but some Communists are Illuminati. (1) Monarchism (thesis) faced democracy (antithesis) in WWI, which resulted in the formation of communism and the League of Nations (synthesis). (2) Democracy and communism (thesis) faced fascism (antithesis) in WWII and resulted in a more powerful United Nations (synthesis). (3) Capitalism (thesis) now faces communism (antithesis) and the result will be the New World Order, totalitarian socialism (synthesis).

The 1953 report of the California Senate Investigating Committee on Education stated: "So-called modern Communism is apparently the same hypocritical world conspiracy to destroy civilization that was founded by the illuminati, and that raised its head in our colonies here at the critical period before the adoption of our Constitution." The California Senate understood that communism is the work of the Illuminati. They failed to realize that the Council on Foreign Relations and the Trilateral Commission are also the work of the Illuminati. You MUST begin to think correctly. The enemy is not communism, it is Illuminism. The Communists are not going to be much happier with the New World Order than we.

I hope to show that most modern secret societies and especially those that practice degrees of initiation, and that is the key, are really one society with one purpose. You may call them whatever you wish—

the Order of the Quest, the JASON Society, the Roshaniya, the Qabbalah, the Knights Templar, the Knights of Malta, the Knights of Columbus, the Jesuits, the Masons, the Ancient and Mystical Order of Rosae Crucis, the Illuminati, the Nazi Party, the Communist Party, the Executive Members of the Council on Foreign Relations, The Group, the Brotherhood of the Dragon, the Rosicrucians, the Royal Institute of International Affairs, the Trilateral Commission, the Bilderberg Group, the Open Friendly Secret Society (the Vatican), the Russell Trust, the Skull & Bones, the Scroll & Key, the Order—they are all the same and all work toward the same ultimate goal, a New World Order.

Many of them, however, disagree on exactly who will rule this New World Order, and that is what causes them to sometimes pull in opposite directions while nevertheless proceeding toward the same goal. The Vatican, for instance, wants the Pope to head the world coalition. Some want Lord Maitreya to head the New World Order. Lord Maitreya is the front runner, I believe, since witnesses say he was present on the ship at Malta with Bush, Gorbachev, and the ten regional heads of the New World Order. "Approximately 200 dignitaries from around the world attended a major conference initiated by Maitreya in London on April 21 and 22,1990. Representatives of governments (including the USA), members of royal families, religious leaders and journalists, all of whom had met with Maitreya previously, attended the conference." Quote from "Prophecy Watch" column of Whole Wheat No. 8, Minneapolis.

Someone has also spent an awful lot of money announcing his presence. The Pope will have to approve him if Maitreya is selected, however, and that would fulfill the Bible prophecy in the Book of Revelation that states that the first beast will be given his power by Rome. If you can interpret Revelation as I can, then you know that the Pope will ultimately win out and will reign as the second beast.

In 1952 an alliance was formed, bringing them all together for the first time in history. The Black Families, the Illuminati (the Order), the Vatican, and the Freemasons now work together to bring about the New World Order. All will protest their innocence and will do everything within their power to destroy anyone who suggests otherwise. I will undoubtedly become a target when this book is published.

You may notice that some of those listed in the preceding paragraphs do not, or so it appears, practice degrees of initiation. That is the public view. Look at the Council on Foreign Relations. Many members—in fact, the majority—never serve on the executive committees. They never go through any initiation of any kind. They are, in fact, the power base and are used to gain a consensus of opinion. The majority are not really members but are made to feel as if they are. In reality they are being used and are unwilling or unable to understand. The Executive Committee is an inner core of intimate associates, members of a secret society called the Order of the Quest, also known as the JASON Society, devoted to a common purpose. The members are an outer circle on whom the inner core acts by personal persuasion, patronage and social pressure. That is how they bought Henry Kissinger. Rockefeller gave Kissinger a grant of $50,000 in the early '50s, a fortune in those days, and made dear old Henry a member of the CFR. Anyone in the outer circle who does not toe the mark is summarily expelled and the lesson is not lost on those who remain. Do you remember the human desire to be a member of the elect? That is the principle at work.

The real power are men who are always recruited without exception from the secret societies of Harvard and Yale known as the Skull & Bones and the Scroll & Key. Both societies are secret branches (also called the Brotherhood of Death) of what is otherwise historically known as the Illuminati. They are connected to parent organizations in England (The Group of Oxford University and especially All Souls College), and Germany (the Thule Society, also called the Brotherhood of Death). I learned this when I was with Naval Intelligence. I was not able to explain why some members of the Executive Committee were not listed under the "Addresses" of Chapter 322 of the Skull & Bones Society until I read The Wise Men by Walter Isaacson & Evan Thomas, Simon and Schuster, New York. Under illustration #9 in the center of the book you will find the caption "Lovett with the Yale Unit, above far right, and on the beach: His initiation into Skull and Bones came at an air base near Dunkirk." I have found that members of these two societies were chosen on an ongoing basis by invitation based upon merit post-college and were not confined to only Harvard or Yale attendees.

Only members of the Order are initiated into the Order of the

Quest, the JASON Society that makes up the executive members of the Council on Foreign Relations and, in fact, the Trilateral Commission as well. The executive members of the Council on Foreign Relations are the real elect in this country. George Bush is a member of the Order. Surprised? You shouldn't be. His father was also a member who helped finance Hitler.

It is important that you know that the members of the Order take an oath that absolves them from any allegiance to any nation or king or government or constitution, and that includes the negating of any subsequent oath of allegiance which they may be required to take. They swear allegiance only to the Order and its goal of a New World Order. George Bush is not a loyal citizen of the United States but instead is loyal only to the destruction of the United States and to the formation of the New World Order. According to the oath Bush took when he was initiated into Skull & Bones, his oath of office as President of the United States of America means nothing.

The Trilateral Commission is an elite group of some 300 very prominent business, political, and intellectual decision-makers of Western Europe, North America, and Japan. This enterprise is a private agency that works to build up political and economic cooperation among the three regions. Its grand design, which it no longer hides, is a New World Order.

The Trilateral Commission was the idea of its founder, American banking magnate David Rockefeller. The real reason for its formation was the decline of the Council on Foreign Relation's power as a result of the people's dissatisfaction with the Vietnam War. The reasoning behind the move toward the Trilateral Commission was the same as entering two horses in the same race. It doubles the chances of winning. The real power has always remained solidly in the hands of the Council on Foreign Relations. The Rockefeller family was, is and always will be the benefactor of both organizations. Rockefeller, though powerful, is not in control in this country or anywhere else. The key to the REAL power is the fact that Rockefeller had to put out feelers at a Bilderberg Group meeting in 1972 about forming a private group of trilateral leaders. The Bilderberg Group gave the nod and Rockefeller's man Zbigniew Brzezinski gathered up a membership and organized the Trilateral Commission in 1972, not in 1973 as the Commission claims.

David Rockefeller & Zbignew Brzezinsky -founders of The Bilderbergers and the Trilateral Commission -

A key to the danger presented by the Trilateral Commission is its "Seminal Peace," written for them by Harvard Professor Samuel P. Huntington in the mid '70s. In the paper Professor Huntington recommended that democracy and economic development be discarded as outdated ideas. He wrote as co-author of the book, The Crisis of Democracy, "We have come to recognize that there are potential desirable limits to economic growth. There are also potentially desirable limits to the indefinite extension of political democracy. A government which lacks authority will have little ability short of cataclysmic crisis to impose on its people the sacrifices which may be necessary."

.....Remember that George Bush was a member of the Trilateral Commission and only resigned as an expediency to get elected. He believes wholeheartedly in the Commission and its ideas and ideals. We have elected a President who believes that democracy and economic development must be discarded- I tell you now that he is working toward that end. Bush is still a member of the Order and the CFR.

The JASON Society, or JASON Scholars, takes its name from the story of Jason and the Golden Fleece, and it is a branch of the Order of the Quest, one of the highest degrees in the Illuminati. The golden fleece takes on the role of truth to JASON members. Jason represents the search for the truth. Therefore the name JASON Society denotes a group of men who are engaged in a search for the truth. The name Jason is spelled with capital letters when used as the name of the JASON Society. Lower-case letters are never used when referring to this secret group. The name may even have a deeper meaning, as the name "Jason" and the Golden Fleece appear throughout history in relation to various other secret societies. In these instances the story represents man (Jason) looking for himself (Golden Fleece).

Top Secret documents that I read while with Naval Intelligence stated that President Eisenhower had commissioned the JASON Society to examine all of the evidence, facts, lies, and deception and find the truth of the alien question.

Founders of the JASON Group (not the same as the JASON Society) include members of the famous Manhattan Project, which brought together almost every leading physicist in the nation to build the atomic bomb during World War II. The group is made up mostly of theoretical physicists and is the most elite gathering of scientific minds in the United States. As of 1987 the membership included four Nobel Prize winners. Today JASON continues to offer scientific help the government cannot find anywhere else. They are probably the only group of scientists in the United States that know the true state of highest technology.

JASON is shrouded in what appears to be unnecessary secrecy. The group refuses to release its membership list. None of the members list JASON membership on their official resumes. Working completely behind the scenes, JASON has guided the nation's most important security decisions. These include, but are not limited to, Star Wars, submarine warfare, and predictions about the greenhouse effect. The JASON members are each paid a $500 per-day consultant's fee.

In the documents that I read while with Naval Intelligence the JASONS predicted that the greenhouse effect would lead ultimately to an ICE AGE.

According to the Pentagon, the JASONS hold the highest and most restrictive security clearances in the nation. They are given the protocol rank of rear admiral (two stars) when they visit or travel aboard ships or visit military bases. The only other reference to the JASON group that I have been able to find is in The Pentagon Papers. The papers stated that JASON was responsible for designing the electronic barrier between North and South Vietnam for the purpose of sealing off infiltration of the South by North Vietnamese regulars during the Vietnam War. I was stationed on the DMZ and I can tell you that it did not work.

The veil of secrecy drawn around the JASON Group has been so tight and so leak-proof since its conception that those who think the government cannot keep a secret need to reexamine that position. The government was able to contain the JASON secret except for the one leak; but the JASON Group itself, a civilian group, did even better. No leaks have ever occurred from within JASON. JASON is administered by the Mitre Corporation. Government contracts allotted to the Mitre Corporation are in reality allotted to the JASON scientists. This is done so that the name JASON does not ever appear in documents which may come under public scrutiny.

What is the difference between the JASON Scholars or JASON Society and the JASON Group? The documents that I read referred to the JASON Society in exactly those words. In public documents the only JASON reference is to the JASON Group, administered by the Mitre Corporation. I believe the JASON Society is one of the highest degrees above the Skull & Bones and the Scroll & Key in the Illuminati. In other words, it is a higher level of initiation. The JASON Group is a scientific organization formed and hired by the JASON Society and the U.S. Government for obvious reasons.

I know a lot more about the JASON Society and the JASON Group, but I do not want to injure Mr. Grant Cameron, who has done extensive research on these subjects. He will publish his research in the coming months. I guarantee his findings will amaze you.

The Council on Foreign Relations has been the foremost flank of America's foreign-policy establishment for more than half a century. The Council on Foreign Relations is a private organization of business executives, scholars, and political leaders that studies global problems and play a key role in developing U.S. foreign policy. The CFR is one of the most powerful semi-official groups concerned with America's role in international affairs. It is controlled by an elect group of men recruited from the Skull & Bones and the Scroll & Key societies of Harvard and Yale, which are both chapters of a secret branch of the Illuminati known as Chapter 322 of the Order. The members of the Order make up the Executive Committee of the Council on Foreign Relations after undergoing initiation into the Order of the Quest, also known as the JASON Society.

The Council on Foreign Relations is an off-shoot sister organization to the British Royal Institute of International Affairs. Their goal is a New World Order. Although it existed as a dinner club in New York, it did not take on its present power until 1921, when it merged with the Royal Institute of International Affairs and received its financial base from J. P. Morgan, the Carnegie Endowment, the Rockefeller family, and other Wall Street banking interests.

The Council on Foreign Relations controls our government. Through the years its members have infiltrated the entire executive branch,

State Department, Justice Department, CIA, and the top ranks of the military. Every director of the Central Intelligence Agency has been a member of the CFR. Most presidents since Roosevelt have been members. The members of the CFR dominate ownership of the press and most, if not all, of America's top journalists are members. The CFR does not conform to government policy. The government conforms to CFR policy.

I read Top Secret documents while with Naval Intelligence that stated that President Eisenhower had appointed six of the Executive Committee members of the CFR to sit on the panel called Majesty Twelve also known as Majority Twelve for security reasons. Majesty Twelve is the secret group that is supposed to control extraterrestrial information and projects. The documents stated that Eisenhower had also appointed six members from the Executive branch of government who were also members of the CFR. The total membership of Majesty Twelve was nineteen, including Dr. Edward Teller and the six members from the JASON scientific group. Again, whether this is true or disinformation depends solely upon the existence of aliens.

The Knights of Malta play a powerful role in this scenario. In the 1930's General Smedley Butler was recruited to help take over the White House. He was told that he was needed because of his general popularity with the military. General Butler blew the whistle and named several prominent Americans as part of the plot. At the top of the list was John J. Raskob, who was a founding member of the U.S. branch of the Knights of Malta. He was board chairman of General Motors. He was, at the time, the U.S. Treasurer of the Knights of Malta. Congressional hearings were held to investigate the plot, but none of those named, including Raskob, was ever called to testify and nothing ever came of the hearings. Although you will find this in the Congressional records, you will never find it in any history book anywhere.

It is significant that the Iran-Contra episode has many similarities to the 1930s plot. William Casey was a member of the Knights of Malta. William Casey, with the help of Vice President Bush, Anne Armstrong and Donald Regan, caused the President's Foreign Intelligence Advisory Board to be emasculated so that Bush, Casey, North and others could carry out their dirty deeds without oversight. They had also developed a plan to suspend the Constitution of the United States and were preparing to implement the plan when they were caught. These facts emerged from the hearings but were suppressed by the committee chairman, Senator Daniel Inouye of Hawaii. You must understand that tremendous power was involved in both attempts to overthrow the United States Government.

William Casey was the Director of the CIA. He was a member of the CFR. Casey was a Knight of Malta. He was the head of Ronald Reagan's political campaign. He was head of the Securities and Exchange Commission. During the Nixon administration he was head of the Export-Import Bank.

Casey arranged financing for the Kama River truck factory in the Soviet Union with 90% of the funds guaranteed or furnished by the U.S. taxpayer. This factory built military truck and tank engines for the Soviet Army. It was, and may still be, the largest factory in the world and could produce more heavy trucks than all U.S. factories together. I believe Casey was murdered.

The Knights of Malta is a world organization with its threads weaving through business, banking, politics, the CIA, other intelligence organizations, P2, religion, education, law, military, think tanks, foundations, the United States Information Agency, the United Nations, and numerous other organizations. They are not the oldest but are one of the oldest branches of the Order of the Quest in existence. The world head of the Knights of Malta is elected for a life term, with the approval of the Pope. The Knights of Malta have their own Constitution and are sworn to work toward the establishment of a New World Order with the Pope at its head. Knights of Malta members are also powerful members of the CFR and the Trilateral Commission.

The Vatican has been infiltrated over many years by the Illuminati. This is easily proven by the fact that in 1738 Pope Clement XII issued a Papal Bull which stated that any Catholic who became a Mason would be excommunicated, a very serious punishment. In 1884 Pope Leo XIII issued a proclamation stating that Masonry was one of the secret societies attempting to "revive the manners and customs of the pagans" and "establish Satan's kingdom on Earth." Piers Compton, in his book The Broken Cross, traces the infiltration of the Catholic Church by the Illuminati. He has found the use of the all-seeing eye in the triangle by leading Catholics and by the Jesuits. It was used in the seal of the

Philadelphia Eucharistic Congress in 1976. It was on a special issue of Vatican stamps in 1978, announcing the final Illuminati victory to the world. Mr. Compton claims that Pope John XXIII wore the "all-seeing eye in the triangle" on his personal cross. Compton is adamant that several hundred leading Catholic priests, bishops and cardinals are members of secret societies. He quotes an article in an Italian Journal that lists more than 70 Vatican offIcials, including Pope Paul VI's private secretary, the director general of Vatican radio, the Archbishop of Florence, the prelate of Milan, the assistant editor of the Vatican newspaper, several Italian bishops, and the abbot of the Order of St. Benedict. Those are only the ones that are known and only the ones known in Italy. It is widely believed that this Pope, John Paul XXII, is a member of the Illuminati. I believe, according to my research, that it is true. The best indication of infiltration is that on November 27,1983, the Pope retracted all of the Papal Bulls against Freemasonry and allowed Catholics, after several hundred years, to again become members of secret societies without fear of excommunication. The goal of the Illuminati to elect one of their own to the Papacy appears to have come to fruition. If that is the case, the New World Order is just on the horizon. Now is the time.

The first U.S. Ambassador to the Vatican was William Wilson, a Knight of Malta. His appointment was probably illegal and, for a fact, was highly unethical. Wilson could not possibly have represented the U.S. when his allegiance was sworn to the Pope.

Wilson, if you will remember, took an unauthorized trip to Libya and met privately with Libyan officials at a time when travel to Libya had been banned by the President. President Ronald Reagan had called Col. Khadafi "a mad dog" and made a few strong threats. The U.S. had been resolute in bombing Libya even though civilians were killed. Following Wilson's trip, Khadafi issued a press release stating that "an American diplomat had been sent to reduce tensions with Libya." The State Department denied that any such thing had taken place. Ambassador Wilson closed his mouth and refused any comment. To this day he has said nothing, even though his actions made a liar of the United States and embarrassed us worldwide.

A clue to what was happening is the fact that while we had cut off Libya and even bombed them and while travel by U.S. citizens to Libya was forbidden, five huge oil conglomerates were filling their pockets dealing with Khadafi. One of the companies was headed by J. Peter Grace, President of W. R. Grace. Eight members of the W. R. Grace Company are members of the Knights of Malta. According to an article by Leslie Geld in the New York Times, administration officials had expressed concern about Mr. Wilson's activities. These actions, they said, often seem to revolve around his contacts and interest in the oil business.

Wilson should have been fired, but instead nothing happened except that he and his wife attended a Papal Easter Mass and stood next to George Schultz and his wife. In diplomatic language this indicated private approval of his actions. George Schultz, of course, is a member of the CFR, the Bohemian Club and the Bechtel Corporation, all of which have close ties to the Order and the Knights of Malta.

Wilson engaged in several other improprieties during his ambassadorship. Again, in each case nothing happened. Finally he resigned. Later, if you will remember, President Reagan suffered a fall from a horse on William Wilson's ranch in Mexico. Do you seriously think that President Reagan would have visited Wilson's home in Mexico if he had not approved of Wilson's actions while he was the U.S. Ambassador to the Vatican?

Knight of Malta Myron Taylor was President Roosevelt's envoy. Knight of Malta John McCone was President Kennedy's envoy and he was also the Director of the CIA during the early '60s. A former mayor of New York City, Robert Wagner, was President Jimmy Carter's envoy. Frank Shakespeare replaced William Wilson. Frank Shakespeare is a Knight of Malta, and so it goes. President Reagan spoke at the annual Knights of Malta dinner.

The Knights of Malta all have diplomatic immunity. They can ship goods across borders without paying duty or undergoing customs checks. Does that ring any bells? In any case, that is power.

The Knights of Malta is held up by a backbone consisting of nobility. Nearly half of the 10,000 members belong to Europe's oldest and most powerful families. This cements the alliance between the Vatican and the "Black Nobility." The Black Nobility is mostly the rich and powerful of Europe. The head of the Black Nobility is the family that can claim direct descendancy from the last Roman emperor. Maybe now you can see that things are beginning to fall into their proper place.

Membership in the Knights of Malta entails obedience to one's superior in The Order and ultimately to the Pope. Therefore, a U.S. ambassador who is also a member of the Knights of Malta faces a conflict of interest. Why is this fact ignored? President Bush appointed Knight of Malta Thomas Melledy to the post of U.S. Ambassador to the Vatican.

The Vatican has founded the Pope John Paul II Center for Prayer and Study for Peace at 1711 Ocean Avenue, Springlake, New Jersey, in a mansion overlooking the ocean. The mansion was given to the New York Archdiocese by the estate of Elmer Bobst, who died in 1978. He was a multimillionaire and chairman of Warner Lambert Company. Richard Nixon was a frequent visitor. Directors of the Center were Kurt Waldheim, former Secretary General of the United Nations and ex-nazi war criminal; Cyrus Vance, former Secretary of State under Carter and member of both the Council on Foreign Relations and the Trilateral Commission; Clare Booth Luce, a dame of the Knights of Malta; and J. Peter Grace of W. R. Grace Company, who is head of the Knights of Malta in the United States.

The Center was set up by the Vatican as a part of the Pope's new peace plan, which will bring the world together. The Center has two roles: (1) Educate Catholics and their children to accept the New World Order. (2) Provide residence for the world-peace-solution computer and an ongoing study for peaceful solutions to any future problems which may endanger world peace. The computer is hooked to the world capitals via satellite. All nations have agreed to relinquish sovereignty to the Pope and submit future problems to the computer for solution. Of course, this will not go into effect until the New World Order is publicly announced. I believe that the New World Order was born in secrecy on January 19,1989. Now you know, The Vatican has stated at various times that "the Pope is for total disarmament; the Pope is for elimination of the sovereignty of the nation states; the Pope is also stating that property rights are not to be considered true property rights. The Pope believes that only the Vatican knows what is right for man."

In the early 1940s, the I. G. Farben Chemical Company employed a Polish salesman who sold cyanide to the Nazis for use in Auschwitz. The same salesman also worked as a chemist in the manufacture of the poison gas. This same cyanide gas along with Zyklon B and malathion was used to exterminate millions of Jews and other groups. Their bodies were then burned to ashes in the ovens. After the war the salesman, fearing for his life, joined the Catholic Church and was ordained a priest in 1946. One of his closest friends was Dr. Wolf Szmuness, the mastermind behind the November/78 to October/79 and March/80 to October/81 experimental hepatitis B vaccine trials conducted by the Center for Disease Control in New York, San Francisco and four other American cities that loosed the plague of AIDS upon the American people. The salesman was ordained Poland's youngest bishop in 1958. After a 30-day reign his predecessor was assassinated and our ex-cyanide gas salesman assumed the papacy as Pope John Paul II. 1990 is the right time with the right leaders: ex-chief of the KGB Mikhail Gorbachev, ex-chief of the CIA George Bush, ex-Nazi cyanide gas salesman Pope John Paul II, all bound by an unholy alliance to ring in the New World Order.

The Pope has challenged world leaders by claiming that the people of the world already recognize the absolute authority of Rome because they observe the Sunday Sabbath that was ordered by the Pope in the Council of Laodicea (A.D. 364). The original Ten Commandments given to Moses ordered that we should: "Remember the Sabbath day, to keep it Holy. Six days shalt thou labor, and do all thy work but the seventh day is the Sabbath of the Lord thy God; in it thou shalt not do any work, thou, nor thy son, nor thy daughter, thy man servant, nor thy maid servant, nor thy cattle, nor thy stranger that is within thy gates: for in six days the Lord made heaven and earth, the sea, and all that in them is, and rested the seventh day: wherefore the Lord blessed the Sabbath day, and hallowed it."

The seventh day, the Sabbath as handed to Moses is Saturday. The celebration of Sunday as the Sabbath is verification that the people recognize the Pope as superior to God. The only whole people who have not recognized the authority of the Pope are the Jewish people, and that is why the Vatican has not and will not recognize the state of Israel. The Vatican refuses even to call it Israel. Instead the Vatican says Palestine when talking about Israel. Again, I must remind you that what you believe makes not one bit of difference. The important thing to understand is that if they believe this, it is going to give you nightmares.

"The Pope has a lot of charisma and in a one world system you need a religious head for power. Khomeini proved that. This Pope has enough following and charisma to make what we consider a great threat in this move." [Quote from The Mantooth Report]

"Pope John Paul II is most anxious to complete his goal. His goal is to reunite the Christian World under the leadership of the papacy. If at all possible, he hopes to reach his goal by the end of this century. This is the primary reason behind the Pope's many worldwide trips." [From an article by Gene H. Hogberg, Nov./Dec. 1989, Plain Truth.]

Were you aware that Hitler and his entire staff were Catholic? Did you know that the Nazis dabbled in the occult? Did you know that the New York Times of April 14, 1990, quotes George Bush as stating, "Let's forgive the Nazi war criminals." I wonder why he said that? Did you know that the Los Angeles Times December 12, 1984, quoted Pope John Paul II as saying, "Don't go to God for forgiveness of sins, come to me." The Pope committed blasphemy, thus fulfilling prophecy according to the book of Revelation. The Pope is telling us that he is God!

Remember, never worship a leader. If you worship a leader, you then no longer have the ability to recognize when you have been deceived!

On July 21, 1773, Pope Clement XIV "forever annulled and extinguished the Jesuit Order." France, Spain and Portugal had independently come to realize that the Jesuits were meddling in the affairs of the state and were therefore enemies of the government. The Pope's action was a response to pressure applied by the monarchies. King Joseph of Portugal signed a decree "by which the Jesuits were denounced as 'traitors, rebels and enemies to the realm...'" Pope Pius VII in August, 1814, reinstated the Jesuits to all of their former rights and privileges.

Ex-President John Adams wrote to his successor, Thomas Jefferson: "I do not like the reappearance of the Jesuits. If ever there was a body of men who merited eternal damnation on earth...it is this Society...." Jefferson replied: "Like you, I disapprove of the restoration of the Jesuits, for it means a step backwards from light into darkness."

The Jesuits are still in trouble today as they have been throughout their existence. On February 28,1982, Pope Paul II told the Jesuits to "keep clear of politics, and honor Roman Catholic tradition." U.S. News and World Report stated that the Jesuits had indeed meddled in the affairs of nations. The article stated: "Jesuits have played leading roles in Nicaragua's Sandinista revolution. Some Jesuits have joined Communist parties. One priest in El Salvador has claimed that his order is working for the advancement of Marxism and revolution, not for God....Jesuits have joined left wing rebel movements in Central America and the Philippines, and have advocated a melding of Marxism and Roman Catholicism in what is called 'liberation theology.'"

When the United States wanted to employ the nastiest forms of the Haig-Kissinger depopulation policy in Central America it was the Jesuits who organized and prodded the people into civil war. Wherever the Jesuits go, revolution quickly follows. I am always sad when I see or hear of people being hurt; but according to my research, the Jesuit priests murdered in Central America probably deserved it.

The most powerful secret organization in the world is the Bilderberg Group, organized in 1952 and named after the hotel where its first meeting took place in 1954. The man who organized the Bilderberg Group, Prince Bernhard of the Netherlands, has the power to veto the Vatican's choice of any Pope it selects. Prince Bernhard has this veto power because his family, the Hapsburgs, are desended from the Roman emperors. Prince Bernhard is the leader of the Black Families. He claims descent from the House of David and thus can truly say that he is related to Jesus. Prince Bernhard, with the help of the CIA, brought the hidden ruling body of the Illuminati into public knowledge as the Bilderberg Group. This is the official alliance that makes up the world governing body.

The core of the organization is three committees made up of thirteen members each. Thus the heart of the Bilderberg Group consists of 39 total members of the Illuminati. The three committees are made up exclusively of members of all the different secret groups that make up the Illuminati, the Freemasons, the Vatican, and the Black Nobility. This committee works year round in offices in Switzerland. It determines who is invited to the annual meeting and what policies and plans will be discussed. Every proposal or plan that has ever been discussed at an annual meeting of the Bilderberg Group has come to pass usually within one or two years following the meeting. The Bilderberg Group is directing the "quiet war" that is being waged against us. How can they do it? These are the men who really rule the world.

The numbers 3, 7, 9,11,13, 39 and any multiple of these numbers have special meaning to the Illuminati. Notice that the Bilderberg Group has core of 39 members who are broken into 3 groups of 13 members in each group. Notice that the core of 39 answers to the 13 who make up the Policy Committee. Take special notice that the 13 members of the Policy Committee answer to the Round Table of Nine. You know that the original number of states in the United States of America was 13. The Constitution has 7 articles and was signed by 39 members of the Constitutional Convention.

The United States was born on July 4, 1776. July is the 7th month of the year. Add 7 (for July) and 4 and you have 11; 1+7+7+6 = 21, which is a multiple of 3 and 7. Add 2+1 and you get 3. Look at the numbers in 1776 and you see two 7s and a 6, which is a multiple of 3. Coincidence, you say? For those of you who still say it's accidental, however, I offer the following evidence. I could write a book just on numerical links, but I won't.

Manly P. Hall, 33rd-degree Mason, probably the most renowned expert on these subjects, wrote in his book, The Secret Destiny of America, "For more than three thousand years, secret societies have labored to create the background of knowledge necessary to the establishment of an enlightened democracy among the nations of the world...all have continued...and they still exist, as the Order of the Quest. Men bound by a secret oath to labor in the cause of world democracy decided that in the American colonies they would plan the roots of a new way of life. The Order of the Quest...was set up in America before the middle of the 17th century....Franklin spoke for the Order of the Quest, and most of the men who worked with him in the early days of the American Republic were also members....Not only were many of the founders of the United States Government Masons, but they received aid from a secret and august body existing in Europe which helped them to establish this country for a particular purpose known only to the initiated few." I found these quotes in a book on page 133. When added together, 1+3+3 equal the number 7—coincidence?

We can get a little insight into the Order of the Quest from Franklin D. Roosevelt's Secretary of Agriculture, Henry Wallace, the man directly responsible for the printing of the reverse of the Great Seal of the United States on the one-dollar bill. Mr. Wallace, a member of the Order of the Quest, wrote in a letter to the Russian mystic and artist Nicholas Roerich: "The Search, whether it be for the lost word of

Masonry, or the Holy Chalice, or the potentialities of the age to come, is the one supremely worthwhile objective. All else is karmic duty. But surely everyone is a potential Galahad? So may we strive for the Chalice and the flame above it." The Holy Grail has a way of popping up on a regular basis in the writings of secret societies.

In the Great Seal of the United States we see the ancient symbol of the Brotherhood of the Snake (or Dragon), which as you already know is the all seeing eye in the pyramid representing the form of wisdom.

Just below the pyramid you will note "Novus Ordo Seclorum" which translated means, "New World Order" There are: 9 tail feathers on the eagle; 13 leaves in the olive branches; 13 bars and stripes; 13 arrows; 13 letters in "E Pluribus Unum; 13 stars in the green crest above; 13 stones in the pyramid; 13 letters in "Annuit Coeptis"

First version of the US flag. (Note the All-Seeing Eye)

All of these mystical numbers also have special meaning to the Freemasons. You would have to be a devout skeptic to miss the tremendous significance of all of these supposed coincidences. Who among you can still say that there is no link?

I read while in Naval Intelligence that at least once a year, maybe more, two nuclear submarines meet beneath the polar icecap and mate together at an airlock. Representatives of the Soviet Union meet with the Policy Committee of the Bilderberg Group. The Russians are given the script for their next performance. Items on the agenda include the combined efforts in the secret space program governing Alternative 3. I now have in my possession offlcial NASA photographs of a moonbase in the crater Copernicus.

This method of meeting is the only way that is safe from detection and/or bugging. The public outcry that would result would destroy everything should these meetings be discovered. A BBC-TV documentary program entitled "Science Report" revealed these same facts but subsequently issued a retraction. In their retraction they stated that the show had been fiction. It must be noted here that "Science Report" was a very respected documentary, nonfiction program in Britain.

Never in its history had it ever aired fiction. This subject is explored in depth in another chapter. There is no other method that I know of to verify these meetings short of somehow becoming a crew member on one of the submarines. Is Alternative 3 true, or is it a part of the plan to ring in the New World Order? It really doesn't matter, because either way we're screwed. The quicker you understand that, the wiser you become.

The members of the Bilderberg Group are the most powerful financiers, industrialists, statesmen and intellectuals, who get together each year for a private conference on world affairs. The meetings provide an informal, off-the-record opportunity for international leaders to mingle, and are notorious for the cloak of secrecy they are held under. The headquarters office is in The Hague in Switzerland, the only European country never invaded or bombed during World Wars I and II. Switzerland is the seat of world power. The goal of the Bilderberg Group is a one-world totalitarian socialist government and economic system. Take heed, as time is running short.

You must understand that secrecy is wrong. The very fact that a meeting is secret tells me that something is going on that I would not approve. Do not ever believe that grown men meet on a regular basis just to put on fancy robes, hold candles, and glad-hand each other. George Bush, when he was initiated into the Skull & Bones, did not lie naked in a coffin with a ribbon tied around his genitalia and yell out the details of all his sexual experiences because it was fun. He had much to gain by accepting initiation into the Order, as you can now see. These men meet for important reasons, and their meetings are secret because what goes on during the meetings would not be approved by the community. The very fact that something is secret means there is something to hide.

John Robison wrote Proofs of a Conspiracy in 1798, and I believe he said it best in the following passage from the book. "Nothing is so dangerous as a mystic Association. The object remaining a secret in the hands of the managers, the rest simply put a ring in their own noses, by which they may be led about at pleasure; and still panting after the secret they are the better pleased the less they see of their way. A mystical object enables the leader to shift his ground as he pleases, and to accommodate himself to every current fashion or prejudice. This again gives him almost unlimited power; for he can make use of these prejudices to lead men by troops. He finds them already associated by their prejudices, and waiting for a leader to concentrate their strength and set them in motion. And when once great bodies of men are set in motion, with a creature of their fancy for a guide, even the engineer himself cannot say, 'Thus far shalt thou go, and no farther.'"

Is the common man really as stupid as the elite seem to believe? If he is, then maybe the average citizen is better off ignorant, being manipulated this way and that, whenever the elite deem it necessary. We will discover the answer very quickly when the common man finds that his ticket to Fantasy Land has just expired.

"U.S. President Bush and Soviet President Gorbachev arrived yesterday on this Mediterranean island for a summit conference beginning today during which both hope to start the search for a New World Order." -New York Times December 1, 1989

Exclusive Interview With Jessica Cooper

Daughter Of The Late William Cooper

(Please Note Reservations About Some Of The Content)

By Timothy Green Beckley

Recently we received an unexpected email from Jessica Cooper requesting that we get in touch her as she was anxious to talk about her father, whom she understood we knew relatively well having published *DEATH OF A CONSPIRACY SALESMAN*, following what some were saying was a government organized "assassination." There were some issues she wanted to have clarified and some things she wanted to discuss. We asked if we could record the conversation and print a transcript of it in this volume.

Jessica readily agreed and we spoke for a little over an hour. She admitted that she was uncertain about some parts and so we offered her the opportunity to read over the transcript and make any necessary factual changes. We explained that we had a deadline and had to get this in to the printer on a specific date. Unfortunately, the time has come and gone and we have not received any changes, though Jessica told us that she wanted to make some alterations in what she had said so as to clarify some points and perhaps to correct others. We are running the interview without these changes because Jessica has been leading a complicated life lately, which we understand.

We will update this interview if necessary and will continue our discussion hopefully in future issues of our two publications *Bizarre Bazaar* or *Conspiracy Journal.* In any case, the interview contains some very fascinating information that friends, associates and perhaps those not so pleasantly disposed to "Wild Bill" will find of immense interest. So here we go. Let's say hello to Jessica Cooper.

******

Timothy Green Beckley: Jessica, how old were you when you last saw your father Bill Cooper and under what circumstances?

Cooper: I think I was nineteen. I had gone to meet him and I was going to stay with him for fifteen days, at his house in Eagar, Arizona.

Beckley: Now what were the circumstances of that visit?

Cooper: Well, I had found him online. I found his website and I sent him an email saying "You're my Dad and I'm your daughter." He emailed me back and we communicated several times through email and then he called me. We spoke over the phone for a while and he bought—not too much time passed—me plane tickets to go and meet him. So I went.

Beckley: Now, previous to that, when had you separated? When I met Bill he was married to a different lady and had another child that I originally had thought was you but obviously it wasn't. When had you left him or parted company as a child?

Cooper: I was three and a half.

Beckley: So you had had no communication with him from the age of three and a half to nineteen?

Cooper: Absolutely none.

Beckley: What had you heard about him? Anything at all?

Cooper: I had heard that he was in the military and that he loved my Mom very much but that he was abusive and an alcoholic and that's why she left him. And I didn't really want to hear those things, but I just didn't really ask because that seemed to be all my mother could say.

Beckley: When you went to visit him in Arizona, did you realize the pressure that he was under or who he was? Obviously, he had quite a bit of notoriety. He was quite a controversial person. People tended either to like him and think he was very sincere, but on the other hand there were people who didn't think too much of him at all. What had you heard about him as far as his controversial nature goes?

Cooper: I had really learned about him from his website and speaking to him. I'd never heard of him or his infamy in his areas of work and expertise before I found him. And I found him via his website so I only learned positive things because that was his forum. Not somebody else's who was critiquing him. But when I got to Eagar, I definitely realized that it was real. I mean, I was never into any of that, conspiracy theory, anything like that. He had to have someone else run all his errands for him (because he would have been arrested if he had left his secluded retreat). To me, he seemed like a very intelligent man, so he wasn't just paranoid. I could see a basis for his paranoia, just all around. There were people watching him and I could see this with my own eyes. I wasn't in to any of this so I wouldn't have seen it if it wasn't there. This told me it was all very real. (not just a mental aberration).

Beckley: So did you say to him upon your arrival, "Pops, what's going on here?" Would you describe it as a fortified compound?

Cooper: No, it was a house. I would describe it as "well-defended," not fortified. It was on top of a hill, so he had a great view of anyone approaching. You really couldn't approach him without him knowing it unless you were dropped from a helicopter. And he had guns everywhere, so that basically if anybody approached through any area of the house, he would be armed and able to defend himself and put up a fight.

Beckley: You say guns. Are we talking about semiautomatic, automatic—

Cooper: No, I didn't see any automatics or semiautomatic weapons. I don't know anything about handguns. They might have been semiautomatic, but I wouldn't know. But they just looked like handguns, revolvers, shotguns or rifles or whatever. I'm not a gun expert so I wouldn't quote me. They were of different shapes and sizes.

Beckley: In other words, there was more than one gun lying on the coffee table?

Cooper: Well, he didn't have multiple guns in one area, but there was a gun here in this room, a gun here in that room. He always had one with him when he left the house. And the law enforcement agencies knew that.

Beckley: Did he tell you why he was under siege?

Cooper: Sort of. At least half of our conversations encompassed that type of stuff. The other half was just patching up things as father and daughter.He sort of said, "The government has federal warrants out for my arrest, and the warrants technically are for tax evasion." His thought was that they would like to apprehend him because of the things that he said and the things that he knew. And no one can know for sure, but he had a very real fear and a very real reason to be afraid. They definitely wanted him.

Beckley: Was he the sole occupant of this house? Were there other people that were there defending his freedom?

Cooper: There was a man—I don't use this word often, but I will literally say I hate that man. He didn't live there, but he practically did. He may as well have. He did everything for my father. He was wonderful to my father. He got his mail for him. I think he did his grocery shopping. Anything that my father would have had to leave the house for, where he could have possibly been apprehended by the police, This person helped him with his website and his work (in the patriot movement) and all of that. So he was there a lot, but he didn't actually live in the house.

Beckley: Why would you dislike him so much, if he was doing all this for your father?

Cooper: Because of how he treated me when my father died. It was horrific. I had letters coming from people I didn't even know who were at his funeral who were commenting on it.

Beckley: Now how many children did Bill have altogether?

Cooper: He had first, my sister Jennifer. She lives in Italy and I talk to her. And he had her with a woman named Angie. Then he had my brother Tony.I'm very close with Anthony.He lives in California. I can't remember his mom's name. Robin perhaps. And he had me, with my mother, Dolly. And then he had Dorothy and Allison, with Annie.

Beckley: Annie is the lady that I met and the little girl I assumed was you. So getting back your dad's "associate," why would this gentleman dislike you so much? You're a legitimate child of Bill's. You didn't come there looking for anything in particular, am I right?

Cooper: No, I didn't. But once my father died and I was the only family member at the funeral, I posed a legitimate threat in the eyes of these people. And it was very clear that that's how they say saw me. Because they even put traffic cones, blocking off the driveway to my father's house, so I couldn't get there.

Beckley: What revelations would you have, though, that would be so upsetting to them?

Cooper: I didn't have *any*. They were just afraid, I don't know, probably that I could take everything if I wanted, if I went to court. Saying I'm the only child who was close to him or something. Maybe I could get his house. I didn't want any of that. I think they were just afraid of that. I went to the house and I saw his will. And each separate page was for a different person. So I don't know if I was in it or not.

Beckley: I knew Bill fairly well. I don't think you could describe him as a wealthy individual.

Cooper: I don't know. I don't care. I didn't want any of that. All I wanted was a set of books he promised me so I'd have something from him to hand down to my kids.

Beckley: How long were you actually there for? How long did you stay on the property?

Cooper: That's a tough one. Let me think. My memory's really bad time-wise, and I don't have any way to—

Beckley: Well, are we talking about three days? A week? More than that?

Cooper: I'm thinking it was about a week. It was probably five to seven days. We had a really wonderful time together until the day all hell broke loose.

Beckley: Were you there when the confrontation with the police took place?

Cooper: Yes, I called them.

Beckley: You called them?

Cooper: What do you think happened?

Beckley: You tell me. I wasn't there. I mean the newspaper reports basically—

Cooper: Oh, no, no. We're not talking about that confrontation. No.

Beckley: So did <u>you</u> have a confrontation with him?

Cooper: Here is the way it went down. . . we were watching a movie and he'd been drinking straight vodka. And he started yelling at me over whether or not some movie was **Blackboard Jungle**, and I got upset because he was yelling and it was starting to scare me. I said, "Okay, I thought we were just talking about a movie. I'm going to go in my room." I went in my room and he came outside the door and was yelling and screaming at me. I was very afraid because my whole life, all I'd heard was that he when he was drunk, he was violent. So I was very frightened, and I tried to call my friend and he got on the line and said, "Why are you making this phone call?" Blah, blah, blah. So I blocked the door with the dresser and I know that the only thing you can call when someone's on the line, the only thing that will go through is 911. So I called the police. One of the people who worked at the police station is the girlfriend of my dad's associate.So I didn't know how safe I was with them either but I called them. And I said, "He's not threatened to hurt me and has not hurt me. He hasn't touched me at all. I'm only afraid. Don't do anything to him. I would just like you to come so that I can safely get out of the house. Please take me away from the house." Well, they did and he was very upset about that, because to him involving the police at all is a huge form of—this is a bad thing to do.

Beckley: Was that the only time you saw him then?

Cooper: That week I was there, yeah. I talked with him forever after that. I spoke with him a lot. I had a relationship with him over the computer and over the phone. He sent me a computer and he set me up with an email account. And he set it up as "Daddy Loves Me" at hotmail.com, and my password was "mdemms," which is "My Daddy's eyes, my Mother's smile." And he got an 800 number so I could call him anytime from anywhere for free. He was a very loving Dad.

Beckley: When you went to visit him, how long was this before the final incident that took his life?

Cooper: About two years.

Beckley: And that would be what year then?

Cooper: I think I visited him in 1999.

Beckley: You were there for about a week. You said you had read about him on the internet, so you must have known then that he had some interest in UFOs, the Kennedy assassination, different conspiracy theories. He was known as a patriot. I'm not sure exactly what that—I guess that has different definitions to different people. But he was a world class speaker. In fact, I was just thinking tonight, Jessica. There's a place in Rachel, Nevada, called the Little A-Lee Inn—you've probably seen that on TV—which is near Area 51. And I sponsored Bill out there for a weekend seminar and skywatch.I was going to say we packed the place but the Inn only holds about forty people. It's in the middle of the desert, and in those days people had just started traveling out there. And of course we did sponsor him at some conferences in Phoenix and San Diego. On a hot summer evening, when the temperature was probably close to 100 degrees, he packed, on a Monday night, well over one hundred people, and they stayed for five and a half hours, to hear him converse about all of these subjects. Did he take you into his confidence and tell you about any of these things? About his military career? I know one of his claims, in **Behold, A Pale Horse**, is that he had a UFO sighting while he was in the Navy.

Cooper: That's true. He told me that. One rose up right out of the ocean. He told me—I'm going to be perfectly honest with you, because it's my goal that any lies on the part of the government or my Dad— because I'm sick of it. He told me that there was a truthful basis for everything he said. That some things he elaborated on, mostly alien stuff. He saw that saucer rise up out of the ocean when he was in the military. But some of the things he said he sensationalized to make people want to hear it, basically, like any good writer would. Hypothesize things..

Beckley: He did say, while he was in the military, he had seen some top secret papers, the *MJ-12 papers* or some documents that purported to tell about aliens who were collaborating with the government —

Cooper: I know that's true, because when I was a little girl my mom and I—she packed up everything when she left my father, including some of his things. One of which was a set of encyclopedias. And when I was ten, we were unpacking a storage locker and we found a set of encyclopedias. In one of them were a bunch of government papers that actually said "Top Secret" on them, which I thought they only actually wrote that on Top Secret papers in the movies. But apparently not. I guess we were hiding them for him and we still have those somewhere.

Beckley: You think you still have these papers?

Cooper: They're somewhere in a storage locker with black widows in California. That is if my mom didn't get rid of that stuff. So it's a possibility.

Beckley: What else did he tell you about his military career?

Cooper: His military career, he was a little bit sneaky about. He was a deep sea diving instructor. After he lost his leg he couldn't do the actual diving anymore so he became an instructor.

Beckley: How did he lose his leg?

Cooper: That he lied about. He drove under a semi and lost his leg. It had nothing to do with the government or anything else.

Beckley: In other words, it was a traffic accident. What else about his military career? Where was he stationed? What did he do while he was in the military?

Cooper: Unfortunately I don't know much about when he was in the military. All I know is that he was a deep sea diving instructor, and that he was in the army as well, I believe, and the navy. I don't know anything else about his military career.

Beckley: So he got interested in UFOs and all because of his sighting?

Cooper: Yes. That and seeing things that he was lied to about that were supposed to be secret and not being allowed to say anything and being treated like he didn't see anything. . . or that he was crazy when he could see these things with his own eyes. It made him very suspicious. When you go into the military, you're supposed to have this sense of—that you believe everything they say and you don't question anything and yes sir, yes ma'am and that's it. But he started to question that and to become upset. Then he started to look into things and he started to learn more and more. Like the JFK assassination. He became interested in (who wanted Kennedy dead or what the reason was for Kennedy being killed).

Beckley: When did he started doing this -- how long had he been out of the military?

Cooper: I tried to ask my mother, and she said it was—he was only just starting to be interested in this stuff when he left us.

Beckley: He was a friend of John Lear. Do you know who John Lear is?

Cooper: No.

Beckley: Well, you know, the Lear aircraft. John Lear's his son and lives in Las Vegas and is involved in the UFO cover-up mystery as well.

CONSPIRACY SUMMIT DOSSIER

I guess somehow Bill and John hooked up, and Bill started telling him about some of these things that he'd seen in the military. And John Lear posted some of this on the earliest versions of the internet bulletin boards. Also, your dad had published a position paper which involved what had happened to him in the military that revealed a lot. He was immensely interested in the various secret societies. Did he tell you anything about that?

Cooper: No. He didn't tell much except for the things that I've told you. It's really what the government tried to do that I know about.

Beckley: Okay, so you're there for several days, probably a week or so. Then you leave after this incident with Bill involving his drinking and so forth. Did you return to California then? Is that where you were living?

Cooper: Yes, in California.

Beckley: And at this point he was under surveillance by the FBI? When you went to visit him?

Cooper:I mean I can't be sure, but there was a white van with dark windows that was always parked down at the end of the road leading up to the house. It was like the vehiclenever left, if you know what I mean. My assumption is that it could have been keeping surveillance on him. What agency were they with?I can't say for sure.

Beckley: You mentioned to me that you were approached by the FBI—

Cooper: Federal marshals.

Beckley: Under what circumstances was that, and how did you find out that there was a problem with the IRS and the feds?

Cooper: I already knew about the IRS. But can I just clear one thing up?

Beckley: Absolutely.

Cooper: Annie and Dorothy and Alison, they weren't sent out of the country for any vacation. Annie turned witness against my Dad. She left him. The government hid her.

Beckley: You mean the government hid her? They put her in some kind of a witness protection program? I don't believe Bill would be the type of person—like a gangster or anything like that!

Cooper: What I mean is that there are some fanatics into my dad who might search her out.

Beckley: Tell us about the incident with the federal marshals.

Cooper: Okay. I was home. I was living with my mother. I had to live with her because I had just had my second back surgery and I was recuperating and couldn't really work at the time. And they just searched me right out because they had obviously been tapping my phone. They knew everything about me, my life . . . everything! They sent a young, good looking man. I'm sure they did it on purpose because I was a young twenty-year-old girl. And they said that they knew I had gone to visit my father. They knew that while I was there to visit him, he had taken me to eat at a restaurant in another town. And that he never left his house except when I was there to visit him. He also took me to the grocery store and let me pick out a bunch of groceries. I wanted to cook for my dad while I was visiting him.

The Feds wanted me to go and visit him again. They wanted me to take one of their agents undercover working as my friend. To go and visit him under the guise that because of what happened last time I didn't feel safe going alone, which seemed to be a very plausible explanation. And have him take me out to the same restaurant again. And excuse myself to use the restroom. While I would be in the restroom, perfectly safe and out of harm's way, other agents, disguised as customers in the restaurant, would arrest my father. And the agent with me would never break cover. The reason they wanted to do it this way was because, in his words, quote, "We can't afford another incident like Ruby Ridge or Waco."

I didn't even know what Ruby Ridge was. I knew what Waco was, and because I knew about Waco, I knew he must have been talking about two such incidents of bad publicity where they just wanted to arrest them based on some little warrant for some little thing like taxes and ended up shedding some innocent blood.

Beckley: A lot of people don't pay their taxes under various other circumstances.

Cooper: Tax evasion.

Beckley: Bill didn't make tons of money. They don't normally send anybody if they owe the government a couple of thousand dollars off to jail . . . OR SHOOT THEM!

Cooper: My dad had some money. Not a lot, but he had plenty. He could say one night on his radio show that he didn't have the money for this or his CD changer was broken. I swear to God, the next day, overnight mail, he would have a brand new five-disc changer sent to him by a fan. There were checks, there were money orders. He had a radio station in his house that he broadcast out of. Many cars. He had two dogs, Sugar Bear and Crusher. Crusher was shot by the police. The bastards! He had a big house on the top of the hill. He had a huge satellite dish. A truck, an old 50s car. He was fixing up a limo for me, which I didn't want. He had money. Ask and you shall receive in his business. And when people love you in that business . . . I'm serious.

Beckley: So obviously you told the Feds you weren't about to do this.

Cooper: Well, wait. I'm not finished saying what they said.

Beckley: Okay.

Cooper: They also told me that my father had made the statement that he would never be taken alive. That wasn't all they said to me. They asked me questions. They wanted me to tell them the complete layout of his house, all the rooms, how big they were, and where every gun I had seen was. And I told them, "Don't go try and arrest him. He always has his guns. When he leaves the house, there's a gun in his car. Just don't do it. Because if you don't want it to end bad, don't even try." That's why they wanted to do the restaurant thing because that would be one place I hadn't seen him take his gun, was into the restaurant.

Beckley: When I first visited him in Verde, Arizona, we met at the Dairy Queen and he had a gun with him. He had it on the seat of the car next to him all the time he was driving. I didn't really blink. I figured he is trying to show me he is packing. Well in Arizona you can pack legally as long as the gun is kept in full view.

Cooper: He had a wooden leg, and that's a pretty good place to hide a gun. But you know, I'm his daughter, and he might not have wanted to have the gun in the restaurant around me in case something happened. He was different around me. He was different. There was

Bill Cooper the conspiracy theorist and there was Bill Cooper the father. And they were two very different people. And I hate them so much for taking him away from me. But that's another issue altogether.

So they wanted to know where all the guns were and what the layout of his house was. I said, "I'll tell you that he has a gun everywhere. I'll tell you that so you don't go try and arrest him." And they said, "We know you hate your life here with your mom. We know that you hate living here, that you don't like how messy it is, and that because of your recent back surgery you can't go back to work right at the moment and save up the money you need to go and get out on your own." Which just floored me, just dropped my jaw and I didn't know what to say, because they had obviously been monitoring my conversations.

Beckley: I was just going to say that's obvious.

Cooper: That's a little bit before the Patriot Act, isn't it?

Beckley: Yeah. Well of course they have the ability to do that. There could have been other ways they could have gotten to him. What would have brought their attention to you exactly?

Cooper: Because I am the only person he had left his house with. Since he'd been living in that house having other people do everything for him.

Beckley: But it seems from what you've told me that they were watching you or monitoring your activities even before that.

Cooper: Oh, it looks like they were monitoring me the whole time I was with him. They knew exactly where he took me, what we did. I take it back. I do know who's in the damn van. (laughter)

Beckley: Well, your dad must have known who was in the van as well.

Cooper: I don't even know how they followed us to the restaurant out of town. This was a tiny restaurant in a town that closed down in the winter. It's so tiny and up in the mountains. There's only one road in and out of it, and I saw no other cars. None. There was nobody following us. They must have been in the sky or—

Beckley: We just published a book called *Mind Matrix* that has a lot of patents forinventions that people have developed that are usedto snoop on Joe Q Public. They don't have to be very close to your premises at all. They can point something at your windowpane and pick up the vibrations of the conversation that's going on in the room.

Cooper: Well, I want to say one thing. You don't go to all that trouble, using that kind of man hours and technology and time to get someone for frigging tax evasion. There are a lot of people spouting crazy ideas out there. Unless something he was saying was true, they wouldn't have cared.

Beckley: Now, what do you think that might have been?

Cooper: I know that the things he saw were true. Because he wanted to be honest with me. He flat out told me the things he lied about. The things I know he lied about are because he told me so. So I believe that the things he told me were true *were true*. And I saw those documents with my own eyes when I was a little girl.

Beckley: Do you know the details of what was in the documents?

Cooper: They just were typed pages and I didn't have time to read anything in them except the big Top Secret at the top.

Beckley: Couldn't they have been copies of other documents that might have been falsified?

Cooper: Sure, they could have been. How could I possibly say they couldn't have been faked? I didn't get to read them, I didn't know what they were and anything is possible. However, why would he hide them with us? Why would he be hiding some fake papers?

Beckley: Yeah, you're absolutely right, because the MJ-12 papers were published. I have a book that Sean Casteel and I worked on called **MJ-12 and the Riddle of Hangar 18** which has supposedly classified documents in there. So you're right. There's no reason to hide copies of something that's been printed in a million different places. Did he take you into his confidence about anything else? The Kennedy assassination for example? I remember he gave a lecture for us one time on the subject and said that the secret service agent in the car had been involved in the assassination and actually had fired one of the guns.

Cooper: I'm pretty sure he believed that. I don't know. He knows it's a theory. He can't prove it. We had a long discussion. I said, "Tell me about your work," and he said things about this and about that. He basically just said what you said. "I have a theory about this, and dah dah dah, and I have a theory about that." He was very honest with me. He never spoke to me like he was speaking to a crowd that he was trying to win over. He spoke in truth and lies. "This is true. I said this and it wasn't true. I fudged this, it sounds better that way. To get people's attention so they'd listen to the things that are really important, that I'm trying to tell them true things I've seen." He was very honest with me. But I've told you the main things he told me. The other things were personal.

Beckley: Did he seem concerned for his life? Did he think that something untimely was going to happen?

Cooper: He had a premonition that he was going to die soon, that they were going to come after him soon. And he was right. Shortly before they killed him. Who actually killed him? The local cops.

Beckley: This was pretty widely reported in the newspaper, even back here in the East. I remember I heard it on the radio the morning that it happened. And it was in the **New York Post** and probably the **New York Times**. It received certainly a great deal of attention. As if it were a warning to other people, don't try this because it could happen to you as well.

Cooper: Back to the U.S. marshals that came to see me. We kind of got waylaid. They offered me $500 and to set me up in an apartment. To go with an agent to get my dad. I just thought that part might be important.

Beckley: Now what did you feel about that, though? Did you feel like these guys were being scumbags?

Cooper: I was disgusted . .. I was so disgusted that they would dangle in my face what I wanted more than anything in the world. But I had to betray my father, who I'd wanted my whole life, who I had just met again, who I loved, who loved me, or I couldn't have it. I hated them. I hated them for it. What a horrible thing to do. It was a horrible thing to do.

Beckley: So you told them obviously that you weren't going to be a part of this?

Cooper: Yes. I told my father immediately what they did, too.

Beckley: And what was his reaction to that?

CONSPIRACY SUMMIT DOSSIER

Cooper: He wasn't surprised. I called him and he just was not at all surprised. He asked me about the conversation and I told him every word. What they knew, what they had seen. And when I told him, I said, "I would never do that to you, daddy. I know you'd rather be dead than be in jail. I would never betray you."

Beckley: And this was about two years before his death?

Cooper: I think about a year, a year and a half.

Beckley: At that point, when you refused to do this, did the federal agents back off because they didn't want to create an incident?

Cooper: I don't know if they backed off of him, but they backed off of me. My father and I didn't talk for a few months after I got back because the night I left, when the cops came to get me, I was in my pajamas. And he said I could only come to get my things if I came into the house without anybody else. And I was afraid so I wouldn't. So the cops put me in a safe house for three days. I had no toothbrush, no hair brush, no change of clothes. And we haggled with the airport to get my ticket changed and then we drove for four hours to wherever the airport was and I got on the plane. My friend got me immediately and brought me a whole new wardrobe. I had been planning to stay in the crazy weather of Arizona for fifteen days so everything I owned was with me at his house. And eventually my mom sort of put me back on the phone with him and we smoothed things over and became closer than ever.

Beckley: They had no reason to approach your mom, though, because at this point she wasn't—

Cooper: I don't know if they approached anyone else. What I don't understand is one of his associate's girlfriend was a police officer in Eagar, Arizona. Isn't it illegal for her to be associating with my dad?Why wouldn't they approach her? She was a cop. If there's anybody they could use against him, it would be her. She could get inside information like that.

Beckley: Was she there at the house?

Cooper: She was at the police station the night the police picked me up.

Beckley: I mean in general, had she been at the house?

Cooper: She'd been there, yeah.

Beckley: Now what were the circumstances that led to your dad being shot?

Cooper: Well, this is a story that I've really had to dig to get the facts here. And apparently what happened is one Fourth of July a young couple went up onto the circular driveway in front of his house on top of the hill to watch the fireworks. He came out of the house with a gun, because anybody coming to the front of his house posed a threat, even though they were just a couple of young kids. And just using the gun as an "influence," told them to get off his property. So they did, but they went to the police and reported it because he scared them. The police sort of filed this away. I'm sure the U.S. Marshals did contact them somehow because they knew he was wanted, and decided that since they were little know-nothing cops in Eagar, Arizona, and the intelligent U.S. Marshals wouldn't go and arrest him that they should be stupid and go and try to arrest him. So they sent two officers up there. I think it's entrapment or something. But they sent two officers up there disguised in plainclothes, like regular people up there for the view to lure him out of his house. When they tried to arrest him, SWAT was around the corner. And SWAT came from around the corner—

Beckley: Well, let's go back a bit. According to the newspaper accounts, they were just two local—a sheriff and a deputy. Is that correct?

Cooper: That's what I heard at first too.

Beckley: Now you're saying there was a SWAT team there?

Cooper: I looked into it further and was told that SWAT was there. If you were those cops—think about it—and you were going to arrest him, with information about him, and all the guns and who knows who's in there, wouldn't you have a SWAT team there for backup? Just in case all hell broke loose and there was a firefight?

Beckley: They had gone there under the pretense as I understand it that somebody had complained that he had drawn a gun on them and threatened them. It was a neighbor?

Cooper: Wasn't he killed in November? That complaint was from the Fourth of July. How does that add up to you? They went up there posing as two people because they had heard that when two people went up on his property for the view he had come out with a gun by himself just kind of innocently telling them to leave. Just so they could see the gun so they knew he meant business. And they thought, well, gosh, this is a great way to get him out and get him arrested. Dress in plainclothes and go up there. I'm not sure what they were wearing, but they were just posing, creating the appearance of two people—

Beckley: He died November 5, 2001.

Cooper: Yeah. So he turned around when they tried to arrest him. I believe it was the sheriff and a deputy. He turned around as if to go back inside the house. Which was a trick. When he turned around he was actually getting his gun out. He turned back around and shot at them. And to put an ironic and completely un-comedic twist on this whole thing, shot the deputy I believe, shot the sheriff. And they shot his dog, Crusher. Sugar Bear ran away, never to be found again. And they killed my father.

Beckley: Did you attend the funeral?

Cooper: Yes. I went through hell to get to that funeral. I got up there, very tired and cranky and everything from my journey. I wanted to go to my father's house first, and they had coned off the driveway. Once the "important" people got there. Apparently this girl who was his girlfriend or something, she lived in another state, I don't remember her name . . . There was a man who identified himself as my father's lawyer. I'd really like someone to find out if he's got a law degree. I wanted to see my father's will, and they showed me. Each page pertained to a different person and was signed by him at the bottom. But if you wanted to get rid of a person in the will, all you'd have to do is get rid of one page. And so everybody in the room had a page that was in his will, and I wasn't, even though my father told me I was. And I said, "It's okay. I just want that set of books." Like gothic novels, where you look at the edges of the page and they're gold. And I wanted to hand them down to my kids. I had nothing of my father's to hand down and I wanted part of him, something from him to hand down to my children. And for their children and so on. And they said it was fine, I could have those books. And they never gave them to me. They lied. I've emailed them and called them a thousand times.

But after that, we went up to the building, I don't know whether it was a church or not. I didn't pay much attention to that, you know.

There were so many people and I was furious that the FBI was there. And that's fine that they're going to be there, but they were so rude. They wore those tacky FBI jackets that are like on **The X-Files**. They actually wear those. And they wore those to my father's funeral. They didn't wear a suit or something appropriate. They couldn't show a hint of respect.

They cut me out of everything. And my father had dedicated a song to me. He played it on his radio show and I had a tape of it. I asked the emcee if he would play it at my father's funeral and he did. And it's like, "You said you loved me, you'd never leave me, I wish that you won't go, most of all I miss you so." It's a really sweet song. And I got to play that for him at his funeral and they played **Amazing Grace** and all these people spoke. There were things that I really wanted to say because everybody was talking about Bill Cooper the conspiracy theorist, and I was the only family member there and I was the only one who could talk about him as a father. I felt like it needed to be said. I had held it together so far without crying and I got up there and started to talk. "It's really hard for me to come up here, but I know that if my dad was here, he'd want me to do this. I wanted to tell you there's a father part of my dad that you didn't know. He loved me very much and I've only got him for two years. But he loved all his children, and I miss him a lot. He called me 'princess.'" Then I lost it. I totally started crying. So I went to sit down and about ten people went up after that and they were saying, "I wasn't going to say anything but the little girl was so brave and she was right. That's exactly what Bill would say." Then my mother went up and talked, and I could have killed her. She was so inappropriate.

Beckley: Why was it inappropriate?

Cooper: Well, first of all, his girlfriend is sitting there and she knows it, and she's saying how Bill always said she was the most beautiful woman he'd ever seen and while everybody knows that he was a drunk and had such alcohol problems and of course he'd knock her around when he'd been drinking, and he could be violent. I was mortified. I was absolutely mortified. We then went to the cemetery and we buried him. Are you supposed to give the flag to the family member?

Beckley: I'm not sure.

Cooper: Well, they didn't give me the flag. That's okay. It's just that it felt wrong. Like I was just shunned.

Beckley: There were no representatives of the military there I take it?

Cooper: I don't know. There were a lot of people there. One guy said that he was a very famous rock musician, and he looked really familiar to me. But he didn't want to give his name. The funeral wasn't about him, it was about my dad. I remember one man who was a good friend of my father's, I don't remember his name, went up and said, "My friend!" and then he burst into tears when he saw my father in the open casket. There were so many people there. It made me feel so good that they all loved my father so much. And when I got home, after seeing how I was treated, all these strangers started sending me pamphlets from the funeral and programs. And they pressed flowers and sent them to me in a beautiful box with a glass front. A shadowbox they made for me with some of the memorabilia from the funeral. And they sent me letters. "We're so sorry that they treated you that way and you were so brave and yadda, yadda." And I was like, wow, it was amazing and moving and I couldn't believe these people did this. I emailed the family a hundred times just about the books and they won't even acknowledge that I exist.

Beckley: We probably ought to wrap this up. Is there any kind of summing up statement you'd like to make?

Cooper: I'm only just now starting to learn about what my father's work was and the things that he said. I'm very interested in it. I really want everybody to know that, for all his faults, he was a very good man. And an intelligent man. And there is truth behind so much of what he says. He really inspired a lot of conflict and negative feedback. But anyone who says anything controversial does. That doesn't mean he was bad or wrong. So try and remember that.

EDITORS NOTE: At the point where Jessica starts telling of the circumstances of her father's death she seems hesitant and unsure and indicates there is probably more she needs to say, meaning she will research the matter more. In order to provide balanced reporting we are reprinting a copy of the official police report concerning Bill Cooper's death. The mystery deepens and we hopefully will hear more from Jessica. Coast to Coast AM has indicated they would like her to appear on the show which we will try to arrange.

ARIZONA DEPARTMENT OF PUBLIC SAFETY
I. SYNOPSIS

DR NUMBER:	2001 - 070756

On November 6, 2001 at approximately 0005 hours, the Apache County Sheriff's Office (ACSO), Special Response Team (SRT), was involved in an "Officer Involved Shooting." The suspect, William Milton Cooper, critically wounded an ACSO deputy and was mortally wounded by another sheriff's deputy.

In the summer of 2001, the Chief of the Eagar Police Department (EPD) contacted the ACSO and asked for assistance developing a plan to arrest Cooper, an Eagar, Arizona, resident. The EPD advised Cooper was wanted on federal tax charges from 1998 as well as felony aggravated assault and felony endangerment charges in Apache County. The felony charges in Apache County were a result of an incident that occurred July 11, 2001.

The ACSO contacted the Maricopa County Special Weapons and Tactics (MCSO/SWAT) and asked for assistance developing a tactical plan to effect Cooper's arrest. The MCSO/SWAT responded and developed an arrest plan.

The ACSO/SRT and the MCSO/SWAT initially planned to arrest Cooper on September 11, 2001, but that attempt had to be canceled because of a possible security breech.

On November 5, 2001, the ACSO developed their own tactical arrest plan and conducted a briefing outlining that plan. Following the briefing, the ACSO/SRT practiced several arrest scenarios utilizing three ACSO vehicles.

On November 6, 2001 at approximately 0005 hours, during the ACSO/SRT tactical operation, Cooper critically wounded ACSO Deputy Rob Marinez and was fatally wounded by ACSO Deputy Joseph Goldsmith.

ACSO Deputy Rob Marinez was flown to Phoenix, Arizona, where he was admitted in critical condition to the Barrows Neurological Institute.

Cooper was pronounced dead at the scene.

Apache County Sheriff Brian Hounshell requested the Arizona Department of Public Safety, Special Investigations Unit, respond and conduct the criminal investigation.

Detective Name	ID No.	Location	Date	Supervisor
Kevin Wood	2613	32030200	04/04/02	Lieutenant Tim Chung #4609

THE TESLA-NAZI UFO CONNECTION

SECRET HISTORY REVEALED!

AVAILABLE IN:
❏ **VHS** or ❏ **DVD FORMAT**
Check Preference

MAY NOT PLAY OUTSIDE NO. AMERICA

VIDEO #1: HITLER'S SECRET FLYING SAUCERS Aerospace writer and engineer William R. Lyne offers striking testimony that · Adolf Hitler had at least seven body doubles and was able to escape, with other Nazis, from his Berlin "death bunker" to South America in order to begin the Fourth Reich · The true history of flying saucers is a big lie, full of deceit and government disinformation, created to conceal one basic truth: that most UFOs are man-made craft based upon German World War Two anti-gravity technology as first developed by Nikola Tesla · Werner von Braun, top German rocket scientist, was present in New Mexico as early as 1937, and the "Roswell Crash" may have been a staged hoax to hide the truth about U.S. government's knowledge in alternative methods of propulsion, including free energy. History books and the mass media have lied to us for over 50 years to cover up the true nature of the UFO phenomena.—**$21.95**

VIDEO #2: NAZI UFOS: HOW THEY FLY Aerospace writer William R. Lyne, who had a Top Secret clearance in Air Force Intelligence, says we not look to space for the origins of flying saucers. Residing in New Mexico for over 30 years, Lyne has seen several formations of flying saucers and has concluded that the UFO crash at Roswell was an elaborate government disinformation hoax meant to convince the American public that these objects are interplanetary in nature when, in fact, they are manufactured right here on earth! Revelations in this shocking video include the facts that German scientists developed a series of circular and boomerang shaped craft based upon the research of electrical genius Nikola Tesla, and flew them during the 1930s and 1940s · That the Germans may even have built a "flying submarine" that was observed and reported throughout Europe, and capable of reaching very high speeds · That, after the war, more than 1,000 Nazi scientists and engineers were allowed into this country to continue working on the antigravity and free energy programs that had begun with the financial aid of the Nazi regime · That the U.S. continues to keep the "flying saucer" phenomena shrouded in mystery for their own unsavory purposes, while they continue to foster the idea that there are "aliens among us." During this 90-minute presentation, the viewer will see the actual parts of what Lyne claims is a U.S. developed UFO based on combined Tesla and Nazi technology.—**$21.95**

PLEASE SPECIFY ❏ DVD or ❏ VHS

VIDEO #3: MORE TESLA-NAZI UFO SECRETS Vladimir Terziski has gathered a vast collection of anthropological stories about antigravity craft from different cultures. Being fluent in Japanese, Russian, German and English has enabled him to penetrate the global veil of secrecy of the NWO. Now missing from his post as chairman of the American Academy of Dissident Sciences, the well-respected engineer gave this presentation before he quite suddenly and mysteriously vanished. Vlad believes the Germans began seriously exploring the South Pole in huge carrier ships in 1937 and that evidence indicates they built a secret underground base to pursue human genetic and space travel efforts while the world believed their craft were being piloted by friendly ETs. A frightening scenario to the uninformed!—**$21.95**

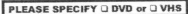

I am anxious to have this amazing information. Please send the following:
❏ ALL THREE VIDEOS showing the Tesla-Nazi Connection—$50.00 + $5.00 S/H
❏ Hitler's Secret Flying Saucers—$21.95 + $5.00 S/H   ❏ Nazi UFOs: How They Fly—$21.95 + $5.00 S/H
❏ More Tesla-Nazi Secrets—$21.95 + $5.00 S/H
We accept USA bank checks, money orders, VISA, MasterCard, Discover. NO CASH. Credit card orders use our secure 24-hour hotline at 732-602-3407. All foreign customers add USA $10 S/H with payment via international money order. *May not play outside North America.*

GLOBAL COMMUNICATIONS • Box 753• New Brunswick, NJ 08903

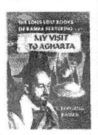

Printed in Great Britain
by Amazon